Books by Edward S. Wallace

GENERAL WILLIAM JENKINS WORTH,
MONTEREY'S FORGOTTEN HERO

THE GREAT RECONNAISSANCE

With Major General John K. Herr

THE STORY OF THE U. S. CAVALRY

The Great Reconnaissance

The Great Reconnaissance

SOLDIERS, ARTISTS AND SCIENTISTS ON THE FRONTIER 1848–1861

by
EDWARD S. WALLACE

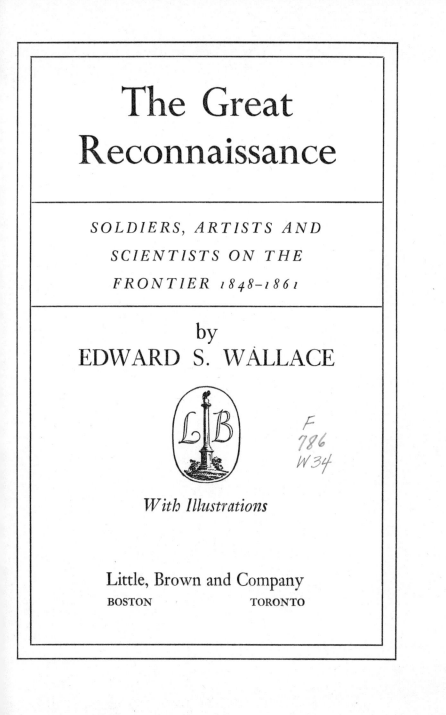

With Illustrations

Little, Brown and Company
BOSTON   TORONTO

21137

To the U. S. Corps of Topographical Engineers

who in their short life of twenty-three years as a
separate corps probably did more, in proportion to
their small numbers, toward the winning of the
West than any other group in our history. With
them it was always quality over quantity, and their
pioneer accomplishments on the frontier were the
lasting foundations for all the following settlement
and civilization.

Acknowledgments

I WANT to express my sincere gratitude for the help received from the staff of the Yale University Library, where almost all the research was done, and, in particular, to the librarian, Mr. James T. Babb, to Mr. Henry M. Fuller, and to Mr. Archibald Hanna, the librarian of the Yale Collection of Western Americana (of which the William R. Coe Collection is the backbone); also, I want to mention a neglected clan, the elevator operators, who carried me for many perpendicular miles, up and down, in that somewhat murky Gothic edifice.

I am most grateful to Mr. Lawrence C. Wroth of the John Carter Brown Library in Providence, Rhode Island, for his guidance in combing through the John Russell Bartlett papers; to Mr. Charles Childs of the Childs Gallery of Boston, Massachusetts, for his advice about artists of the 1850's; to Mr. Walter Whitehill and Miss Margaret Hackett of the Boston Athenaeum for their interest and help; and to Mr. Henry P. Rossiter of the Boston Museum of Fine Arts for showing me its collection of sketches by Edward M. Kern. Also I am greatly indebted to Mr. T. R. Hay of Locust Valley, New York, for his information about the Ives family during the Civil War; to Mr. A. H. Greenly of Hoboken, New Jersey, to Mrs. Philip Dana Orcutt of Boston, and to Mr. Chris Emmett of San Antonio,

Texas, for their special help in finding material about the camel experiment; to Mrs. Katherine Edsall of the Peabody Museum, and to Mr. Thomas F. O'Connell of the Harvard College Library, both of Cambridge, Massachusetts, for their co-operation; to Colonel J. Franklin Bell of the U. S. Corps of Engineers for information about the Topographical Engineers; and to that mentor of Texas history, Colonel Martin L. Crimmins of San Antonio, for his expert and unique assistance. Especial thanks are due to Edward Eberstadt and Sons of New York City for generously allowing me to inspect the William H. Emory papers in their possession. And, finally, my heartfelt gratitude goes to Miss Sherry Hawkins of Boston for her constant skill and patience in typing a much revised and confusing manuscript.

Edward S. Wallace

Washington, Connecticut

Preface

THIS is the informal story of the men who explored, surveyed, and mapped our new boundary with Mexico after 1848, and then the huge area within it, before the outbreak of the Civil War in 1861; and of those who blazed the trails for wagon roads and railroads through this land to the Pacific Coast. Also, it tells of the accompanying artists who sketched, painted, and photographed the Indians, the landmarks, and the scenery; and the scientists who collected, classified, and meticulously illustrated the flora and fauna in those vast regions. It was nearly all unknown country and their activities in these lines were probably greater than similar ones in any other decade of our history, but their achievements were historically blanketed by the great gold rushes to California, Colorado, and Nevada, and by the political excitements leading to the Civil War, so that these unusual pioneers have been undeservedly forgotten.

Some of the official reports of the Topographical Engineers were of necessity highly technical and are to a lay reader repetitious, and dull in their scientific jargon, and so only the more colorful accounts have been chosen to present the high lights, although nearly all the reports are mentioned in one way or another. The Mormon War and the experiments with camels in the Southwest are included because these were reconnaissances of a sort in the land ceded by Mexico and fall into the general picture of the probing and prying in these regions by the military.

The narrative has been footnoted only for some direct quotations and for specialized statements, but general sources have been given for the book as a whole and for each chapter by itself.

Contents

CONTENTS

Illustrations

ILLUSTRATIONS

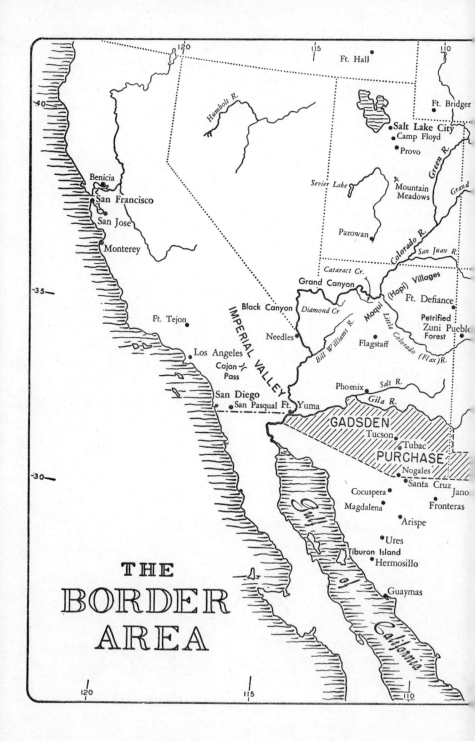

THE
BORDER
AREA

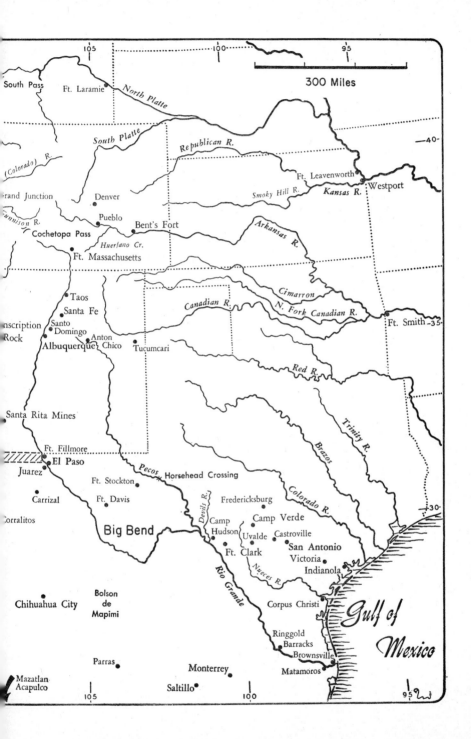

The Great Reconnaissance

CHAPTER I

A Puritan on the Border

AFTER the outbreak of the Mexican War in May, 1846, a column of American troops, mostly mounted, which was called "The Army of the West," invaded New Mexico (which then included the present Arizona) and California. Colonel Stephen Kearny, a remarkable soldier, had assembled this small force, of less than two thousand men, at Fort Leavenworth, Kansas, and led it into New Mexico to capture the town of Santa Fe in August. From there he pushed on at the head of one hundred picked dragoons, mounted on mules, and guided by the frontiersman Kit Carson, up through the Rocky Mountains to the headwaters of the Gila River, which he then followed to its junction with the Colorado River. Thence the small cavalcade rode through the desert, ascended the Sierras, where they were nearly wiped out by attacking Mexican lancers, and finally arrived at San Diego, the first American military force to reach the Pacific coast. California had previously surrendered to a naval force commanded by Commodore Robert F. Stockton, aided by the men of an exploring expedition under Lieutenant Colonel John C. Frémont, but the native Californians soon afterwards rebelled and Kearny's men arrived in time for the last skirmishes and final pacification of the country.

Right behind Kearny came another small American col-

umn, the Mormon Battalion, which was commanded by one
of Kearny's dragoon officers, Captain Philip St. George Cooke.
This unusual battalion consisted of volunteers recruited at Council Bluffs, Iowa, where thousands of that persecuted faith had
assembled, after having been driven from Nauvoo, Illinois, with
the plan of settling in Mexican territory, probably in California.
This was an infantry column with a wagon train and was unable
to follow Kearny's way through the rough mountain passes.
Cooke took it on a wide arc, considerably south of the Gila
River, captured Tucson, Arizona, without firing a shot, and
pushed and hauled the heavy wagons up over the Sierras into
California. The only conflict it had was a bizarre battle with a
herd of wild bulls which charged the caravan, disemboweled
many mules and horses and wounded several men. The Mormon
Battalion was the first expedition to reach the Pacific with wagons south of the Oregon Trail, and was especially important because it blazed the way for the only possible wagon road or
railroad along our later southern boundary. This route was overlooked when the treaty of peace was signed with Mexico, an
omission which caused many complications as we shall see.

At the end of this war in the spring of 1848, which was certainly our most profitable conflict, the United States acquired
about a half (if Texas is included) of the territory of the Republic of Mexico by the terms of the Treaty of Guadalupe
Hidalgo. The land gained by this treaty amounts to almost a
third (including Texas again) of the present area of the continental United States. Outside of eastern Texas, the upper Rio
Grande, and the coast of California, it was almost unknown,
for it was populated by wild beasts, mostly bison, and roaming
and savage Indians; and very few Americans had ever entered
it before the conquering columns of Kearny and Cooke.

It was imperative that this huge area be explored and mapped;

and the first step, naturally, was to survey and define the new boundary line. According to the terms of the treaty, each of the two countries was to appoint a commissioner and a surveyor, and these four officials were to meet in San Diego, California, and proceed with this job. This joint commission met in 1849, as required, but the whole business was completely upset by the discovery of gold in California and the consequent rush to the diggings of most of the personnel of the American party, especially by the soldiers assigned as escorts, who deserted in droves. The officials then adjourned in February, 1850, and agreed to meet again the following November in El Paso del Norte (now Juarez, Mexico), far from the madding gold-rushers. But despite the frantic distractions, the joint commission had succeeded in running the line eastward to the confluence of the Colorado and Gila Rivers, where Yuma, Arizona, stands today.

On this first American commission, Andrew B. Gray of Texas, the official surveyor, was assisted by two young army officers with the title of "astronomer," William H. Emory of Maryland, and Amiel Weeks Whipple of Massachusetts. Both were West Pointers and members of the U. S. Corps of Topographical Engineers, a unique organization and a crack outfit to which the highest-standing members of each graduating class at West Point were assigned. It was a veritable military brain trust whose primary purpose became the exploration, surveying, and mapping of the vast new Western territories. Its roster of officers became resonant with the names of men of distinction, for, at one time or another, it included such officers as Stephen H. Long, whose explorations of the Rocky Mountains in 1819–1820 and consequent pessimistic report developed the myth of the "Great American Desert"; and later it included George B. McClellan, John C. Frémont, Joseph E. Johnston, John Pope, William B. Franklin, William H. Emory, George Gordon Meade, and many others who rose high in both armies of the Civil War. It had been a branch of the Corps of Engineers from 1813 to 1838, when it was made a separate corps, and it continued as such until 1863, when it was again consolidated with the Engineers. It was commanded in the 1850's by Colonel John J. Abert, a distinguished officer, a native Virginian who had graduated from West Point in 1811 and who remained its head for thirty-two years, from 1829 to 1861. Incidentally, his son, James W. Abert, West Point 1842, had accompanied General Stephen Kearny as far as Santa Fe in 1846, and his reports about New Mexico are well known to students of Southwestern Americana.[1] The Topographical Engineers, after 1838, were active in many civil engineering works directed by the government, but their most colorful and adventurous achievements were in the exploration of the Far West, in which they played the major part, and they were the constant background motif of that great drama.

Officers of other branches, however, including the Navy, and the accompanying scientists and artists on many of the military expeditions performed important missions as well in this great probing and searching out of these vast new lands during the 1850's, until the Civil War ended this decade of wonder and discovery. While politicians and extremists fanned the evil flames of sectionalism back in civilization, these officers, artists, and scientists, from all parts of the country and from Europe (most of the artists were Germans), worked together against hardships and hostile Indians to mark the ways for the oncoming emigrants.

The first American boundary commissioner, acting in San Diego, was John B. Weller of Ohio, but he was soon removed when the Whigs came into office in 1849 under President Zachary Taylor, and replaced by the "Pathfinder," John C. Frémont,

---

[1] Contained in Lieutenant Colonel W. H. Emory, *Notes of a Military Reconnaissance, etc.* (Washington 1848).

who, however, resigned the office without serving when he was elected a United States senator from California. John Russell Bartlett, a stanch New England Whig, was then appointed as the boundary commissioner in June, 1850, and our story really begins with him.

Bartlett was a bookish man, a scholar of considerable prominence, and his appointment to the rough-and-tumble job of running a border survey through a wild and savage country was largely political. He desired the appointment for, as he quite sensibly noted in his unpublished memoirs,[2] he had led a sedentary life and wanted to travel for a change, and besides, he had a great interest in the American Indians. For two and a half years, this bookseller and ethnologist wandered at great lengths, and at considerable expense to the American taxpayers, back and forth along the Mexican border and, more often, up and down far away from it, usually attended by a sizable entourage. To such an extent and to such far places did he roam that his trips have been disrespectfully referred to as the original junkets which set the tone and pace for later travels by restless government officials. The matter is probably debatable. Bartlett always furnished plausible reasons for his wanderings, and at least wrote an interesting book with a title nearly as long as his journeys: *Personal Narrative of Explorations and Incidents in Texas, New Mexico, California, Sonora, and Chihuahua, Connected with the United States and Mexico Boundary Commission, During the Years 1850, '51, '52, and '53* — and this became a mine of information for later travelers on the southwestern frontier.

His family was an old and respected one in Rhode Island but young Bartlett, although born in Providence, had been reared in Canada. He returned when a young man to Providence, where he worked as a clerk in his uncle's dry-goods store, and then

[2] At the John Carter Brown Library, Providence, Rhode Island.

became a bank cashier. In his spare time he studied natural science, helped form the Providence Athenaeum, and joined the Rhode Island Historical Society in 1831. The Royal Society of Northern Antiquaries of Copenhagen, Denmark, made queries in 1834 about Dighton Rock on the Taunton River in Massachusetts, a rock which was first observed by the colonists in 1680 to bear many mysterious inscriptions, and which became the subject for more weird speculations than any other subject of antiquity in America. These blurred and esoteric inscriptions were attributed in the nineteenth century to the Phoenicians, Norsemen, and some thirty other unprovable sources, but modern photography has shown that they were probably mostly meaningless scribblings by Indians, sober or otherwise. Anyway, the Royal Society of Copenhagen wanted to know more about them, on the theory that they might be Norse runes, and Bartlett obliged the Danes with two carefully drawn sketches. This began an international pen-pal friendship which Bartlett later sought to develop by obtaining the post of minister to Denmark.

Two years after his Dighton Rock researches, young Bartlett, who was not yet thirty, moved to New York, where he became a partner in a bookstore, dealing mostly in imported foreign books. He became the corresponding secretary of the New York Historical Society and a great friend of old Albert Gallatin, who had been Secretary of the Treasury under Presidents Jefferson and Madison and, at times, the minister to France and to Great Britain. Bartlett and Gallatin founded the American Ethnological Society in 1842, Bartlett's particular attention being a study of the origins and customs of the American Indians. His bookstore became a center for people interested in the natives of the Americas and he is credited with arousing the curiosity of E. G. Squier and John L. Stephens in Central America, both of whom became pioneer explorers in that long neglected region and started the ball rolling for the later great activities in Mayan archaeology. If only for guiding these two men, Bartlett deserves the gratitude of archaeologists.

But Bartlett also had a claim to recognition in his own right, for during these busy New York years he produced three books of his own, one of which, a *Dictionary of Americanisms* (1848) ran to four editions and was a sort of trail-breaker for H. L. Mencken's work along the same lines nearly a century later. So it can be seen that Bartlett had made his mark as a scholar of some note before he turned toward the American West.

In 1849, he returned to Providence from New York, where he had found it increasingly difficult to support a wife and four children. The Whigs had won the presidential election of 1848 and Bartlett went to Washington to see President Zachary Taylor about the appointment as minister to Denmark. He bore along a letter from "my venerable friend Mr. Gallatin" to John C. Calhoun, who introduced him to Senators Jefferson Davis of Mississippi and Thomas Hart Benton of Missouri. He also obtained the backing of Senator Stephen A. Douglas of Illinois. It seems strange that a man seeking a Whig appointment should have called on these leaders of the Democratic opposition, and perhaps it did him no good, for he was unsuccessful in his quest. At that point John C. Frémont resigned as boundary commissioner and Senator John H. Clarke of Rhode Island secured the position for Bartlett. Bartlett found a place for the senator's son on the commission, which had sad consequences, for the boy was later murdered near El Paso.

Bartlett no sooner received this appointment, on June 15, 1850, than his troubles began. It seemed as if every ambitious and adventuresome young man in the East wanted a job with the commission which had such promise for excitement and romance in its exploration of the unknown Golden West. The gold fever was at its height and the commission was headed for regions which were believed to have the promise of another Eldorado, possibly even greater than California. Hundreds of applications, endorsed by influential members of Congress, poured in and Bartlett had the disagreeable task of boiling down the number to a hundred-odd picked men, most of whom, alas, like Senator Clarke's son, it was necessary to choose for political reasons rather than for experience. Among his best choices were Dr. Thomas H. Webb as secretary and surgeon, who was also the secretary of the Massachusetts Historical Society, and John C. Cremony, a journalist then working on the *Boston Herald*, who was made Indian interpreter because of his previous experience in the Southwest.[3] Besides these white-collar appointees, the expedition was overmanned with all sorts of craftsmen, such as tailors, bootmakers, and saddlers, of which number Bartlett's surveyor, A. B. Gray, later estimated about four fifths were utterly useless. But the pressure from Washington was probably too great for the inexperienced Bartlett to resist and he was loaded down with the government boondogglers of the time.

The next step was to outfit the expedition, and again Bartlett was burdened with ill-chosen gear and supplies. It was assumed that the astronomical and surveying equipment of the old commission in San Diego would be brought on to El Paso and so but little attention was given to procuring additional or better instruments — an omission which later caused great delays. His brother, George Bartlett, was appointed commissary and bought general supplies, clothing, wagons and ambulances in huge quantities, and even obtained four iron boats, which could each be disassembled into four pieces, for use on the Rio Grande and

---

[3] John C. Cremony later wrote an interesting book, *Life Among the Apaches* (San Francisco 1868), in which he relates many of the adventures of the Bartlett commission.

the Gila River. One of these was shipped around Cape Horn to San Diego, but none was ever used. Lieutenant Isaac G. Strain of the United States Navy was attached to the expedition to supervise this flotilla, and although he never launched a boat, the lieutenant later earned his salt by organizing and commanding the cavalry detachment of the expedition in Texas. Another civilian quartermaster was sent ahead to Texas to buy horses and mules, which, however, nearly all proved unfit when the main party arrived. And so it went to prove that the ivory tower of scholarship and book selling was a mean preparation for surveying the wild and woolly West.

Besides the workaday personnel, a small but esoteric brain trust of species-mongering scientists was attached which included botanists, zoologists, and geologists to collect and report upon the flora, fauna, and formations of the country to be explored; also surgeons, and a full-time draughtsman and artist, Henry C. Pratt of Boston, a landscape painter of some reputation. Bartlett, of course, served as the expedition's ethnologist, and he seemed to take this duty more seriously than the business of establishing a boundary line. It became woe to any stray Indian within range because he was ruthlessly submitted to an hours-long quiz on how to pronounce two hundred fundamental words in his language, which Commissioner Bartlett meticulously wrote down in phonetic English while the hapless victim squirmed. Two large collections of specimens were garnered by these scientists, one for the Smithsonian Institution, the other for Harvard College, and these probably lie in dusty vaults to this day. This precedent was later followed by all sizable government exploring expeditions, and the reports on the flora, fauna, and geology of the unknown West were of great interest to the contemporaneous public and to posterity.

In August, 1850, the commission, with its supplies and equipment, sailed in two detachments from New York for New Orleans. Its total strength was one hundred and eleven civilians and officers, accompanied by a military escort of eighty-five men of the 3rd Infantry under the command of Lieutenant Colonel L. S. Craig, a gallant officer who became a stanch friend of Bartlett, and who met a violent and tragic death, as did several others, during the course of the survey. All reshipped from New Orleans to Indianola, Texas, then the main seaport for San Antonio and the interior of Texas.

There the party reassembled and were met by the advance quartermaster, who had bought about one hundred horses and mules which, alas, were mostly found below standard, as were the wagons which had been brought along from New York. While waiting for these deficiencies to be filled, the party moved thirty miles inland to the pretty little town of Victoria. The teamsters and blacksmiths kept busy breaking in and shoeing the unbroken Texas mules as they arrived, and many of the Eastern tenderfeet got their first bite of Texas dust after somersaulting from the back of a bucking native mule.

The engineers and their assistants were commanded by the expedition's astronomer, Brevet Lieutenant Colonel John McClellan of Pennsylvania, a West Pointer and a member of the elite Corps of Topographical Engineers, who had won promotion for gallantry during the Mexican War, but whose addiction to strong liquors was soon to bring about his recall. These engineers were formed into a cavalry corps under the command of the lone naval officer, Lieutenant Isaac G. Strain, and the men were uniformed in blue flannel shirts, dark pantaloons, and broad-brimmed white felt hats. By careful drilling Strain brought this corps to a state of "very respectable appearance." The mechanics and other laborers formed a rifle corps on foot, with the same uniform except that they wore red flannel shirts. All were armed with rifles or carbines, and many of the cavalry with Colt's revolvers, called six-shooters.

The party suffered from the famous Texas September heat, when it seemed as if the blistering summer was increasing rather than waning and the thermometer reached 102° in the shade, and this especially affected the bibulous Colonel McClellan, whom Bartlett tactfully referred to as being seriously ill. Finally the colonel recovered enough to report for duty, and the new mules and horses having been shod and semibroken to harness and saddle, the expedition moved out toward San Antonio on September 21.

On the fourth day of this trek the first of a long series of murders occurred when one of the Texas teamsters, hired at Indianola, shot and killed a Mexican who had ordered him off his property. Bartlett promptly paid the expenses of the deceased's funeral and placed the murderer under arrest in a tent; but he escaped that night, stole a horse from the picket line, and disappeared into the darkness, never to be seen again. The killing of a Mexican in Texas was only considered a misdemeanor and little effort was made by the local authorities to catch the fugitive.

The party arrived in San Antonio before the end of the month and marked the event by another murder, again by a Texas teamster, who shamefully cut up the unarmed butcher of the commission with his bowie knife in a particularly brutal and cowardly attack. The murderer then seized a nearby horse and dashed out into the brush and chaparral, but he was quickly pursued by some of the mounted engineers, captured at pistol point, and turned over to the civil authorities. Bartlett, hearing that there was a plot among the other Texas teamsters to free him, detailed six men of the commission to guard the jail, and the culprit was later tried and sentenced to fifteen years' im-

prisonment. But, when Bartlett returned on his way home, he
learned that the murderer had escaped after serving only two
years. Life was cheap in Texas but the commissioner seemed to
take it all in his stride.

It was in San Antonio that the capable naval officer, Isaac G.
Strain, finally had his fill of the hard-drinking habits of Colonel
McClellan, with whom he was forced to associate closely, and,
resigning his position, he returned to Washington, where he
preferred charges against the colonel of habitual drunkenness
and conduct unbecoming an officer and a gentleman. These
charges later caught up with McClellan after the expedition
reached El Paso and caused his recall to Washington. Incidentally, Strain afterwards achieved some note by exploring the
Isthmus of Panama,[4] and died from the results of his hardships
there.

They remained for about two weeks in San Antonio, where
they bought additional mules and wagons, and a hundred head
of beef cattle to drive on the hoof on the long trek of over six
hundred miles across the little known plains and deserts to El
Paso. Bartlett then decided to divide the rather cumbersome
party into two parts and to proceed forward himself with about
thirty men, lightly equipped, along the new and shorter, but
less known, northern trail through Fredericksburg, so as to arrive as nearly as possible to the agreed meeting day with the
Mexican commission on November first. The rest of the expedition, with all the big wagons and heavy equipment, followed
along the usual southern route, through Castroville and on westward.

The advance party set out in style, all well mounted on horses
and mules and armed to the teeth with rifles and Colt's revolvers.

---

[4] See *A Paper on the History and Prospects of Interocean Communication
by the American Isthmus*. Read before the New York Historical Society, June
17, 1856, by Lieutenant Isaac G. Strain, U.S.N.

Six light wagons, each drawn by five mules, carried the supplies and equipment, and Commissioner Bartlett led the way in a fancy vehicle, drawn by four mules, which was "called in New York a Rockaway" and which could be turned into "an excellent sleeping place." It could also have been dubbed an armory, for Dr. Thomas Webb, who as surgeon and secretary shared the Rockaway, the driver, and Bartlett himself were armed with several rifles and pistols apiece, with more hung on the sides and top of the carriage. The commissioner noted that he "occasionally resorted to a mule by way of variety," for being slowly dragged along in a cramped carriage was a dull way to travel, and he always made a point of walking a few miles every day at the start, a practice good for man and beast, which example was followed by the others. The train seldom moved faster than a walk and set out every morning at seven o'clock so as to make a daily average of about twenty miles by two in the afternoon, when it halted and turned out the animals to graze. At night the seven wagons were formed into a semicircle and the tents of the party closed the gap to form a corral for the animals. All were under semimilitary discipline, guards were regularly posted, and young Edward C. Clarke, the son of the Rhode Island senator, was appointed acting quartermaster in charge of all forage and provisions.

The party passed through the thrifty frontier German settlements around Fredericksburg and on into Indian country where the Comanches, Lipans, and Apaches held almost complete sway and had prevented the German pioneers from entering. They traveled for two days through a huge prairie dog town with the usual parasitic rattlesnakes and small owls sharing the burrows of the industrious owners. Upon leaving this, Bartlett met his first bona fide wild Indian in the person of an elderly, benevolent, and rather corpulent Lipan chief who bore a striking resemblance to General Lewis Cass, the unsuccessful Democratic presidential candidate in the last election. The chief shattered the commissioner's ideal of the noble red man by immediately asking for a drink of whisky and was nonplused when Bartlett truthfully asserted that he always drank water and carried no whisky with him. The chief, however, was well informed about the amenities when men of distinction met on the plains and must have considered the commissioner a mean fellow indeed; and this belief was strengthened the next morning when the poor old fellow, shivering in the dawn, after spending a cold night on the ground, tapped on the window of Bartlett's carriage and chattered through his teeth, "*Mucho frio — poco de visky*," and was unchristianly tendered a cup of hot coffee. During all his Western travels, Bartlett never gave liquor to the Indians — which probably prevented petty disorders about the camp but incurred the long-range hostility of the thirsty savages, who never believed him and showed their disapproval by repeatedly stampeding the expedition's livestock.

The small party crossed the Concho and the Pecos Rivers, the latter at the famous Horsehead Crossing, so named from the skulls of horses and mules which lined the bank, and ran into the usual difficulties in finding good water in the arid country beyond. Their provisions ran low, for the hard bread was found to be riddled by weevils, but luckily an occasional stray ox or cow, abandoned by some earlier emigrant train, was found and shot for food. Indian signs were seen and the tension of continual vigilance and the rigors of a howling norther, bringing snow, added to the general exhaustion of the plodding caravan.

This advance party reached the small military post at Franklin, across the Rio Grande from the Mexican town of El Paso del Norte, on November 13, Bartlett arriving in his de luxe carriage, which had been shoved and hauled by manpower through the rough mountain passes just to the east. The journey of about six hundred and thirty-five miles from San Antonio had taken thirty-three days, of which twenty-seven were spent in traveling — which was good going. The commanding officer at Franklin, Major Jefferson Van Horne, a West Pointer of the class of 1827, received them hospitably and assigned them all to comfortable quarters about the garrison. Bartlett's arrival was nearly two weeks late for the appointed meeting date of the joint boundary commission, and his sense of punctuality had fretted him along the way. But he need not have worried, for the Mexican commissioner, General Garcia Condé, was calmly waiting for him in the comparative comfort of the city of Chihuahua, far to the south.

CHAPTER II

Collations and Controversies

THE name El Paso is confusing. At the time of Bartlett's arrival it properly applied to the Mexican town of about three thousand inhabitants, El Paso del Norte, on the south side of the Rio Grande, but this name was later changed to Juarez, which it holds today. To compound the confusion for the present-day reader, that international river below El Paso was then usually called the Rio Bravo by the Mexicans. Across the river, the tiny American settlement of Franklin later became El Paso, Texas, and thus gained the original Mexican name.

In Franklin was the warehouse of James Magoffin, a famous trader with Chihuahua and Mexico, who had given great help to the invading Americans during the late war with Mexico, and whose wife, Susan Shelby Magoffin, wrote that delightful classic of the frontier, *Down the Santa Fe Trail and into Mexico.* Magoffin cashed Bartlett's drafts, helped him replenish his supplies, and generally made himself invaluable as was his wont with newly arrived American officials.

Bartlett sent word of his arrival to General Condé and used the interim to explore the surrounding country and attend a round of banquets and collations — what a shame that word has been succeeded by "cocktail party." He must have just missed one of the almost fabulous characters of the Southwest, "The

Great Western," for it is certain she had been in El Paso the
year before and Bartlett would surely have mentioned such a
flaming personality in his narrative if she had been around. Probably she had joined one of the emigrant trains and moved on to
California before his arrival.

The Great Western was a giant of a woman, over six feet
tall, with a man's stalwart frame, who, old Rip Ford, a Texan
forty-niner, said "had the reputation of being something of the
roughest fighter on the Rio Grande; and was approached in a
polite if not humble manner . . ." [1] She was one of those interesting but tantalizing persons about whom there are brief snap-
shot descriptions in various personal memoirs but no continued
account of her unusual career. She was evidently a sort of moth-
erly amazon who had been an integral and official part of our
long-ago army, a formidable virago on occasion, but an extremely brave and kind woman who had made a splendid record
in the Mexican War and had become a great favorite with the
officers and men. She seems to have begun her military career
as the wife of a soldier in the 7th Infantry and was employed
as a laundress, under which calling a certain number of enlisted
men's wives were allowed to accompany their husbands in the
field. She ran a mess for the younger officers of that regiment
at Corpus Christi, Texas, when General Zachary Taylor concentrated his forces there in the winter of 1845–1846.

The following spring Taylor moved his small army southward
to the Rio Grande, a move which brought on the war with Mexico. The Great Western accompanied the troops across the
plains of south Texas, which were teeming with game and colorful with the wildflowers of the season. A halt was made at the
Arroyo Colorado, where the Mexicans, hidden in the brush of

---

[1] "From Texas to California in 1849. Diary of C. C. Cox," edited by Mabelle
Eppard Martin, *Southwestern Historical Quarterly*, October 1925.

the opposite bank, made a show of resistance with much shouting and many bugle calls. These guerrillas were quickly scattered by a charge led by General William Jenkins Worth, the Achilles of Taylor's army, but not before The Great Western had offered to charge and clean out the enemy, saying that if the general would lend her a pair of tongs she would wade the river and whip every scoundrel Mexican that dared show his face. The chances were strong that she probably would have.

Later, after Taylor had left a small detachment on the Rio Grande opposite Matamoros, while he led his main forces down the river to its mouth to secure a base for seaborne supplies, The Great Western set up her mess for the officers of this detached group. The Mexicans opened an intense artillery bombardment from across the river and the other half-dozen or so American women were rushed to the comparative safety of one of the underground magazines. But not The Great Western! She had begun to prepare breakfast when the firing began and neither hell, high water, nor bursting shells were going to interfere with that duty. She continued her cooking over an open fire, served breakfast, with plenty of hot coffee, to all the officers, and then carried more coffee to the artillerymen serving the guns. She did the same for lunch and dinner, under shellfire, and kept up this routine for a week with the meals always ready on time, until Taylor returned, fighting his way through the main Mexican army, to relieve the beleaguered garrison. At one time, when the situation looked particularly grim and desperate, she had applied for a musket and ammunition and announced she would defend herself to the end.[2]

Later on in the war, Dr. A. Wislizenus, "a German by birth but an American by choice," who had accompanied Colonel

---

[2] Brantz Mayer, *History of the War Between Mexico and the United States*, Vol. 1 (New York and London 1848), pp. 185–188.

William Doniphan's famous Missouri Volunteers from Chihuahua City to Saltillo, wrote that in the latter city: "I stopped for
some hours in the hotel of the 'Great Western,' kept by the celebrated *vivandière*, honored with that *nom de guerre*, and whose
fearless behavior during the battle of Buena Vista was highly
praised; she dressed many wounded soldiers on that day, and even
carried them out of the thickest fight." [3]

A Texas veteran of this same battle gave another account of
her activities which was just as creditable to her although it
placed her a few miles away in her hotel in Saltillo. However,
as that dingdong battle lasted for over two days, she may well
have been in both places during the fighting. The Mexican
lancers, at one point, actually chased a regiment of Indiana
volunteers off the field and some of them into Saltillo, which was
about seven miles to the north. This Texan, years later, said:

There is a story the boys tell, I don't know whether it is true or
not. There was a big woman they called the Great Western. She was
a great nurse, and always went with Taylor's army. She stood six
feet two; she was a great nurse and would always get up at any time
of night to get one something to eat — kept a sort of restaurant; they
all knew her, and the boys tell about one of the Indianans, that when
they broke through, two of Miñon's cavalry made a dash at them on
horseback, and after running them about two hundred yards they
found this fellow was leaving the horses so badly he threw up his
hands, says "My God! It is no use running that fellow any longer."
It was about three hundred yards to Saltillo, and a jack-rabbit broke
up, and he passed the jack like he was standing, went into Saltillo and
rushed right down to sort of headquarters for everybody, the Great
Western's, and he came running in breathless and told the Great
Western that General Taylor was whipped and the army was all cut
to pieces, and the Mexicans under full headway for Saltillo. She just

[3] A. Wislizenus, M.D., *Memoir of A Tour to Northern Mexico Connected
with Col. Doniphan's Expedition in 1846 and 1847*, Sen. Exec. Doc. Misc. No.
26. 30 Cong. 1st Sess. (Washington 1848), p. 75.

drew off and hit him between the eyes and knocked him sprawling; says, "You damned son of a bitch, there aint Mexicans enough in Mexico to whip old Taylor." She says, "You just spread that report and I'll beat you to death." You can imagine how tall she was, she could stand flat-footed and drop these little sugar plums right into my mouth, that way. She was an immense woman, would whip most anybody in a rough and tumble fight.[4]

Her husband appears to have evaporated during the war, perhaps killed in action, for she attached herself to a squadron of the 2nd Dragoons, under Major L. P. Graham, which was ordered, in July 1848, after the treaty of peace, to ride overland from Monterey,* Mexico, to California. There was a rather unreliable report that she had to marry (at least temporarily) one of the dragoons to obtain the official status necessary to accompany the detachment, and she was said to have appeared before the troopers carrying her blanket roll and cooking utensils and demanded a man to share her bed and board. She was immensely popular and had a reputation as a wonderful cook so she probably had her pick of the squadron — without any special benefit of clergy. On the way, she became ill and was left at the city of Chihuahua. Later, after much privation, suffering, and hardship, she somehow reached El Paso.

In April, 1849, Lieutenant Henry Chase Whiting, a topographical engineer, who had just explored a route from San Antonio to El Paso, met her and wrote in his journal:

As I went down in the evening with Lieutenant Smith and Howard to cross to El Paso, the first person we met, passing in the dug-

---

[4] This account was originally dictated to the historian Hubert Howe Bancroft or one of his aides and is now in the Bancroft Library at the University of California. Excerpts were published as "George Washington Trahern: Texan Cowboy Soldier from Mier to Buena Vista," edited by A. Russell Buchanan, in the *Southwestern Historical Quarterly* of July, 1954.

* The town in the state of Nuevo Leon near Texas. Then spelled with one *r* and not to be confused with Monterey, California.

out, was the celebrated Great Western. Never was anyone more
delighted at the sight of American officers than she appeared. Her
masculine arms lifted us one after another off our feet.[5]

Old Rip Ford also reported that she had opened a hotel on
the American side of the river by July, 1849, and was recalled
with gratitude by many of the more than four thousand forty-
niners who passed through El Paso that year, because she treated
them with much kindness.

The real name and later fate of this stanch amazon seem unknown. A pity, because The Great Western sweated out a
whole war in contrast to the one-day stand of the famous Molly
Pitcher. And after The Great Western's war, women were never
again officially allowed to accompany their husbands in a campaign.

But to return to the border commissions, General Condé
reached El Paso in early December and Commissioner Bartlett
crossed the Rio Grande with a small staff to call upon him and
his assistants, an agreeable mission as they found the Mexican
engineers to be graduates of the Chapultepec Military School
and gentlemen of education. The interpreter was Don Felipe
de Iturbide, the youngest son of Mexico's late and only emperor
to that time. A Swedish soldier of fortune, Colonel Langberg,
was in command of the Mexican military forces which had just
arrived from Chihuahua City to protect the frontier against the
mounting Indian attacks; for northern Mexico had been desolated by the Apaches and Comanches since the withdrawal of
the Spaniards in 1821, and these attacks had intensified during
the disruptions of the defeats and losses of the war with the
United States. The joint commission of the two countries (minus
the official American surveyor, A. B. Gray, who had not yet

[5] "Journal of William Henry Chase Whiting, 1849," *Exploring Southwest Trails 1846–1854*, edited by Ralph P. Bieber (Glendale, California, 1938).

appeared) then got down to serious business and had frequent meetings to arrange the actual matter of surveying.

About a week after the first meeting with General Condé, the main body of the American commission arrived and went into quarters at two small villages down the Rio Grande from El Paso. Its heavy wagons carrying supplies and surveying equipment had creaked slowly along the southern route, guarded by the military escort under Colonel Craig. On the way there had been another murder committed when a cashiered army officer, a West Pointer named Stephen Decatur Dobbins, who had been employed as a guide and hunter by his old friend Colonel McClellan, shot and killed the train's wagon master. Dobbins surrendered to the authorities upon arrival and was tried and acquitted on the grounds of self-defense, but soon afterwards committed suicide with a pistol in McClellan's quarters.

Bartlett had received word from Washington of the recall of Colonel McClellan, stemming from the charges of Lieutenant Strain, and of his replacement by Brevet Lieutenant Colonel James Duncan Graham, another topographical engineer and West Pointer, who had previously surveyed the final boundary between Maine and Canada. The commissioner's immediate problem was to break the news gently to McClellan, who had been a topographical engineer since 1838. That organization was extremely sensitive about its dignity and reputation and Bartlett had been requested by Alexander H. H. Stuart, the Secretary of the Interior, under whose authority the commission worked, "to wound as little as possible the high-toned and gentlemanly corps of which he is a member" and to permit the colonel to leave on the score of illness. McClellan again became indisposed after his arrival and kept to his quarters, where he was well covered by his loyal aide, Lieutenant Amiel Weeks Whipple, who answered his correspondence and refused to commit the colonel to any appointments on the ground of illness. Bartlett tactfully suggested to McClellan that he resign because of ill-health. The colonel wrathfully refused, and Bartlett was then compelled to notify him that he had been officially recalled because of the charges preferred against him but did not reveal their source. McClellan evidently blamed the guiltless Bartlett and left for the East with several other disaffected men to initiate a stream of complaints against the commissioner.

Other troubles broke out in the immediate vicinity. The Indians (probably Apaches) drove off many of Mr. Magoffin's mules one night under the noses of several men of the commission who were sleeping in wagons in the corral from which the animals were taken, but so quietly and expertly was it done that the loss was not discovered until the morning. A less quiet and more serious outbreak was the murder, in January 1851, of young Edward C. Clarke (the son of Bartlett's personal friend the United States senator from Rhode Island). Young Clarke was knifed to pieces at a Mexican dance, or fandango, by a gang of border ruffians who had kept the Mexicans, on the American side of the Rio Grande, in a state of terror. But this unprovoked murder was the last straw, for a posse of Mexicans and Americans arrested eight or nine of the desperadoes, although the leader of the affray escaped.

The accused were tried in one of the adobe houses; the judge, clerk, attorneys, and the mixed jury — half Mexican, half heavily bearded Americans — were all armed with pistols or rifles and all smoking pipes or cigarettes. The reckless unconcern of the prisoners, who treated the affair as a farce, and the armed spectators, also smoking and dressed in serapes and overcoats, made the scene remarkable for a courtroom. Three of the accused, all of whom had been with the boundary commission, were found guilty and promptly hanged the same afternoon in the village plaza. The escaped leader was soon afterwards caught, tried, found guilty and hanged from the same tree. The rest of the local ruffians then made a speedy exit from the district.

In the meanwhile Colonel Craig and the military escort had moved up to the abandoned Santa Rita copper mines, about ninety miles northwest in the mountains of New Mexico, because of the lack of forage and provisions around El Paso; Lieutenant Whipple had temporarily assumed the duties of chief astronomer while awaiting the arrival of Colonel Graham, who was coming to replace McClellan, and had sent out several small parties to survey the vicinity of El Paso; and Bartlett, between trips to nearby Indian ruins, met with the Mexican commissioners and made a fateful agreement with them.

The Treaty of Guadalupe Hidalgo had placed the boundary between the territory of New Mexico, which was ceded to the United States, and the Mexican state of Chihuahua along a line running west from a point on the Rio Grande eight miles north of El Paso del Norte as shown on Disturnell's *Map of Mexico and Texas*, published in New York in 1847.[6] The purpose of this line was to leave the town of El Paso del Norte in Mexico and yet allow room for a wagon road or railroad to California within the new southern boundary of the United States. It so happened that Disturnell's map was incorrect about the latitude of El Paso, which was placed about forty miles too far south. Bartlett, on his own responsibility, then made a deal with the persuasive General Condé in which he swapped latitude for longitude. His argument was that the latitude of El Paso del Norte had been incorrectly shown on Disturnell's map and therefore this should be corrected on the survey, a course, as he wrote

<hr />

[6] John Disturnell was a New York compiler and publisher of popular guidebooks, which included the *Western Traveller, Emigrants' Guide*, and *Summer Resorts*. His famous but inaccurate *Map of Mexico* was reputed to have been pirated.

Secretary of Interior Stuart, "that any geographer would have pursued if unbiased by any sinister motive." Also he claimed that for making this concession to the Mexicans, they, in return, had allowed the southern boundary line to run farther west before turning due north to the Gila River (or to its nearest branch as the treaty read), and thus had allowed the inclusion of the famous and valuable Santa Rita copper mines in American territory.

This agreement was strongly opposed by Lieutenant Whipple, the only topographical engineer on the spot, by Mr. A. B. Gray, the official surveyor, a native Texan, who had also been the surveyor of the original commission in San Diego, when he arrived with Colonel Graham; by Colonel Graham when he finally appeared the next July; and by Major William H. Emory, who succeeded all of them, and finally successfully completed the survey. Their counterargument was that the controversial map had been used solely because it was the only one available to the peace commissioners in the town of Guadalupe Hidalgo when the treaty was drafted. They admitted that it was incorrect as to the latitude of El Paso del Norte, but claimed this error was immaterial as the map had been used only to show that the line should run eight miles north of the town, regardless of latitude. They seemed to suspect that Bartlett's compromise with Condé was a case of a New England Yankee blithely disregarding the needs of Texas and the South for a way to California, following the road opened by Philip St. George Cooke and his Mormon Battalion during the Mexican War, which was largely through the disputed area.

But Bartlett overrode Whipple's opposition and ordered him to establish an initial point for the westward survey from the Rio Grande about forty miles (instead of eight) north of El Paso del Norte. The young lieutenant obeyed but wrote a letter to the commissioner in which he stated his opposition to this point, which, at least, put his opinion on record.

Both sides had plausible arguments but the decision of time seems to be that Bartlett was wrong. As a matter of hard fact, they all were wrong except Emory, because it was soon found that the only suitable route was south of both lines, which Emory, who had ridden with General Stephen Kearny in his famous dash to California in 1846, knew and had vainly tried to impress upon his superiors. Fortunately this additional needed land was obtained by the Gadsden Purchase in 1853, and so all ended happily. Probably there was a modicum of truth in the belief that Bartlett was inclined to favor the Mexicans. The opposition to the Mexican War had been deep and intense among the Whigs in New England, where it was looked upon as a plot to gain more territory for the expansion of slavery, and Bartlett, possibly subconsciously, may have shared this prejudice.

In April, 1851, Bartlett moved the headquarters of the over-manned and idle commission, at a standstill until the arrival of Colonel Graham and Mr. A. B. Gray, to the more salubrious Santa Rita copper mines, which had once been profitably worked but had been abandoned by the Mexicans in 1838 because of the fury of Apache attacks; today these famous mines are still worked by a subsidiary of the Kennecott Copper Company. On the way, Commissioner Bartlett dashed hither and yon from the line of march of the long caravan to explore Indian ruins and examine geological formations which he sketched in detail. While skittering ethnologically about, he was thrown by a mule and then kicked in the shoulder as well, which stopped his sketching and confined him to his cot or chair for two weeks, while his friend Colonel Craig nursed him with the care of a mother. General Condé and the entire Mexican commission ar-

rived shortly afterwards and both parties set up the usual round
of collations in the cool air and green fertility of this mountain
site, where Craig and his soldiers had been for several months.

Bartlett recovered quickly from his injury and decided to
visit the Mexican state of Sonora while awaiting the arrival of
the tardy Colonel Graham, who was by then several months
overdue. He nicely rationalized this trip as serving the useful
purposes of inspecting Philip St. George Cooke's original wagon
road to the Pacific, of inducing the people of Sonora to renew
their old trade with the copper mines, and, above all, of establishing sources of food supplies for the future surveying parties
on the Gila River.

So, on May 16, 1851, Commissioner Bartlett and Colonel
Craig, with eight members of the staff, accompanied by four
wagons drawn by six mules each, with the attending drivers and
helpers, set out to follow the trail over which Philip St. George
Cooke had brought the first wagons through to California south
of the Oregon Trail. Bartlett's arm caused him to ride in his
tried and true carriage but the others were all mounted on horses
or mules. The way led at first through a waterless and barren
country and Bartlett noted that Cooke deserved great credit for
his bold and successful pioneering in this unknown and difficult land, a feat which had not been sufficiently appreciated by
his countrymen.

The little band rode happily on, with Bartlett noting the
change in flora and fauna as they descended into the hot desert
country. The party encountered herds of wild and ferocious
cattle, abandoned by their owners because of the Apaches, the
same breed which had actually charged Colonel Cooke's column
in 1846 and caused much damage. One wild bull treed Bartlett's
carriage driver, and, at night, their bellows and mooings, with
the unearthly barkings and yelpings of the coyotes, made an

uncanny cacophony under the moon which disturbed the slumbers of the party. Bartlett's other complaint was about a Mexican teamster named Jesus who acted as a very inefficient guide. The commissioner grumpily noted that this name was common in Mexico, especially among the lower classes, and that there were two working for the commission, "both of whom . . . proved entirely unworthy of it."

Turning south off Cooke's old road, the column plodded on through rough chaparral until they entered a well-watered and fertile valley in which lay the Mexican town of Fronteras, Sonora. They were greeted by General Carrasco, who had recently arrived with a detachment of ragged and barefooted soldiers to try to re-establish the town, abandoned because of Apache attacks. The general had taken the aggressive against these hated savages and had led an attack upon them at the town of Janos in the neighboring state of Chihuahua, much to the rage of the military authorities in the latter state, who had made a separate peace with the Apaches, and eagerly bought livestock and goods stolen in Sonora — an example of the chaotic condition of the Mexican frontier.

After a few repairs and a short rest the small band pushed on southward along rough mule paths, through an upland valley which reminded Bartlett of the scenery of Vermont and New Hampshire. His carriage was somehow shoved and hauled through this scenic but difficult mountain country.

The Mexicans met on the way had a stock answer to all questions about distances, locations, population, customs, and in fact about anything at all, "*Quien sabe?*" (Who knows?). Finally they reached the town of Arispe, in a beautiful mountain park where the weary travelers were wined and dined by the officers of the Mexican garrison and the local priest. This place had once been the capital of Sonora, with a population of about

five thousand people, but civil wars and Indian attacks had reduced the number to some fifteen hundred and the state government had been removed to Ures, a town farther south. However, it was the best built Mexican town Bartlett had yet seen,
and he was particularly interested in the church, whose proportions were unpleasing, as its length, as in most churches of that
frontier, where long timbers were unobtainable, was too great
for its width. He attended Mass and was interested to hear the
orchestra, largely clarionets, play several "popular Ethiopian
airs, such as 'Dearest May,' " and in the singing by two girls
who seemed to have learned "under the tuition of the Chinese."

Provisions were as scarce in Arispe as in the other frontier
Mexican towns, and the Americans were unable to load their
wagons, as they had hoped, with fresh vegetables and fruits, one
reason being that they were not in season, which Bartlett seemed
to have overlooked before setting out on his quest. However,
they enjoyed what few vegetables and fruits were available and,
in return, entertained the Mexicans by their use of toothbrushes,
which was considered a very droll habit indeed. After three
days in pleasant Arispe the party started on the back track to
the copper mines in the first week of June, 1851.

The usual mishaps with broken wheels, wagon tongues, and
other gear of the vehicles were experienced on this return trip,
and these troubles were endemic and constant in that rough
country, so that the party was forced to stay over for four days
in Fronteras for repairs. We are prone to romanticize today our
ancestors who went West in covered wagons but, in truth, it
must have been largely monotonous drudgery, interspersed with
moments of terror from attacks and stampedes by the ever-
threatening savage Indians.

In Fronteras the party ran head on into a full-scale local fiesta
which culminated in a grand fandango. Everybody in the town

and a fair share of the Americans proceeded to get gloriously drunk for the occasion, but evidently no harm was done, for Bartlett commented favorably on the Mexican tendency for fun and frolic when intoxicated in contrast to the belligerency of the Irish in the States when in the same condition. At the fandango the American tunes of "Oh, Susannah" and "Dan Tucker" were in high favor with all.

After this respite they again passed through the range of the bellowing and belligerent wild cattle and finally clattered into the camp at the copper mines about the middle of June, to find that there was still no word of Colonel Graham and Mr. Gray, who were by then about eight months overdue. Lieutenant Whipple, who was pinch-hitting as both astronomer and surveyor for the commission, two assignments which he was perfectly capable of filling, had been surveying the boundary line west from Bartlett's initial point on the Rio Grande, but he lacked certain necessary instruments and suggested waiting for Graham before continuing, to which Bartlett perforce agreed.

CHAPTER III

Apaches, Engineers, and Excursions

ON the day of Bartlett's return to Santa Rita, he received a state call from the great Apache chief Mangus Colorado (Red Sleeve), who was attended by about a dozen of his warriors, from the most deadly and dangerous of all the Western tribes. Mangus Colorado was an important leader who had met General Kearny on his way to California, near this same spot almost five years before, to offer his help against the Mexicans. Kearny's guide, the famous Kit Carson, had said to this with insight, "I would not trust one of them." Mangus Colorado told Bartlett that he and his men had shadowed the small American party for days on its trip to Sonora and considered their abstention from hostilities or livestock stampeding as the acid test of friendship, which should unquestionably be royally rewarded by nothing less than much whisky. Bartlett gave his truthful stock answer to thirsty Indians, that he had none, and offered presents of shirts and beads instead. The Apaches didn't like that alternative at all nor did they believe that any Americans could possibly be without that indispensable beverage, and proceeded to sample all the catsup and vinegar bottles in the camp until convinced of the commissioner's word.

At the end of June two events broke the dull monotony of the idle commission. The first was the arrival of a party of New Mexican traders with a beautiful and young Mexican captive girl, named Inez Gonzalez, and a number of stolen horses and mules, all of which they had bought from Indian raiders into Mexico and were taking north to sell at a profit. Bartlett promptly impounded the girl, who was "quite young, artless, and interesting in appearance, prepossessing in manners, and by her deportment gave evidence that she had been carefully brought up," for he deemed it his duty, "and a pleasant one it certainly was, to extend over her the protection of the laws of the United States." He took no action about the horses and mules. Bartlett then sent word of his good deed to General Condé, who warmly approved and requested him to keep the girl under his protection (and expense) until she could be restored to her home. Inez then settled down in a camp of over one hundred men, the only female present, and spent her time in making new clothes for herself and in reading the few available Spanish books.

The other incident was the rescue of two captive Mexican boys, aged thirteen and twelve, from the hands of the Apaches. These boys had suddenly broken away from a large band of the Indians who were visiting the camp, and rushing into the tent of an American, had begged protection. Mangus Colorado, who was present, seemed unperturbed and suggested that Bartlett should settle the matter by buying the boys as was the usual local custom. Bartlett refused to buy or return the boys, and this time the Apaches were really angry and left the camp much offended. To be refused whisky among gentlemen was bad enough, but to have their personal property purloined on a friendly visit was beyond all toleration. Bartlett then sent off the Mexican boys to General Condé and appeased the indignant Apaches, who considered their race as at war with the Mexicans and consequently fully entitled to capture and sell captives of war, by finding a Mexican in the employ of the commission who paid a fair price in trade goods for the captives. The suspicion is strong that no Mexican teamster would or could have been so altruistic and that the humanitarian Bartlett and his friends actually supplied the purchase price for this unofficial transaction.

After this rather tactful solution of a delicate situation, the relations with the Apaches remained outwardly friendly. Bartlett presented Mangus Colorado with a splendid full suit of blue broadcloth which consisted of "a frock coat lined with scarlet and ornamented with gilt buttons, and of pantaloons, which, at the chief's request, were open from the knee downwards with a row of small fancy buttons on one side, and a broad strip of scarlet cloth on the outer side from the hip downwards, all according to the highest Mexican fashion." A white shirt and red silk sash completed the outfit. Mangus Colorado was delighted with this present but vexed the generous Bartlett by insisting on wearing his shirt outside his pants. Bartlett kept tucking the shirt in and Mangus Colorado kept pulling it out until the American commissioner bowed to the inevitable, although this breach of New York custom seemed to offend him more than the kidnaping of young Mexicans.

Bartlett, pursuing his course of concilation, often invited the Apache chiefs, particularly the resplendent Mangus Colorado, to dine with him, but he was disturbed by their habit of gorging themselves and then, after refilling their plates, beckoning to one of their friends who stood outside the tent to take the seat and finish the last, large helping. But the well-fed Apaches at least remained quiet and peaceful and made no attempt to run off the livestock of their generous hosts and providers. Certainly a meal on the plate was worth several on the hoof.

The commissioner's hospitality, or possibly gullible philan-
thropy, was evidently bruited abroad in the Indian world, for the
next visit was from a band of four hundred Navajos, distant blood
relations of the Apaches, who were a nomadic, warlike, and more
numerous tribe than the Apaches, and whose bailiwick was in the
north central part of the Territory of New Mexico. Bartlett was
impressed with their hand-woven blankets, which were far superior to other native fabrics and whose fame still continues,
but firmly refused them whisky in exchange. Some believed that
the Navajo visit was for the main purpose of spying out the
ground, the numbers of available livestock, and the strength of
the American guards — a supposition which was sadly confirmed
when the Navajos returned shortly afterwards at night to stampede and run off most of the commission's herd of horses and
mules, which was indeed a serious loss.

Shortly after this calamity, more trouble came, this time with
the Apaches, when one of the two Mexican employees whom
Bartlett had said were so unworthily named Jesus shot and seriously wounded an Apache brave. The result was almost an
armed clash, for the Indians, who had had tragic experiences in
the past in treacherous massacres by the whites, gathered fully
armed behind Mangus Colorado and prepared for battle. Colonel
Craig saved the situation by courageously walking unarmed toward them alone, reaffirming the friendship of all the Americans,
and inviting them to the questioning of the murderer, who had
been placed in irons; and the Apaches became convinced that
the shooting was a personal affair in which the Americans were
not involved. The wounded brave died from his wounds about
a month later and the real showdown then came. The Indians
finally agreed that the murderous Jesus should be punished, not
by hanging, but by the payment of his monthly wages to the

murdered man's wife, and that he should be kept in captivity indefinitely under this plan.

About the middle of July, 1851, the long awaited official surveyor, Mr. A. B. Gray of Texas, arrived at Santa Rita, accompanied by Lieutenant Ambrose Everett Burnside, later to win fame for his peculiar type of side whiskers, which have immortalized his last name as was and with the syllables reversed. Young Burnside became a thorn in the side of Bartlett, and one wonders if they later met on more friendly terms in Providence, in which city both resided after the Civil War, Burnside becoming a United States senator and a governor of Rhode Island. These men had arrived at El Paso with Colonel Graham, the tardy official astronomer, but the latter had remained in that town.

Lieutenant Colonel James Duncan Graham was one of the senior officers of the Corps of Topographical Engineers, a Virginian, a West Pointer, class of 1817, who had been with Major Stephen H. Long on the famous exploring trip to the Rocky Mountains in 1819–1820. He had resurveyed the Mason and Dixon line, and had won promotion for valuable and highly distinguished service in surveying the controversial boundary between the State of Maine and the bordering Canadian provinces. As can be seen, he had had a great deal of experience in the field and had at one time worked with and instructed A. B. Gray in surveying the boundary between the United States and the Republic of Texas, when Gray represented Texas. Graham married a sister of George Gordon Meade, the victor at Gettysburg, and was a Virginian who remained loyal to the Union. Today, Mount Graham in southeastern Arizona is named after him. Incidentally, his brother, Major Lawrence Pike Graham, had commanded the detachment of the 2nd Dragoons to which The

Great Western had attached herself in Mexico. Graham had been appointed "Principal Astronomer and Chief of the Scientific Corps" of the boundary commission in October, 1850, but explained his long delay in reporting for duty to the time spent in procuring the proper surveying instruments for the job.

There was something in his explanation. Being a methodical officer, he had first checked in Washington on all of Bartlett's correspondence for information about the equipment and instruments of the commission, and had found this a mess with no available data. He realized that the survey of about twenty-five hundred miles along the boundary would be the biggest project of its kind, up to that time, in the world, and became convinced from the evidence that Bartlett had left in great confusion without the proper equipment. Then he learned that the original commission had left most of its instruments in San Diego and that new ones would be absolutely necessary for any work performed out of El Paso. So Graham, quite properly as it seems, remained in the East, buying and testing new instruments, which were shipped from New York to Texas in January, 1851. He followed these to San Antonio, whence he accompanied the first available government train to El Paso, arriving there in June, about eight months after his appointment the previous October. Bartlett blamed Graham's tardiness for the delay in starting the border survey, and Graham blamed Bartlett for his failure to bring the proper instruments with him in the first place. It was a vicious circle of blaming but probably Graham was right, for a little more care at the start would have allowed Bartlett to supply the competent Lieutenant Whipple with the proper equipment; Whipple could have begun the survey at once; and his senior officer, Graham, would have arrived much sooner.

When Graham arrived at El Paso, he wrote Bartlett a polite letter announcing his presence and stating that as he understood

Bartlett planned to be in El Paso in the near future, he would meet him there as a matter of mutual convenience. Unfortunately, by a clerk's error a pencil copy of the letter was sent to Bartlett instead of the original written in ink, and this informal missive in that day of high-flown punctilio and formality (the redundant letters were always signed "your obedient servant") rubbed the commissioner's fur the wrong way at the start. Graham added further irritation by ordering Lieutenant Whipple to report to him in El Paso for a conference without informing Bartlett of this order, and Whipple, who well knew on which side his bread was buttered for the long haul, immediately obeyed.

Graham was thoroughly disgusted with the situation as he found it and noted that most of Bartlett's employees were incompetent, superfluous, and politically appointed, and that the commissioner sat, except for the junket into Mexico, with about one hundred and twenty of his men at the Santa Rita copper mines from April to August, 1851, all doing absolutely nothing but drawing their pay. As it so happened, Secretary of the Interior A. H. H. Stuart, back in Washington, had become as much annoyed as Bartlett at Graham's long delay in reporting for duty and had already requested that Major William H. Emory replace Graham. This request was granted, but of course nothing was known of this change in far-off New Mexico at the time.

Within a week after surveyor A. B. Gray's arrival, he sent Bartlett a letter in which he protested against the initial point on the Rio Grande for the westward survey as agreed upon by Commissioner Bartlett and General Condé, using the same argument as Whipple had, that it violated the intent of the Treaty of Guadalupe Hidalgo by not following Disturnell's map. Because of this incorrectly chosen initial point, Gray, a patriotic native son of the Lone Star State, who must have hated to see a southern route from Texas to the Pacific blocked by Bartlett's personal opinion on a questionable point, recommended that all surveying based on that initial point be immediately halted, and refused to sign the official documents as surveyor of the American boundary commission.

Bartlett replied that he was satisfied as to his own decision about this point, and, at the same time, wrote the Secretary of the Interior about this disagreement. The secretary then wrote Gray telling him to sign and get on with the job but Gray, in turn, was removed before he had a chance to obey this order.

Other troubles came from the military. Bartlett's answer to Graham's penciled note announcing his arrival was curt and cold. Then, behind the scenes, the "West Point Protective Association" must have swung into concerted action. Lieutenant Burnside and another youthful officer, Lieutenant W. F. Smith, who had both arrived with Graham, began to throw roadblocks into the path of the harassed Bartlett; very probably they had also heard distorted stories of his treatment of their fellow officer, the bibulous McClellan. Anyway, they obviously tried to give Bartlett a hard time. It began when Bartlett requested Burnside, who had assumed the duties of quartermaster and commissary of the commission, to furnish the artist, Henry C. Pratt, and his son John with subsistence. Burnside refused to do this under orders from Graham, and the latter backed up his subordinate on the technicality that the Pratts had not yet been admitted to the scientific corps which Graham headed with the resounding title of "Principal Astronomer and Chief of the Scientific Corps." Burnside, however, was soon sent back to Washington with personal dispatches from Graham to Colonel Abert, the head of the Topographical Engineers, in which the "Chief of the Scientific Corps" griped long and loudly about Bartlett's management of the commission's affairs.

The real showdown came with Lieutenant Smith, who evidently succeeded to Burnside's job. Bartlett wrote Smith a mild reprimand about the shortage of supplies at the copper mines and received a reply which for contumacious sassiness to a superior officer set some kind of record. Smith said among other things "you have not the slightest right to reprove anyone to whom you cannot give an order" and suggested that Bartlett adopt a "more manly course." [1] This, of course, was absurd, as Bartlett, after all, was the boundary commissioner and all others, military or civilian, were subordinate to him. Bartlett immediately and quite rightly fired young Smith, who then added his complaints to the growing anti-Bartlett chorus. Incidentally, Smith, in after years, became a major general of volunteers in the Union Army and, later, the police commissioner of New York City.

There were other petty squabbles as well. Graham was aggrieved because Bartlett did not give him his full title as "Chief of the Scientific Corps" when later introducing him to General Condé and other members of the Mexican commission and complained bitterly about this affront to Bartlett and to Washington, and he and Gray quarreled because he would not furnish Gray with some of the new instruments he had brought from New York. The net result of these disputes was that all involved were eventually recalled.

The one man who seemed to mind his own business was the quiet, industrious, and capable Lieutenant Whipple, who remained on with Major Emory after all the others had left. But even Whipple had his detractor in the jealousies of the service, for when he had run the boundary survey, under Emory's direction, from San Diego to the confluence of the Gila and Colorado Rivers, in the autumn of 1849, the commander of his mili-

[1] The details of all these quarrels are in Sen. Exec. Doc. 119. 32 Cong. 1st Sess.

tary escort had been Lieutenant Cave Johnson Couts of the
2nd Dragoons, two years behind him at West Point. Couts kept
a private journal in which he declared that Whipple was a prig,
"modest as a young maiden," who was embarrassed by the
bawdy talk of the campfires, and that "Washington City dan-
dies with white kid gloves, etc., don't like roughing it . . ."
And "take him away from his books, and he is not worth a
tinker's d--n for anything under God's heaven. I now doubt
his capacity for determining the position of the mouth of the
Gila." [2]

The brash Couts was a Tennessean who soon afterwards married a California heiress and resigned from the army; Whipple,
from Massachusetts, was worth enough of a tinker's damn to locate accurately the mouth of the Gila, to make subsequently an
extraordinary record as an explorer and surveyor of the West,
and to die gallantly as a Union major general at Chancellors-
ville in May, 1863.

Just as the hassle between Bartlett and Graham, a forerunner
of the later constant disputes between the Department of the
Interior and the Army, was starting up in low gear, who should
descend upon the camp at Santa Rita and in a series of hit-and-
run raids run off almost all the remaining mules, horses, and cattle of the commission and its military escort but the well-fed
and pampered Apaches! Evidently the dullness of the Bartlett
temperance regime had become unbearable, and if they couldn't
have whisky they were going to have other excitement, which
they profitably found in stampeding the camp's livestock. The
camp then underwent a state of siege from their former friends
and it was necessary to postpone an official meeting with the
Mexican commission. This, and the long delay in the arrival

[2] *From San Diego to the Colorado in 1849. The Journal and Maps of
Cave J. Couts,* edited by William McPherson (Los Angeles 1932).

of Gray and Graham, were grist to the Mexican diplomatic mill, for they completely turned the usual tables for accusations of habits of procrastination and the *mañana* spirit against the gringos; and the Mexican ambassador in Washington happily bombarded the State Department with charges of American tardiness and delay in the border survey.

Finally enough new horses and mules were assembled for the Americans to start to meet the Mexican commission, which was then thought to be on the Gila River. Along were Colonel Graham, Surveyor Gray, Lieutenant Whipple, the Bostonian artist Henry C. Pratt, and the beautiful young Inez Gonzalez, "who was placed on a very gentle mule," and a number of engineers, muleteers, cooks, and interpreters which brought the total strength up to about seventy people. For the first time most of the equipment and provisions were carried on pack mules, for this was to be no trip across the open and level plains and deserts but a journey into the rough and rugged Rocky Mountains to the Gila River, through which country General Stephen Kearny had also been forced to drop his wagons in his dash to the Pacific coast nearly five years before.

Bartlett remarked on the novelty of the pack mules and the high skill of the Mexican *arrieros* or muleteers in handling those difficult beasts. The Mexican prisoner, Jesus the murderer, accompanied the party as a muleteer, and Bartlett freed him of all obligations of turning his wages over to the Apaches, as the Indians had certainly forfeited all claims on him by their outrageous behavior.

The way, at first, was through wooded and beautiful mountain country, but the summer sun beat down with such an intensity that Inez Gonzalez suffered from sunburn. Possibly to cheer her up, Bartlett named a bubbling spring at which the party camped Inez's Spring, although the Mexicans had previously known it as Hawk Spring. Pushing on south and west through a drenching rainstorm which soaked everyone to the skin and turned the ground into sticky and almost impassable gumbo, they finally arrived at the deserted camp of General Condé, where a note on a pole informed them that the Mexican commission had moved to the north in search of a better water supply. Following on through rough mountain country, word was received that the elusive Mexican general had again moved his camp about twenty-five miles farther to the west in order to be nearer the Mexican settlements. Much alarm was caused in the American party by the continued absence of John O'Donoghue, one of the astronomical computers, who had been lost a day previous, and a small searching party was dispatched to search for him. All prayed that the Apaches would not find him first. Fortunately he had wandered into General Condé's camp and was safe with the Mexican commissioner. Finally, after much rough and tough chasing, the pursuing Americans caught up with the mercurial General Condé and his party of some seventy men. The Mexicans had been attacked once by the Apaches, and those wily savages had stampeded the saddle horses but had failed to drive off the herd of mules which were the transportation mainstay of the expedition.

An important meeting of the joint border commission was then held with, for the first time, all key officials present. Mr. A. B. Gray, the official surveyor, went on record as dissenting from the agreement previously made between Bartlett and Condé about the southern boundary of New Mexico. General Condé remarked that this had all been settled and the decision could not be reversed. Gray accepted this as a temporary decision and plans were then agreed upon whereby Gray and Whipple were to run the survey down the Gila River to its junction with the Colorado River and the chief astronomer, Colonel Graham, was to work down the Rio Grande from El Paso to the Gulf of Mexico. The Mexicans were to divide their party accordingly to work with the Americans and General Condé chose to accompany Gray and Lieutenant Whipple down the Gila. This plan was satisfactory to all as there were no disputes whatever about these two sections of the boundary. The debated southern boundary of New Mexico was thereby temporarily shelved, and nearly one year after Bartlett's arrival the joint commission became a going organization.

General Condé then announced his intention to go to the Sonoran town of Santa Cruz for supplies. Bartlett, who had not turned over the beautiful Inez to the Mexican commissioner, as was his original plan, decided that he too was in need of mules and provisions and that a trip to Santa Cruz would allow him to obtain these and also to deliver the long-delayed Inez Gonzalez to her parents in that town. Why he kept her from the care of the polished General Condé is not explained, but perhaps he had an inkling of her penchant for Mexican army officers which he afterwards discovered with puritanical dismay. But was it quite fair to Inez? Certainly she would have been better off with a general than with the mere captain with whom the horrified commissioner, after all his efforts, later found her living in sin. So Bartlett took leave of Gray, Whipple, and Graham, who were supposedly going back to work, and headed due south, after Condé, with thirteen followers, among whom were Dr. Webb and the artist Henry C. Pratt, all escorting the beauteous Inez homewards.

Soon the small party found that General Condé's trail mysteriously turned northwest, in a direction away from Santa Cruz, but Bartlett kept his party headed south. For the first time they met a herd of mustangs, or wild horses, and many deer and antelope were seen. The country was fertile and watered but the expedition became lost in a dead-end valley, with no visible exit toward the south, where, to their surprise, they were joined by Colonel Graham's party, who had received word that Bartlett and his small party were lost and starving. All were low in provisions and worried about their predicament. Graham was much disgusted at the whole situation and later acidly commented in his official report about the waste of time in returning one young Mexican girl to her home while the boundary survey was forgotten for forty-four days! Finally, by retracing their steps, they arrived at the ruins of a large hacienda — one of the many monuments to the depredations of the Indians — and here they encountered two Mexican soldiers with a letter from the good General Condé, who, taking Bartlett in hand, led him and his party safely down the valley of the Babocomori River toward Santa Cruz.

This fertile valley had once contained one of the largest cattle ranches in Mexico and had counted not less than forty thousand head, besides a large number of horses and mules, but the Indians had ruined all this, as they had the other ranchos, haciendas, and villages in northern Mexico since the independence of that country in 1821. The herdsmen had been murdered, the buildings burned, and the livestock driven off by raid after raid, and the desolate countryside was a depressing commentary on the benefits of an independent republic. Herds of mustangs and wild cattle were the only reminders of the former peace and prosperity under Spanish rule.

When they arrived at Santa Cruz, a crowd of Mexican men, women, and children milled excitedly about the young girl who rode beside Bartlett and, as he described it:

Each in turn (rough and half-naked as many of them were), embraced her after the Spanish custom; and it was long ere one could utter a word. Tears of joy burst from all; and the sun-burnt and brawny men, in whom the finer feelings of our nature are wrongly supposed not to exist, wept like children, as they looked with astonishment on the rescued girl. . . . The members of the Commission who witnessed this affectionate and joyful scene, could not but participate in the feelings of the poor child and her friends; and the big tears as they rolled down their weather-beaten and bearded faces, showed how fully they sympathized with the feelings of our Mexican friends.[3]

When about a half-mile distant, all dismounted and escorted the attractive Inez to the village church, which she and her native welcomers entered to give thanks for her deliverance from the savage Apaches. The Americans waited respectfully outside until the devotions were over, when they led their horses and pack mules outside the village walls and pitched their tents, preferring the great outdoors to the adobe houses which the Mexicans offered.

For several days the Americans enjoyed an unusual burst of emotional hospitality from the natives and, in return, Dr. Thomas H. Webb, the surgeon of the party, spent most of his time attending to the sick and maimed of the village. But soon things began to disappear from the camp. As Bartlett wrote: "Meat was stolen from the pot in which it was cooking; blankets were taken from the men while asleep; and all the iron stakepins that secured our animals were carried off." A poor reward indeed for returning intact a kidnaped daughter of the village, and Mr. Bartlett, bibliophile and ethnologist, was considerably disillusioned about the capacities of Mexican gratitude.

There were no needed mules and provisions available in Santa Cruz, so Bartlett decided to proceed further south into the interior of Sonora to buy these. Actually this trip extended itself for him into a mammoth sort of junket with its end in San Fran-

---

[3] John Russell Bartlett, *Personal Narrative of Explorations and Incidents, etc.*, 2 Vols. (New York 1854), I, p. 410.

cisco, but that was caused by later circumstances which were un-guessed at the time. The fed-up Graham, who had found the constant ringing of the village church's cracked bell and the howling of the native curs bad for sleep, left to go back to work. But Bartlett headed for the town of Magdalena, seventy-five miles to the south; and a cavalcade of Santa Cruzans, of both sexes, took advantage of this unusual protection against Apache raiders to join the party to go to the annual fiesta of San Francisco which was soon to take place there.

These Mexicans were picturesquely dressed in holiday garb, the men wearing "roundabout jackets, with pantaloons open at the sides, showing their large white cotton drawers beneath. Some of their pantaloons were lined with pink or sky-blue; and in every case they were decorated with a row of bell-buttons or clasps, extending from the hip to the ankle." A red sash held up the pants and a multicolored serape was gracefully draped over the shoulder. The women wore black *rebozos*, or scarfs, covering their necks and heads, but had nothing else peculiar to their dress to compete with the gaudy males.

The party rode out gaily into a countryside which became more and more fertile and green but remained as much a scene of utter devastation as the haciendas in the arid, brown grazing country to the north. A beautiful but ruined old mission at Cocuspera, which had been abandoned about six years before, was passed and Bartlett remarked that the interior, judging from the faded paintings on the walls, must once have been very attractive. Now it was occupied by bats and swallows, the sole living things in what had been one of the richest missions in Mexico. Its property in cattle had once been so great that the yearly increase amounted to ten thousand calves. The remains of an excellent orchard behind the mission furnished the travelers with peaches and quinces, which were in season and highly welcome.

Many wild and ferocious cattle were seen and one truculent bull chased Dr. George Thurber, the naturalist, who was out exploring the countryside, all the way into the camp. The bellowing of the wild bulls at night caused feelings of apprehension as always.

The first giant cactus, called *petahaya* by the Mexicans, was seen, a plant which was to become as familiar to Bartlett as the elms and maples of Rhode Island but its first appearance caused the usual wonder. Farther on the mixed caravan passed other semideserted hamlets and one old church, built about 1687, in the village of San Ignacio, which Bartlett found worthy of a brief inspection. In its interior he noticed two Chinese wood figures, doubtless intended originally for mandarins, but here metamorphosed into saints, which reminded him of the old connection between the west coast of Mexico and the Far East, for it was from the port of Acapulco that the yearly Manila galleon set forth to the Philippines to return laden with goods from China and Japan. Bartlett asked an attendant about these figures and received the old, old Mexican answer of *"Quien sabe?"* The church, like so many others in Mexico, had been built by the Jesuits and, even years after their expulsion in about 1767, the results of their industry still showed in the surrounding pomegranate orchards. The Americans had heard of the fame of this local fruit and, for once in Mexico, they found something which came up to expectations, for they found it delicious beyond comparison. A strong and fiery sort of *aguardiente* (brandy) was distilled from it and this too was pronounced excellent.

On October 1, they reached their destination, the town of Magdalena, where the alcalde held them for a short time for questioning because the conduct of many of the American emigrants to California, who had passed along this southern route, had been brutal and shameful to the quiet natives; for often these reckless adventurers would enter a Mexican house and take what they wanted at pistol point, and gringos were definitely not popular in northern Mexico. A few days later the fiesta of San Francisco burst with full blast and the town was given over to celebration by the thousands who had flocked there from as far away as California and Sinaloa. After elaborate religious ceremonies and parades, all turned to a street fair and to music and dancing, and Bartlett remarked on the complete absence of drunkenness and the general good and cheerful behavior of the people in a perpetual fandango which kept up day and night. It was a carefree and hilarious atmosphere and the homesick Americans enjoyed it all thoroughly; but Bartlett, who never completely forgot business, was disappointed to find that he could not obtain the needed provisions or mules in the town, which meant a trip further on to the south, to Ures, then the capital of Sonora. Circumstances seemed constantly to stretch the radius of the little ethnologist, and this was but the beginning of his longest junket.

CHAPTER IV

The Grand Circuit

BARTLETT'S party, some with frightful hangovers from the grand parade and climax of the fiesta the night before, set out the following afternoon for Ures along a mule path over which wheeled vehicles had never traveled. Crowds of people leaving the fiesta filled the road, which gave all a feeling of security against the prowling Apaches who infested the country, even this far to the south. Bartlett was suddenly taken desperately ill on the next day, and it was certainly not a reaction from the festivities which hit the always temperate little commissioner. He would willingly have stopped, but the villages were so miserable and squalid that all agreed it was best to push on to Ures, and Bartlett, in much pain, progressed by dismounting from his mule and resting every hour. Finally the party reached that place on the sixth day, and he collapsed in the gloomy rear room of an unoccupied shop, the only quarters available. The governor of Sonora called the next morning and courteously offered his services but Bartlett was too ill to say much or even to listen with attention. A good Samaritan then appeared in the person of an American, a Dr. Campbell, who had lived in Sonora for some twenty-five years. He and Dr. Webb agreed that Bartlett would not be able to leave the place for a long time, and they carried him into more comfortable quarters. Bartlett then sent the rest of the party, except for his personal servant and the artist Henry Pratt and his son, on to the seaport of Guaymas to cash drafts to pay for the needed mules and provisions. They finally returned with the funds, but were not able to secure all the necessary animals and supplies.

Dr. Campbell took over complete charge of the case, assisted by an English and a German physician, so that Bartlett was, at least, well provided in medical attendance. When those who had gone to Guaymas returned, it was agreed among all the doctors that the commissioner was far too ill to make the return trip north to the Gila River and all advised him to recover where he was, and then to proceed by water from a port on the Mexican west coast to San Diego, California, where the engineering parties running the survey westward down the Gila River, under Gray and Whipple, would meet him. Whipple had completed the survey between Yuma and San Diego in 1849, so it was judged that this would not take too long. Under the leadership of Dr. Webb, all the others, except Bartlett's servant, then left for the north to rejoin the American engineers.

So Bartlett was left in Ures with his faithful servant, nurse, and cook, William Turner, and about the middle of December was moved to Dr. Campbell's house, where he enjoyed the luxury of recuperating before an open fire in the town's only fireplace, and receiving the care and attentions of the doctor's kind and amiable Mexican wife, which poor Bartlett gratefully said were "such as can be appreciated only by those, who, having a family and home, are taken sick among strangers in a foreign land." It was a far cry that Christmas from his wife and the four little Bartletts back in his snug New England home in Providence.

Before Dr. Webb and the others left, however, Bartlett was well on the road to recovery, and his acute interest in peoples and their customs led him to poke about the town, which, like the other northern settlements of the republic had started as a Jesuit mission but, like the others, had declined since the expulsion of that remarkable order in 1767. The governor of Sonora, Don Francisco Cubillas, was an accomplished and cultivated gentleman, who had spent many years in Europe and the United States, spoke English fluently, and made Bartlett's convalescence as pleasant as possible. The little capital town was a comparatively civilized and pleasant place and Bartlett happily wandered about, visiting the state legislature, whose assembly had only eight members; reading the weekly *Sonoriense*, the only newspaper in the state; exploring the nearby ranchos and haciendas; and attending the local theater, which was run, somewhat along Shakespearean lines, in a courtyard where the audience stood or brought their own seats. The plays were tedious, for the prompter always read the entire play in an undertone, with the actors repeating their parts after him.

Bartlett had full scope here to indulge his passion for ethnology and he almost pounced on a few Indian victims and wrung them dry of information. The Yaqui Indians were the laborers of the town and he noted, "They fill the same place and perform the same duties as the lower class of Irish do in the United States" — a highly transient observation for both countries. The Yaquis in later years took the places of the Apaches as a destructive menace to northwestern Mexico. But at that time they were in a phase of good behavior before reverting to their former savage truculence and were honest, faithful, and industrious, which was probably a temporary heritage from their Jesuit converters and eventually wore off. Bartlett wanted a Yaqui to catechize and the obliging governor sent him one of whom Bartlett wrote, "He had a mild expression of countenance and was considered a good specimen." This mild Yaqui was first made to sit for a portrait by Mr. Pratt, before the artist left, which so alarmed him that he never returned, and thus escaped the usual cross-examination which Bartlett gave his Indian specimens on the key words of their languages. Luckily, a learned and venerable local priest knew the Yaqui language thoroughly and from him Bartlett obtained the required answers for his formula.

Not so fortunate was Tanori, the chief of the Opate Indians, who were noted for their bravery and fighting ability against the marauding Apaches. This tribe acted as a sort of paid militia for the state and were the mainstay of defense against the forays of the fierce savages from the north. They were a clean and industrious tribe and had long been Christianized. Tanori was pleased to have his portrait painted by Henry Pratt, which Bartlett told him would be sent to Washington, D. C., and hung, among those of other celebrated Indian chiefs, for the President of the United States and other dignitaries to see. Tanori was a light-complexioned, handsome six-footer whose expression was "full of benignity," and he and his wife willingly sat for their portraits for a whole week. Bartlett made ethnological hay during such an unusual opportunity and obtained from the chief a full vocabulary of the Opate language.

Scarcely a week passed during Bartlett's protracted stay in Ures that he did not hear of murders and robberies by small, wandering bands of Apaches in the neighborhood. The Mexicans had become almost paralyzed with fear and made practically no effort to defend themselves. Many Mexican officers told Bartlett that ten Apaches would put a hundred of the *peones*, or lower-class Mexicans, into a panic flight and that this fear had become a sort of contagious mental disease. The Opates and Yaquis seemed to be the only ones who could be relied upon to stand up and fight the murderous invaders.

A band of fifty Coco-Maricopa Indians from the Gila River suddenly appeared in Ures, just before Christmas, to beg firearms from the governor to defend themselves against the attacks from the Yumas and Apaches, for the latter tribe played no favorites, and, like true Ishmaels, their hands were against all men. These Indians informed Bartlett that a party of Americans had recently passed through their villages, and he believed that these were the engineers of the boundary commission working their way westward down the Gila River. Bartlett presented their chiefs with presents but not until they had completed the usual two-hundred–word language quiz. Among the presents were written testimonials, addressed to all concerned, of their good character and friendship toward Americans. A red ribbon and a large red seal were attached to each testimonial, which pleased the Indians greatly. These testimonials were the usual thing to give friendly Indians to show other parties of traveling Americans and were much prized. Occasionally, however, an Indian would proudly flaunt a testimonial to a band of California-bound emigrants which described the bearer as "a damn big rascal. Don't trust him around the corner."

Just before Christmas, Bartlett was walking near the outskirts of the town when he perceived a huge cloud of dust, kicked up by an approaching drove of animals. These were escorted by a body of armed men, mounted and on foot, who seemed to be in high glee and were saluted and cheered by crowds who poured out of the town to meet them. These proved to be the doughty Tanori and his Opate warriors, who had defeated a band of Apaches and recovered eight hundred and sixty stolen animals. This milling herd of cattle, horses, and mules was driven into the main plaza, where the owners were permitted to reclaim their animals upon the payment of three dollars per head for the expenses of driving them in and subsisting them. The Opates thus gave Bartlett a firsthand demonstration of their prowess in contrast to the lassitude and panic fear of the Mexicans.

On Christmas Eve, a Dr. Vassbinder, a Canadian physician attached to the Mexican army, arrived with the sad news of the death of General Garcia Condé, the Mexican boundary commissioner, who had been so congenial with Bartlett. The general had become ill soon after Bartlett had left him in the dirty and miserable little village of Santa Cruz in early September, and had died about the middle of December in his native town of Arispe. Bartlett keenly felt the loss of his opposite in the joint commission, for Condé was an able engineer and a cultivated man whose company he had enjoyed, although the impression of others of the American commission was that Condé had taken advantage of his charm and talents to slip over a rather fast one on the matter of the southern boundary of New Mexico.

By the end of the year 1851, Bartlett was so far recovered as to set out for the port of Guaymas, on the Gulf of California, now a popular resort for gringo deep-sea fishermen, in a two-wheeled Scotch carriage. On the second day, he arrived at the lovely little city of Hermosillo, a place then of about twelve thousand people, and then as now the largest city in Sonora, and now the capital of the state. Here the governor, whom he had met in Ures, called upon him and offered him a seat in his carriage, which was leaving in a few days for Guaymas, an offer which Bartlett gratefully accepted.

This gave him some time in Hermosillo, and he requested the governor to secure for him for the usual vocabulary quiz an Indian of the famous Ceris tribe, whose home was on the large island of Tiburon in the Gulf of California, north of Guaymas. This small but hostile tribe was, and still is at times, the dread of the Mexicans in that area by its habit of murdering and plundering small parties of Mexicans whom they attacked from ambush with poisoned lances and arrows. Their method of securing this poison was simple and effective and showed a super-

Borgian ingenuity. Bartlett quoted a young British naval officer's description of the process. Lieutenant Hardy wrote as follows:

They first kill a cow, and take from it its liver; they then collect rattle-snakes, scorpions, centipedes, and tarantulas, which they confine in a hole with the liver. The next process is to beat them with sticks, in order to enrage them; and being thus infuriated, they fasten their fangs and exhaust their venom upon each other, and upon the liver. When the whole mass is in a state of corruption, the women take their arrows and pass their points through; they are then allowed to dry in the shade.

After that, of course, they were shot into the hide of some unwary Mexican.

The governor sent Bartlett "a good-looking man, about thirty years of age" from this ingenious tribe and he was thoroughly grilled for three hours and wrung dry of his basic vocabulary, which Bartlett, to the surprise of "several young Mexican gentlemen of education" who were interested observers, then read back to the Indian, who readily recognized each word and gave the spellbound audience its Spanish equivalent. Bartlett's reputation as a *simpático* savant became great in Mexico and probably eclipsed his position as border commissioner.

Bartlett left Hermosillo for Guaymas with the governor on January 2, 1852, after spending New Year's Day sketching the beautiful little city from a hill outside the town, surrounded by the same coterie of admiring young Mexicans who had watched his skill in recording the Ceris vocabulary. He remarked on the difficulty of giving any character to a Mexican town in a picture because the houses are generally of one story, the streets narrow, and from an elevation the whole appears an unbroken mass of flat roofs with only the towers and dome of the church rising above the level monotony.

Soon after leaving the small city, a striking party of a hundred and fifty Frenchmen were met, a hard-looking, determined, sunburned lot, wearing long, full beards, and all heavily armed, who had emigrated from California and were marching along on foot toward the ruined mission of Cocuspera to establish a colony there and to reopen some abandoned mines. This was far more of a history-making group than Bartlett realized at the time, for these adventurers were the forerunners of a horde of later filibusters who descended on Mexico, Nicaragua, and other Latin American countries and sought to set up governments and grab land by surprise and force of arms. The ill-fated Narcisso Lopez in Cuba had been the pioneer in these raids into Latin America, two years before, and William Walker in Nicaragua was the most notorious and successful of the succeeding reckless adventurers.

This particular band was led by the Marquis Charles de Pindray, who in the Middle Ages would probably have been called a peerless knight, but in the prosaic mid-nineteenth century was dubbed a wastrel. He and his followers had been recruited in California, which was full of adventurous Frenchmen, and armed by the Mexican government, to fight the Apaches, but before the frontier was reached, friction developed between the French and the Mexicans — and De Pindray was one day found dead with a bullet in his head. His followers started back south across the desert and met a new French expedition, also from California, under Count Gaston Raoul de Raousset-Boulbon, another flaming soldier of fortune. The two parties joined and, the next October, after declaring Sonora an independent republic, under their aegis, they captured Hermosillo. This was an incredible achievement as the Frenchmen numbered only two hundred and forty-three men, while the city had about twelve thousand inhabitants with a garrison of twelve hundred soldiers. These odds were too much against holding the place for long and the French filibusters finally agreed to evacuate the city and return to California. But they had shown the possibilities of filibustering and opened the floodgates for a deluge of later raids and forays.

As Bartlett approached the Pacific coast he experienced the most delightful sensation of inhaling the fresh and soft salt air from the ocean, and it was as balm of Gilead to the Rhode Islander who had spent the last year and a half "on the parched and barren wastes of the interior of our continent." This change in air seemed to have completed his cure.

In Guaymas he noted the only neat cemetery he had seen in Mexico and generally liked this pretty little port, which was enjoying a boom in shipping provisions to the California settlements. He approved of the thriving warehouses and stores, which, however, carried almost entirely English or French goods and practically no American. From here he sailed on a schooner down the coast to Mazatlan, and pleasurably read some New York newspapers, for he had not heard from his family or the government for eight months or seen an American newspaper for over six months.

At Mazatlan he went ashore with a colonel in the Mexican army who had been educated in the United States, and was taken to an excellent hotel run by a Chinese, with a German chef, and a cockpit in the interior patio. This was the most civilized and cosmopolitan place he had yet seen in Mexico. It was impossible, however, to find a passage to California from there on anything but a slow sailing vessel, and he decided to sail six hundred miles farther southward to Acapulco, whence he could board a fast steamer to California, thus getting ever farther away from the boundary survey. He made this trip down the coast in a Mexican vessel which was commanded by a "Captain Nye, a very clever navigator, hailing from New Bedford, Massachusetts." Among his fellow passengers was an absconding United States Army quartermaster who had arrived posthaste from El Paso and who politely gave Bartlett all the latest news from the north.

After a short stop at the rather primitive, then as now, port of San Blas, where the captain of the port was an obliging Swede, and at the even more dreary Manzanillo Bay, the ship arrived at Acapulco on the last day of January, 1852. Again Bartlett found a room at a hotel run by a Chinese, and his pretty Mexican wife, which he called the "very perfection of neatness," and, in fact, the Chinese usually ran the best hotels of the times in Mexico. Bartlett admired the magnificent enclosed harbor from which the Manila galleons had set sail to the Philippines every year during the centuries of Spanish rule, returning laden with the spices, fine silks and other goods of China and the Far East. But he did not like the climate, which bred fevers and cholera, and quoted Alexander von Humboldt, who had spent some time in Acapulco, as saying "the heat is more oppressive, the air more stagnant, and the existence of man more painful at Acapulco, than at Vera Cruz" — which is a damning opinion indeed, and certainly different from anything put out by the Acapulco Chamber of Commerce of today.

In early February, Bartlett boarded the mail steamer *Oregon*, which was jammed to the gunwales with four hundred and seventy-two California-bound passengers. To get aboard he had to pull his rank "as a government officer charged with important duties." After an absence of five months, during which time he had traveled about two thousand miles away from those important duties, it was, perhaps, about time for him to return to work. The trip was hot and uncomfortable but uneventful and its crowded monotony was broken only once, when the whaler *Carlton*, sixteen months out from New Bedford, sent a boat to the steamer with a present of a large turtle, for which the passengers returned a collection of newspapers brought from the States. The coastline of Lower California to the right rose abruptly from the sea in barren and rugged mountains of a most dreary and forbidding aspect, and all welcomed the arrival at San Diego on February 9, 1852.

Bartlett landed and found that the surveying parties from the Gila River, under Gray and Whipple, with the military escort under Colonel Craig, had arrived there about a month before and were snugly encamped outside the town. They had felt anxiety for him, as nothing had been heard about him after he left Santa Cruz about the first of October, and also for the missing Dr. Webb and his party, who had left Ures the middle of December. The surveying parties had been compelled to suspend their work for lack of provisions, when about sixty miles east of the junction of the Gila with the Colorado River, and had hurried on across the desert to San Diego to replenish their supplies.

Two days after Bartlett's arrival, Dr. Webb and his party limped into town, most of them on foot, exhausted and half starved after their trip from Ures.[1] Most of the men had had enough of desert wandering and were keen to join the rush to the goldfields, and Bartlett was busy for a few days in paying them off. Colonel Craig's military escort of twenty-five men also caught the fever and twenty of them, including three non-commissioned officers, deserted in San Diego. Desertion was almost the rule, not the exception, at that time on the frontier, and became so commonplace that it was rationalized as being rather beneficial because it helped to settle the country. The few surviving animals of both parties were in bad shape and there seemed but one thing to do — Commissioner Bartlett should take

---

[1] John C. Cremony describes their hazardous and exhausting journey in *Life Among the Apaches* (San Francisco 1868), pp. 89–128.

another trip to secure equipment and provisions, but this time to the north, up the coast to San Francisco. Before he left, however, he corralled several of the local Indians for his language examination.

By the end of February, 1852, Bartlett was in roaring, bustling San Francisco, which greatly impressed him, and he quite naturally found reasons for several sight-seeing trips. He went across the bay to Benicia, where he called on Brevet Brigadier General Ethan Allen Hitchcock, that strange character steeped in esoteric mysticism, who gave Bartlett an order on the commanding officers at San Diego and Fort Yuma to furnish him with the necessary military escorts as needed. From there he went on to the lush Napa Valley and remarked on how much more work the immigrant New England farmers accomplished there than the natives. He admired the redwood trees and the thriving truck gardens which supplied San Francisco with vegetables, especially large onions, which he believed were the best preventative for scurvy and which he ate with more relish than oranges.

Turning westward, toward the coast, he stopped at the ranch of a Mr. Knight from Vermont, who was so pleased to see a fellow New Englander that he rushed out and rounded up three local Digger Indians who perforce had to take Bartlett's tried and true vocabulary test, not the basic two-hundred-worder but the full and complete vocabulary quiz given to only the more intelligent redskins. Pushing on toward the coast, the party descended the Pluton River in Sonoma County to a valley of active geysers which had been explored and described by Professor Shepherd of Western Reserve College nearly two years before. Bartlett was intensely interested in all these phenomena and quoted the professor's erudite findings at length in his book.

After returning to San Francisco, the peripatetic little commissioner managed to squeeze in a few more trips before buying the needed supplies and returning to duty at San Diego. He visited San Jose, forty miles to the south, which he considered rather dull, but redeemed the trip by discovering a female Indian of the San Luis Obisco tribe, married to an American, whom he found "to be quite an intelligent person" and in no time at all he had pumped her dry of "a most satisfactory vocabulary." From there he went on to the famous New Almaden quicksilver mines, later to be involved in an endless legal wrangle, which produced about a million pounds annually. Bartlett was fascinated by the workings and production statistics and wrote a report in his book which would have done justice to a mining engineer. He had planned to continue on by land to Monterey, but the spring rains had made the intervening rivers impassable and he was forced to return to San Francisco and sail by boat to San Diego, but not before he had met the famous Captain Sutter, on whose land gold had first been discovered in California. He was unable to secure all the equipment and provisions needed, but he had a nice trip.

About the middle of April, Bartlett reached Monterey by water, where he noted the charm of the town and of the *señoritas* of the old native Spanish families who were constantly courted and married by officers of the army. A lovely country and beautiful women, he decided, but, like many another visiting New Englander, he declared the Pacific crawfish so much inferior to the Atlantic lobster "that they would hardly be tolerated on the tables of the Atlantic coast."

He left Monterey on a government revenue cutter and arrived safely at San Diego to receive the news that Mr. Gray, the surveyor, had been removed and replaced by Major William H. Emory, who had originally held that position in the first commission which had met in San Diego in 1849. Also, the position of astronomer had been abolished, which meant that Colonel

Graham had been recalled as well. This compelled Bartlett to pay off and discharge all of Gray's men, which reduced the strength of the party, about to retrace its steps to the Rio Grande, by about forty per cent. As Emory was at parts unknown, somewhere between Washington and El Paso, the responsibility of completing the unfinished surveying gap on the Gila River fell on the reliable wheelhorse Lieutenant Whipple, who from first to last seemed to do the lion's share of the work among that collection of scientific prima donnas. A valuable addition, however, was made to the eastward-bound band when Bartlett hired the famous guide Antoine Leroux of New Mexico, who had conducted Philip St. George Cooke and his Mormon Battalion to the coast during the Mexican War, and had just arrived in San Diego with Captain Sitgreaves's exploring party, who had come from Albuquerque through what is now northern New Mexico and Arizona. Sitgreaves was another topographical engineer, and on this trip roughly blazed the trail for the later route of the Santa Fe Railroad,[2] a route which our Lieutenant Whipple, accompanied by Leroux, was to examine in greater detail, about two years later.

Bartlett finally obtained all the needed provisions and livestock for the return trip, but also characteristically found time to explore all the surrounding country, even including a trip, accompanied by Dr. Webb and the artist Henry Pratt, to the mission of San Luis Rey, forty miles to the north. While in that sylvan retreat, an army sergeant gathered four Indians of the Kechi tribe for the vocabulary test, which they passed with high marks. An ancient chief among them, dressed in a Mexican army officer's uniform — "a blue coat with red facings trimmed with gold lace, and a high military cap and feather" — sadly spoke of the

[2] See Captain L. Sitgreaves, *Report of an Expedition down the Zuni and Colorado Rivers* (Washington 1854), illustrated by R. H. Kern.

good old days under the padres of the mission and of the general degeneration since their expulsion.

Returning to San Diego, Bartlett visited the local mission, the last to be abandoned, which was occupied by United States troops under the command of Colonel John Bankhead Magruder, the colorful "Prince John," a West Pointer and later one of the dashing leader of the Confederate Army. Bartlett does not give his impressions of the exuberant Magruder, with whom he probably had little in common, but expressed his gratitude for the generous help which the colonel gave the expedition. He also visited the monument below San Diego (which still stands) erected on the Pacific at the initial point of the boundary survey begun there over two years before.

CHAPTER V

A Straight Line East

AT the end of May, 1852, the party started back eastward.
The immediate purpose was to survey the unfinished gap of
about sixty miles to the east from the junction of the Gila and
Colorado Rivers, which had been left undone because of lack
of provisions the previous December. Bartlett provided himself
with a small wagon drawn by two good mules which had come
all the way from Texas, and a "fine American horse," which
had belonged to ex-surveyor Gray, and the party and its livestock set out in detachments for Fort Yuma. Bartlett, accompanied by Dr. Webb, drove out in spanking style in his wagon
and spent the night at a hacienda owned by a Mrs. Snooks, the
widow of an Englishman. Passing the battlefield of San Pasqual,
where Stephen Kearny nearly lost his small detachment of
dragoons in 1847, they descended the mountain passes to the
level desert of what is now the Imperial Valley, and Bartlett
noted how good it was to get back to camp life and how much
better the health of all became in the active life in the open
air, and called it the surest preventative to disease.

The familiar heat and dryness of the desert now met the party
of about fifty men, which included Colonel Craig and his five
remaining enlisted men, who had been temporarily reinforced
by a detail of ten men loaned by Colonel Magruder from the
San Diego garrison. Dr. Webb, who was also secretary, George

Thurber, the quartermaster and botanist, and Henry C. Pratt, the draftsman and artist, all original veterans of the commission, were along and, as can be seen, all had duties additional to their scientific pursuits. Night marches to avoid the desert heat now began over a region so barren that even the mesquite and the prickly pear were not seen.

One morning, Lieutenant Sweeney arrived from Fort Yuma in pursuit of two deserters from that post whom he believed to be still behind him to the east and who, he guessed, would probably stop at the camp for water. At evening the party began its march, Bartlett in a wagon with Colonel Craig riding a mule at his side. The colonel dropped back to check on the wagons, and the pack mules, as they always did, pushed by the wagons and went to the front. That night's march was forty-five miles, without a rest, over the desert.

When the column halted at dawn, an excited and exhausted sergeant, his hat gone, rode into camp and reported to Bartlett that Colonel Craig had been murdered by the two deserters, whom he had recognized on the road. The colonel had advised them to return with him and had offered to include them in his command so that they might continue with the survey party and not be detained at Fort Yuma, which was admittedly a veritable hellhole among army posts. To emphasize his good will the colonel had laid aside his arms and advanced to talk with them as he had previously so bravely done with the Apaches at the Santa Rita copper mines. But these men were more treacherous than Apaches, for the deserters shot him down in cold blood as he approached them. He had been accompanied by two sergeants, and one of these, and his mount, had been shot down as well. The survivor had put spurs to his mule and escaped under fire.

A heavily armed party set off at once along the back track,

riding in the daytime heat of 108°, but were handicapped by the weariness of their mounts. They rode for about thirty miles in this blast-furnace temperature and had great trouble in finding the body from the surviving sergeant's excited descriptions, and only by a systematic fanning out over the desert did they finally locate it, carefully covered with a blanket. Dr. Webb reported: "The scene was a sad and sickening one, and produced a strong sensation upon all present, and particularly on the Colonel's body servant. It was evident from appearances that the Colonel did not long survive the wound inflicted, or experience much, if any, severe suffering." This was merciful, for exposure to the baleful sun would have been extreme agony to a wounded man. Not far away they found the dead body of the other sergeant's horse but no signs of the sergeant himself. Placing the colonel's body in an ambulance, they mournfully commenced their return march. About ten miles along they noticed a man resting by the roadside, and this happily proved to be the missing sergeant, who had been only slightly wounded when his mount was killed. The deserters had disarmed him as he lay stunned from his fall, and had asked him if he or the colonel carried any brandy. The sergeant replied, probably not, the colonel not being a drinking man. They then rifled the colonel's pockets, both mounted his mule, and made off toward the mountains to the west.

The camp was much saddened by this atrocious murder, for Colonel Craig was an excellent officer, a kind and humane man, and had been much beloved by all. He had risen from the ranks by ability and gallantry and had made a wonderful record in the Mexican War. Bartlett had found him an unfailing source of strength and a comforting contrast amidst his wrangles with the other army officers. The colonel was buried at sunset in the lonely desert, and Bartlett said that "Wolfe's beautiful lines on the burial of Sir John Moore involuntarily suggested themselves to every mind."

Word of Colonel Craig's murder was sent by special messenger to Colonel Magruder in San Diego, and it is satisfying to know the energetic colonel quickly posted a reward for the capture of the murderers and sent word of this to all the Indians of Southern California, who then established a cordon and soon captured the wanted men, who were tried, condemned, and hanged in San Diego. Both men were Englishmen and were said to have been deserters from the British army.

After burying the colonel, the saddened caravan resumed its nightly march, guided by the moon over the eerie desert. The whitened bones of animals marked the road in many places and abandoned wagons were constantly seen, which were a boon to later-comers who used them for firewood or cannibalized them for needed spare parts. A sharp watch was kept and the company held closely together, for it was now in the country of the Yuma Indians, who were on the warpath. Early one morning they reached the swollen Colorado River, whose waters, charged with mud, had a dark reddish appearance from which came its Spanish name. Major Samuel Peter Heintzelman, later a Union major general, but then commanding Fort Yuma on the California side of the river, welcomed the dispirited travelers and made them as comfortable as the frightful June heat of the place allowed, where the thermometer in the shade read 105°.

The next morning the discouraging news was brought to Bartlett that the Yumas had stolen fifteen of the party's animals, including the splendid Kentucky horse he had obtained from Gray, the former surveyor. The Indians had noiselessly snaked into the camp, unseen and unheard by the two men on guard, had loosed the animals, who were all staked or tied to trees, and had led them away without a sound. It was as expert an example of the fine art of animal stealing as could possibly happen. A halfhearted pursuit was perfunctorily made but all realized it was hopeless. The guide Leroux, an old hand at Indian fighting and pursuit, said that the only possible way to catch marauding Indians was to ride steadily after them from dawn to dusk for several days, resting at night. In time the Indians would slow down from their first headlong pace and the pursuers would usually catch them with time and patience. Bartlett's men did not have the time or patience for a long stern chase like this, and after the token effort was made the losses were resignedly accepted. The men, animals, equipment, and wagons were laboriously ferried across the Colorado River and the long trail struck, eastward into the desert, with every wagon and mule loaded to the utmost because of the loss in animals.

These Yumas were an unusually pestiferous lot, and one forty-niner bound from New York to California, L. N. Weed, called them "bloody villains" and complained bitterly of their indignities to his party, writing in his journal: "The Yumas Indians was troublesome, picking up our spoons & jerking knives out of mens belt – spitting in the water pails." Weed had gone by sea from New York to Galveston, Texas, and thence went overland by the southern route through El Paso. Near Presidio, Texas, on the Rio Grande, a Philadelphian of the party was "bitten by a mad wolf" with shocking results of which Weed wrote:

. . . Henry Lockett showed symptoms of Hydrophiba and began writing a letter to his parents. A spasm coming on ropes were thrown over him till the fit was passed. He would then commence writing the sentence he had left – incomplete and when another was about to occur he would warn them to secure him, one who was present described it as an awful scene, on the third day he died.[1]

[1] L. N. Weed, "Narrative of a Journey to California in 1849." Manuscript in William R. Coe Collection, Western Americana Collection, Yale University Library.

Bartlett, with almost second sight, predicted that the desert over which they had passed in California would some day bloom if the waters of the Colorado were tapped above Fort Yuma for irrigation, which is exactly what is now done by the All-American Canal in the Imperial Valley.

After crossing the Colorado, the industrious Lieutenant Whipple resumed the interrupted boundary survey, and Bartlett, probably with a gleam in his eye, seized the opportunity to sidle off to see the Coco-Maricopa Indians, who lived near where the Salinas (Salt) River flowed into the Gila. They passed hundreds of boulders inscribed with ancient Indian drawings and symbols, which evidently brought back memories of far-off Dighton Rock in Massachusetts, for Bartlett halted the party and copied many of the cabalistic figures. They kept passing the old camps of General Kearny and Captain Philip St. George Cooke, made on the marches of these two officers to California in 1846–1847, and Bartlett again noticed how well things were preserved in that dry climate. The soldiers, who were on foot, made heavy going through the deep sand in the blistering heat and Bartlett slowed the pace. They passed the scene of the terrible Oatman massacre, with fragments of trunks, boxes, clothing, wagons, and human bones and skulls strewn about, where the Apaches had ambushed and murdered a family of four the year before. Finally they reached the first Coco-Maricopa village, just west of what is now Phoenix, Arizona. This spot afforded the first good grazing they had found since leaving California, and they thankfully turned loose their exhausted mules to luxuriate in the grass until the arrival of Lieutenant Whipple and his slow-moving surveying party, who followed behind.

The camp soon filled with visiting Coco-Maricopas, and their close allies the Pimos (Pimas), both friendly tribes, who were glad to meet again various old acquaintances who had spent time with them while surveying the river the previous year. Several of the chiefs spoke Spanish and a thriving barter for fresh vegetables and fruits went on. Bartlett recognized three Maricopas whom he had met in Ures the winter before, and found that they still carefully carried the testimonials which he had given them there. A war party of these Indians set forth against the Apaches and begged him to lend them a few rifles and ammunition, but he refused them and enforced a strict neutrality for his party in this local war. This was probably a gross error, for he had experienced Apache treachery, and if he could have foreseen the horror and devastation which those fiendish "tigers of the human species" were to wreak on the settlers of Arizona for the next thirty odd years, he would probably have given the friendly Indians every available weapon and help to fight this mutual scourge. Despite this sanctimonious refusal, the Coco-Maricopas were magnanimous enough to offer to bring back to him a live Apache boy, and a girl too, if he wished. But this generous offer was refused with dignity. The war party finally left, gaily bedecked in white cotton and red flannel shirts which they had obtained from the Americans but armed only with bows and arrows, although Bartlett had to restrain several eager volunteers of the commission from joining their new friends in this crusade.

Bartlett asked one of the chiefs to a meal and was annoyed, as he had been with Mangus Colorado, the Apache chief, back at the Santa Rita copper mines, by the guest's filling his plate again, after he had finished, and passing it over his shoulder to hungry friends. This fellow also was most importunate for whisky and, as usual, did not believe Bartlett when he was told that there was none on hand, declaring it was the first party of Americans he had ever seen that did not drink whisky. He tasted every bottle in the camp and was finally convinced after swallowing a nauseous medicine for diarrhea.

Bartlett did his usual ethnological investigation into the customs of these tribes and was impressed by the way the women did all the work, including the weaving of cotton cloth and blankets from a high-grade native cotton of which he obtained seeds to distribute among planters on the Eastern seaboard. After thoroughly investigating all the adjoining villages, the commissioner set out up the Salinas (Salt) River to explore some ancient remains. Its waters were rapid and clear in contrast to the muddy and sluggish Gila, and before long they met a band of jolly Pimos fishermen who sold them a fine mess of fish to last a week. They reached the ruins of a prehistoric settlement with its usual elaborate web of abandoned irrigation ditches, and called, as almost all of these mysterious old ruins were, Casas Grandes (large houses). This was a field day for Bartlett and he snooped, pried, and dug around happily, turning up artifacts, and sketching the ruins.

On their return to the Indian villages, they were mistaken at first, from the distance, for a band of marauding Apaches, and a swarm of armed and mounted Pimos galloped out to give battle, but broke into roars of laughter when they recognized their friends. That night Lieutenant Whipple and his surveying party stumbled into camp nearly prostrate from the 120° daytime heat in which they had been working. This completed the job from the headwaters of the Gila River to the Pacific, and the next step was to return to El Paso and join Major Emory, who was working eastward down the Rio Grande. To make sure that Whipple's observations and notes reached Washington safely, duplicates were made and sent to Fort Yuma to be forwarded to the Secretary of the Interior by way of California.

Before leaving the Gila River, Bartlett visited the famous ruins, also called Casas Grandes, near what is now Florence, Arizona, where he made his usual careful observations, notes, and sketches, all of which he expanded in his book. He stated that these ruins and others in the surrounding area were definite proof of a large and quite civilized native population in pre-Spanish times, a conclusion to which later observers all agree. "After three hours spent at the ruins, the hottest, I think, I ever experienced, we set out on our return to camp," Bartlett wrote in the July heat of 119° in the shade.

The evening afterwards, the party began a night's march across the desert toward the town of Tucson. All at once they were engulfed in a terrific thunderstorm which reminded Bartlett of an African simoon. Torrents of rain drenched them as they groped their way by lightning flashes. Suddenly, like ships that pass in the night, they heard the sound of voices in this wild confusion. "Who comes there? Quien vive? were quickly cried by a dozen voices in English and Spanish, and as quickly answered, Friends! Amigos! Who are you? Where are you from? De donde viene? etc. and in a moment we were surrounded by horsemen, pack-mules, and the accompaniments of a large party." The strangers proved to be Missourians and not Apaches and were on their way to California. The two parties stopped for about ten minutes in the raging storm to exchange news about the trails traveled, and all became so mixed in the darkness and rain at this strange meeting that members of both parties mistakenly rode for a way, back along their previous path, with the wrong group.

Tucson was finally reached after exhausting marches, and Bartlett wearily called to pay his respects on the Mexican general in command of the desolated village. The Apache depredations had recently become more frequent and deadly, and these devils of the desert had raided into Tucson, Tubac, and Santa Cruz, killed many Mexicans and stolen much stock. Tucson itself was almost in a state of siege.

Outside the town, Mr. Coons of El Paso held a band of fourteen thousand sheep which he was driving to San Francisco. This was an extremely risky venture and the losses en route were huge, but so were the profits on any surviving sheep, and the more daring and enterprising stockmen were taking the chances. Coons had sixty men, forty-five Americans and fifteen Mexicans, in his party. He had already suffered a serious loss when a party of Apaches rushed him near the town of Janos and ran off fourteen mules and horses, which forced him to return to the city of Chihuahua to replace these animals. Coons was one of the most successful of the early frontier entrepreneurs, a pioneer settler of El Paso, Texas, and his daring deserved high rewards.

After rest and repairs, the party went on, swinging to the south along Philip St. George Cooke's old wagon road, to the old mission of San Xavier del Bac, now restored and a center of tourist attraction. Bartlett found it, after all the Apache raids, "truly a miserable place," but thought the old church the largest and most beautiful of all in the country. He took time to inspect the interior carefully and noticed, once more, wooden statues of Chinese mandarins masquerading as saints, which had undoubtedly found their way to this remote frontier mission by way of Acapulco.

From this mission they plodded on through more rainstorms in the thick, sticky mud and gumbo to Tubac, a small presidio or garrison of dilapidated huts, half of them empty, with another ruined church. Here Bartlett recognized Captain Gomez, in command of the small Mexican garrison, whom he had met over a year before on his first trip into Mexico, but the real shock came, in Bartlett's own words, when:

To our infinite astonishment and regret, we learned that Señorita Inez Gonzales, the Mexican girl whom we had liberated from captivity, and restored to her parents at Santa Cruz in September, was living at this place with the officer just named.

This was a frightful disillusionment to the well-meaning commissioner, who had gone to such great trouble and expense (to the American taxpayer) to return this young maiden unsullied to her parents after rescuing her from the Mexican traders who had bought her from the Apaches, back at the Santa Rita copper mines.

Bartlett finally persuaded the libidinous Mexican captain to let him interview the poor girl at his house, and reported that she was not ill "but evidently felt under some restraint, as the captain remained during the interview." The meeting was very unsatisfactory but the commissioner was a bit mollified by the captain's promise that Inez would return home with her mother, who was then in the town. The mother was probably complacent about the whole affair, which was, after all, an old Mexican custom. The next day the Americans went on, expecting Inez and her mother to overtake them, which, rather predictably, never happened. Poor Bartlett was considerably shaken by this wickedness and Captain Gomez probably was completely baffled by this meddling in his private life. Bartlett's feelings were aggravated when a wagon broke down as his party left Tubac and he was forced to apply to the captain for help to repair it.

Soon another small train of California-bound emigrant wagons hove in sight, consisting of some forty persons, men and women, from Arkansas, who were typical of the Southerners who were pouring along this route, then all in Mexico from El Paso to the Colorado River, to the promised land. The Southern emigrants have never received the notice which has been given those traveling along the Oregon Trail to the north. The exodus from the slave states to the Pacific coast was probably proportionately as large, and the danger from the fierce Comanches and Apaches greater, but no Francis Parkman ever traveled that way to record its sights and scenes. Bartlett did a good job of noting scientific facts, but he missed the human color and excitement of this way to the goldfields. Evidently these people were not of the slave-holding class, for he never mentioned any accompanying slaves, who would probably not have escaped his keen eyes. Train after train of these migrants passed, all using oxen on their wagons, often more than were needed, so as to sell the surplus for beef in California.

Robert Louis Stevenson probably best epitomized the drudgery of the long, long haul to California when he wrote:

Yet one could not but reflect upon the weariness of those who passed by there in old days, at the foot's pace of oxen, painfully urging their teams, and with no landmark but that unattainable evening sun for which they steered, and which daily fled them by an equal stride. They had nothing, it would seem, to overtake. Nothing by which to reckon their advance; no sight for repose or for encouragement; but stage after stage, only the dead green waste under foot, and the mocking, fugitive horizon.[2]

All these people were puzzled by meeting a well-organized party going eastward and exclaimed, "Halloa, strangers, haven't you mistaken the road — you're going the wrong way — this is the way to Californy!" Many of the women and children of these parties were sick, and Bartlett stopped at each meeting to allow Dr. Webb to visit and prescribe for them as best he could, as rarely did the emigrants possess medicines. They had been exposed to constant rains, with no protection but their wagons, and it was pitiful to see these poor emaciated and suffering people

[2] *Across the Plains* (New York 1887), pp. 41-42.

lying beneath the trees at every halt, trying to recuperate. Perhaps it occurred to Bartlett then that he had rather casually bartered away this well-traveled route to California when he succumbed to General Condé's blandishments, but if so, he kept silent about it. The opposition to his agreement, especially among the Texans and other Southerners, was very understandable.

The Americans were joined by a party of Mexican soldiers who attached themselves, probably to get under the wing of such a well-armed group for protection against the Apaches. Again Bartlett emphasized in his narrative the utter desolation of this once fertile and populated land, with ranch after ranch abandoned, the villages in a state of siege, and the old missions in ruins; all because of the constant raids by the relentless Apache savages.

They reached Santa Cruz, the home town of the fair Inez Gonzalez, and Bartlett, remembering the petty thievery on his first visit, encamped the train a mile beyond the village, "where the men would be away from the contaminations of a low Mexican population, miserable, filthy, and poor as this was." The commissioner was occasionally a hardheaded realist. He went to call on his old friend the village priest, and they mutually deplored the fate of Inez Gonzalez, but the priest affirmed that it was beyond his powers to interfere with an army officer's amatory affairs. Bartlett, however, had one shot left in his Puritanical locker and wrote a long letter to his friend the governor of Sonora, requesting his interference in Inez's behalf — with unknown results, for he never mentioned Inez again. The ways of New England were not the ways of Sonora.

Dr. Webb again visited many sick natives in Santa Cruz, presumably free of charge in most cases. In fact, the doctor seemed a thoroughly good Samaritan at all times, and he must have been a great builder of good will for the Americans. He attended a

Polish officer in the Mexican Army who had been wounded in a fight with the Apaches, and also Captain Murphy, in command of the garrison. Always one found European soldiers of fortune, especially from the Catholic countries of Europe, in the Latin-American armies, and especially Irishmen who carried on the tradition of the close bonds between Spain and Erin before the wars of independence. Incidentally, the last Spanish viceroy in Mexico was named O'Donoju, and he was but one of thousands with an Irish name in the old Spanish colonial service.

Despite Bartlett's precautions in pitching his camp a mile away from the iniquities of Santa Cruz, all the teamsters and mule skinners managed to slake their raging thirsts, built up by the miles in the hot, arid desert, and got roaring drunk in town. Jesus Lopez, the muleteer who had killed the Apache back at the Santa Rita copper mines, particularly distinguished himself in the general brawl by beating up a respectable woman into whose house he had broken. Bartlett was delighted to turn him over to the local authorities as he had made trouble all along the line. He concluded, as has many an army officer, that it is impossible to isolate the men from temptations, and that the worst behavers in the fleshpots of a town are often the best and most reliable men on the march.

CHAPTER VI

Full Circle

LEAVING Santa Cruz, the party came again to the beautiful wooded country, the first they had seen since California, which had previously reminded Bartlett of the hills of Vermont and New Hampshire on his first trip into Mexico. They again met several parties of westward-bound Americans, one of which threw Bartlett's men into momentary fear because they approached at a gallop in the distance and were thought to be Apaches. The fear was soon lifted when Bartlett saw through his telescope that the oncoming riders wore hats, some of them black. This showed they were neither Apaches nor Mexicans, for the former never wore hats and the latter always wore distinctive, extra-wide-brimmed sombreros. For years afterwards in Arizona it was the custom for white men to shoot at sight at any hatless human figure, a custom which the despondent hatmakers would probably like to have revived and extended in the present Apachelike age.

They reached the town of Janos in northern Chihuahua, after meeting a miserable detachment of Mexican soldiers supposedly chasing the terrible Apaches, and more and more Arkansans hurrying toward the land of gold. Like the other northern posts of Chihuahua and Sonora, the place was falling into decay and had a desolate and forsaken appearance: its buildings in ruins, and the only apparent inhabitants squatting in the shade of the walls, engaged in gambling. Bartlett went to call on the colonel in command, but that officer was taking his siesta and not receiving callers during that sacrosanct period. They found seven Americans in this Godforsaken hole, the usual backwash from the stream of westering emigrant trains, but only one of these, an "herb" or "Thomsonian" doctor, as they called themselves in Mexico, was a permanent resident, and this physician had left an emigrant party and established a lucrative practice, his fees being high and based on a sort of doubles-or-quits system depending on the cures accomplished.

One of the horses died there from a rattlesnake bite received three days before, and the low mortality from this constant danger was surprising. It is hard to realize how these poisonous snakes simply swarmed over the West a century ago. The early explorers, particularly Lewis and Clark, frequently mentioned their excessive numbers. Their numbers today must be but a small fraction of what they once were; probably automobiles and hard roads, by limiting their areas, have been as destructive to them as any other factor.

About the middle of August, 1852, the party set off on the last stretch to El Paso. Bartlett, who never missed anything of interest along the way, stopped to inspect a silver mine and descended its deep shaft for his usual thorough investigation of everything to be seen. The catholic interest of the commissioner in almost everything was unusual, and he must have been a marked contrast to the Arkansas emigrants and the American army officers who typified the United States in Mexico.

After leaving the mine they came to the Santa Maria River, and were in country which later became the stage for the furious but futile pursuit of Pancho Villa by the American forces under General John J. Pershing in 1916–1917. The country was covered with playas, or dry lakes and sand hills, with little forage, and the intense heat and glare of the sun made all miserable. To pass through the white sand hills it was necessary to hitch double teams of mules to each wagon, whose wheels would sink to the hubs in the loose and shifting sands. Men and animals finally staggered exhausted into El Paso after a journey of eighty-one days from San Diego, half of which time had been in a temperature of over 100° and the other half in drenching rains.

Bartlett learned there that the energetic Major Emory, who had succeeded Colonel Graham, was making excellent progress in surveying the lower Rio Grande (or Rio Bravo) and had sent word that he would complete the line to its mouth by the following March. Bartlett decided to join him on the river but to leave the ever-dependable Lieutenant Whipple to complete the survey of a small gap on the debatable southern boundary of New Mexico.

When all was ready for the start, the commissioner found he could not obtain a military escort, as all the available men had been assigned to Whipple. This meant that it would be extremely dangerous to travel on the American side of the Rio Grande, for the Comanches, in many ways a more dangerous tribe than the Apaches, had recently attacked every small party coming through from San Antonio; and the arrival of a mail party from that place, commanded by the famous Big Foot Wallace, who was about as able an Indian fighter as Texas afforded, with the news that they had been besieged for several days by a large body of Comanches, decided Bartlett to accept the offer of a Mexican escort from his old friend Colonel Langberg, and to travel through the northern Mexican states to Camargo on the lower Rio Grande.

So the scientific brain trust of the border commission — Bartlett, Dr. Thomas H. Webb, the surgeon and secretary, George

Thurber, quartermaster and botanist, and Henry C. Pratt, draftsman and artist — with twenty other assistants, teamsters, and
servants, set out in the first part of October, 1852, from James
Magoffin's storehouse, after a farewell cold collation which
Bartlett said would have done credit to the caterer of a metro-
politan hotel. The commissioner, as usual, rode in a light traveling carriage in which he also slept. They picked up their Mexican escort of only five soldiers on the other side of the Rio
Grande and ascended the tableland, southward toward the city
of Chihuahua, making good and bad going, depending on the
rains and consequent mud and gumbo, to the village of Carrizal,
where years later, in 1916, the Mexicans defeated two troops of
the colored 9th U. S. Cavalry in pursuit of Pancho Villa. Bartlett kept outside the place, for, as he wrote, "we had not been
in one where the *arrieros* or teamsters did not get into a row, or
return to the camp in a state of drunkenness." This town, like
the others, had been devastated by Indian attacks.

Early one morning, on an open plain, the long-dreaded Indian
attack came like a bolt of lightning. Probably the members of
the party had become dulled to the danger, for it was the first
and only time they were attacked in over two years of wandering through hostile Indian country. A band of about forty
mounted Indians, armed with lances and bows and arrows, burst
headlong at full gallop out of a hidden arroyo, and with terrific
screams and yells tried to break the straggling line of march and
stampede the mules. But the teamsters and Mexican soldiers kept
their heads and closed up the line, keeping the savages at bay
by leveling their pistols at them but holding their fire. Bartlett
said: "Had they fired and missed their mark (and the chances
were ten-to-one against their hitting), they would have been
pierced by a lance or an arrow the next moment." Failing to
throw the wagons into disorder, the Indians dashed to the rear

and made a furious charge at the men driving the spare mules and horses, but again they were determinedly met. One Mexican herdsman was lanced to the heart in the melee, and an Indian was fatally shot, but his companions threw his bleeding body across a mule ridden by another Indian and rode off with it.

Unsuccessful in these two attacks, the Indians espied poor Mr. Thurber, the botanist, who had stopped to put some plants in his portfolio, off by himself to the rear. With more screams and whoops they charged at him with their lances, but he, good man, kept his head, and held them off with his leveled repeating Colt revolver, a weapon for which all Indians had learned respect. Fortunately, Bartlett's men were close on the enemies' heels, so that the attackers turned and made for the nearby hills, and Mr. Thurber was rescued unharmed. Despite this valiant stand, ten mules and a valuable horse were stampeded and lost, which was a poor exchange for the horse, saddle, and arms of one Indian.

Bartlett seemed to believe that these attackers were Apaches, in which he may have been mistaken — possibly because he could not give them a language quiz. The Apaches rarely attacked mounted and were but indifferent horsemen at best, using what mounts they had for travel and dismounting to attack, usually from ambush. The Indians, in this case, had all the earmarks of Comanches, who were superb horsemen and experts in the use of lances and bows and arrows from horseback. Also, the train had moved far enough eastward in the Mexican state of Chihuahua to be in Comanche country, close to the famous war trail down which the Indians descended each year in the light of the full September moon to scourge the Mexican settlements as far south as Durango.

The country became more settled and cultivated as the train moved south, following almost exactly the march of Colonel William Doniphan and his Missouri Volunteers in 1847, and they camped one night near the battlefield of Sacramento, where the Missourians had gained a decisive victory over the Mexicans which resulted in the capture of the city of Chihuahua. On October 22, Bartlett's party entered that city amid a tremendous cracking of the teamsters' whips, which always made a good show for a grand entry, and pitched their camp in a large enclosure, within a high wall, which was kept by the city for just such wagon trains.

A rest had been well earned after the 270-mile journey from El Paso, and the gentlemen of the party relaxed in a round of social activities. Formal calls were exchanged with the Mexican officials and several Americans dropped in. General Trias, the governor of Chihuahua, gave a formal dinner for the gentlemen of the commission, at which excellent food and wines were served by soldiers acting as waiters, and patriotic toasts were politely exchanged. Afterwards the party attended a ball at which a number of lovely Mexican ladies graced the dance floor. Bartlett was enthusiastic about their charms, but noticed their unusual custom of smoking cigarettes between dances. However, he said, they exhausted these dainty little cigars with a few puffs, which were not accompanied by the filthy practice of spitting.

Bartlett was much interested in "a singular breed of diminutive dogs which are found only here," and tried unsuccessfully to learn their origin. These, of course, were the famous Chihuahua breed, which, as he described them, "have not the shape of common lap dogs, or of the stunted, dwarfish curs, with large bodies and short legs, which are of common occurrence; but they possess the elegant form of a full-grown mastiff, with small heads, and slender and delicate limbs and bodies." Several were bought and brought home by members of the commission, two by Bartlett which did not weigh over four pounds each, but he was disappointed when the puppies later born to this pair in

Providence "attained a size and weight about four times that of the mother," which seemed to be the usual result when the breed was introduced into the United States.

In November the party resumed a typically Bartlett zigzag course toward the lower Rio Grande. Mr. Flotte, an American mine owner, joined the train with his Mexican wife and eight children, but also brought along several well-armed retainers, so that this addition pulled its own weight through the dangerous Indian country. Again they saw the same sights of abandoned haciendas and ranchos, and general desolation. Everything in the country was in ruin or decay. The villages, the churches and all their furnishings, the roads, the bridges; and even the people themselves seemed sunk in resigned apathy to the Indian scourge.

But now they were in the path of the mounted Comanches, who were even more destructive than the Apaches because their superb horsemanship gave them wider range. Both tribes were wantonly destructive, killing all horses and cattle which they were not able to drive off for their own use and leaving utter devastation in their wakes. Probably never in the history of the Americas have the Indians wreaked more continual and severe damage than that which they did in northern Mexico for over forty years after that country's independence.

The party skirted the famous Bolson de Mapimi, the badlands of northeastern Chihuahua, which were the strongholds of the Comanches and Lipans (a branch of the Apaches), and proceeded south to the state of Durango. Again they entered more prosperous country, too far south to be seriously damaged by the marauding Indians, and passed large cattle and horse ranches, one of which, in the good old days of Spain, had reportedly presented a regiment of dragoons with a thousand white horses, all of the same age and all raised on the estate. The story went that the colonel happened to be a friend of the family of the owner, then a widow, and she casually gave these horses from her enormous herds, as a slight token of esteem.

From Durango they turned east to Parras, in the state of Coahuila, which Bartlett thought a neat and well-built town, and noted its surrounding maguey plantations, the plant from which the drink of pulque was made. He collected there an unusual number of specimens of minerals, reptiles, and insects through the help of the priest, "a courteous and intelligent gentleman." Americans seemed to be unusually popular in Parras because of the favorable impression left by General John E. Wool and his officers, who had stopped there for a time during the Mexican War, on their famous march from San Antonio, Texas, to Saltillo.

Continuing east, they struck the path up which General Santa Anna had marched his army from San Luis Potosi to attack Zachary Taylor and his comparative handful of men at the battle of Buena Vista, on February 22–23, 1847. The party rode directly through the narrow pass of Angostura, in which Taylor's men, outnumbered by about five to one, repulsed the Mexicans in the most desperate and bloody battle ever fought by United States forces before the Civil War. The small party stopped for a while and the men walked about the battlefield, following the general plan of battle from a map which Bartlett produced. Many relics were found, and many still remain there to this day on this almost forgotten field upon which nearly three hundred American soldiers lie in unmarked graves.

In the evening of that same day they rode, with the customary cracking of whips, into Saltillo, the capital of the state of Coahuila, producing the usual sensation in the quiet Mexican towns, as forty long-bearded gringos, armed to the teeth, clattered through the streets with their wagon train. The Americans had held Saltillo for over a year and a half during the Mexican War, and this band of Americans must have stirred recent memories among the natives. Here Bartlett received news of the election, the month before, of the Democrat candidate Franklin Pierce as President, and he must have realized that his days as boundary commissioner appointed by a Whig administration were probably numbered. But any such forebodings did not stop the commissioner from making his usual careful sight-seeing tour of the city, and he was particularly interested in the cathedral, which he decided surpassed any other he had seen in Mexico; its interior abounding in fine pictures, sculptures, and ornaments of much taste, and well preserved. He also was impressed with the city's modern cotton mills, which were managed by a fellow Rhode Islander. Saltillo, he decided, was the finest city he had yet seen in the republic.

From here the party rode on eastward to Monterey (then spelled with one *r*), descending slowly through mountain passes to the lower level of the plain. Just before entering the city, they passed on their left the steep hill on which stood the bishop's palace, the key point of defense, which General William Jenkins Worth's men had carried by storm when Zachary Taylor attacked the city in September, 1846. Monterey, like Saltillo, was a pretty, attractive place, far different from the Indian-desolated towns of northern Chihuahua and Sonora, to the west. Bartlett, as always, did the town thoroughly and rode up to the bishop's palace, from where one can see the beautiful city along the Santa Catarina River, with the mountains enclosing it, except to the north, like a three-sided corral. This city was, and is, the capital of the state of Nueva Leon; today a booming industrial center, often called the Pittsburgh of Mexico.

The party left Monterey on its last lap back to the States and arrived at Ringgold Barracks, Texas, near the present Rio Grande

City, just before Christmas. There Bartlett met Major William H.
Emory, who had succeeded Colonel Graham as chief surveyor.

Emory was another topographical engineer, a native of Maryland and a graduate of West Point, class of 1831, who had accompanied General Stephen Kearny on his dash to California
in 1846 and had written a report of this, *Notes of a Military
Reconnaissance from Ft. Leavenworth, in Missouri, to San Diego, in California,* which was an interesting account of this pioneering trip to the Pacific coast. He had worked on the survey
of the northeastern boundary between Maine and Canada in
1844–1846, had received two brevet promotions for gallantry
during the Mexican War, and had been the original chief astronomer of the first boundary commission, which had met in San
Diego in 1849. Later, during the Civil War, he won four more
brevets and rose to the rank of major general. He married
Matilda Wilkins Bache, a great-granddaughter of Benjamin
Franklin. He was a skillful, fine, and courageous soldier, and
the border survey was at last in competent technical hands.
Emory eventually went on to finish the whole job, including a
new survey of the southern boundary of what is now Arizona
and New Mexico, as soon afterwards acquired under the Gadsden Purchase in 1853.

Bartlett had hardly arrived at Ringgold Barracks before a
dispatch came from Washington which ended his career as
boundary commissioner. His arbitrary decision about the initial
point on the Rio Grande for the survey of the southern boundary
of New Mexico had come home to roost with a dull thud. The
latest congressional appropriation for funds to pay the expenses
of the commission contained a proviso that these funds could not
be used until it was satisfactorily shown that the southern boundary of New Mexico followed the line "laid down in Disturnell's
map." Secretary of the Interior Stuart expressed the desire, in

the dispatch, that Bartlett complete the survey of the Rio Grande if he had the means on hand, but "if otherwise, the commission must retire from the field." Bartlett did not have the means or even enough money to pay the expenses of the officers and men to their homes. There was no choice. The commission had to be disbanded at once. A large part of the field equipment and livestock were sold in San Antonio and the proceeds, with what funds Bartlett had, allowed him to pay off all the personnel, including their necessary traveling expenses.

The falling of the ax on Bartlett had been pretty obviously on the cards for some time. His decision to disregard the boundary line on Disturnell's map was good enough in theory and ethics, but it was against the solid advice of all his experienced advisers, particularly of the topographical engineers. Unquestionably the map was inaccurate, but this was only relative and he should have followed the specific terms of the Treaty of Guadalupe Hidalgo and placed his initial point so many miles "north of the town called Paso" *as shown on that map*. Instead of this he insisted on correcting the latitude of that town and then accordingly moving the initial point so many miles farther north. By doing this he greatly antagonized the Texans and other Southerners who probably believed that the little Rhode Island Yankee was purposely giving the only far-southern wagon road or railroad route to California back to Mexico against the specific terms of the peace treaty. It is almost certain that Bartlett had no such ulterior motive and acted only on the highest principles, but he was in the clouds of high ethics and theory and his fall to the hard ground of reality was inevitable. The way of the theoretical "do-gooder" was hard when it conflicted with the fierce and fanatical sectional interests of the 1850's.

Bartlett, accompanied by Major Emory and most of the personnel of the border commission, then went to the Texas coast, to Corpus Christi. On the way, he had one last bit of Western excitement when an immense herd of wild horses, mustangs of the plains, stampeded some of his loose mules and nearly swept off those drawing the wagons like an avalanche. This disaster was prevented by pulling into a line, locking the wagon wheels together, and then turning the onrushing torrent of mustangs by shots fired at their front. It was a narrow squeak and as exciting an adventure as Commissioner Bartlett had met during all his travels. In early January, 1853, he sailed from Corpus Christi and transshipped at Indianola, but not before he had thoroughly investigated and reported on both towns and the surrounding areas. He landed in New Orleans, went by boat up the Mississippi and Ohio Rivers to Cincinnati, and thence by the railroad cars via Albany to his home in Providence, where it can be assumed that he, carrying a little Chihuahua lap dog under each arm, was joyfully welcomed by his wife and the little Bartletts, after an absence of nearly two and a half years.

Bartlett's after-career was distinguished. He served as secretary of state of Rhode Island for fifteen years, and during this time he arranged and edited a great mass of public papers which he gradually published in ten volumes. He wrote several books on Rhode Island history and he helped John Carter Brown with his famous collection of books on early Americana which are now in the library of that name on the Brown University campus. He compiled the *John Carter Brown Catalogue* of this collection, which was the greatest advance to that time in the bibliography of early American discovery and history and is still most useful to the student of that period. His first wife died in November, 1853, in the autumn of the year of his return, leaving him with the children, but he soon married again and never thereafter left his home. He died in 1886, a leading citizen of Providence.

Bartlett was a kindly humanitarian, an able antiquarian, ethnologist and bibliographer, and an inquisitive and keen observer who reported his findings and experiences in crisp, technical language, and his reports were of great value to scientists and later travelers in the Southwest. Considering all this, he was probably a good investment for the American taxpayers despite his sloppy administration of the border commission and his interminable junkets in all directions. But he was certainly not the man to direct a prompt and efficient border survey. Major Emory, who succeeded him, fortunately had all the experience and qualities needed for the task, and under his direction the survey was brought to a quick and satisfactory termination.

CHAPTER VII

The Final Boundary Settlement

THE recall of Bartlett and Major Emory, of course, left everything in the border survey at loose ends and hanging in mid-air. Naturally, something had to be done — and quickly. The incoming Democratic administration strongly desired to obtain a good southern road, wagon or rail, to California, and it was finally realized that such a route would have to follow approximately Philip St. George's way to the coast in 1846. Part of this, however, lay south of even the line specified in Disturnell's map, a fact which the competent Major Emory had realized and earlier had futilely reported to the powers in Washington. There was only one practical way to obtain this needed land and that was by purchase. Luckily, the avaricious and corruptible Antonio Lopez de Santa Anna was again the president of Mexico and badly in need of money to bulwark his shaky administration. President Franklin Pierce and the Democratic leaders saw that the time was right for striking and chose, as the personification of a hot iron, Colonel James Gadsden of South Carolina.

Gadsden was a scion of a famous Charleston family, a grandson of Christopher Gadsden, who had won distinction in the Revolutionary War. He had graduated from Yale College in 1806, two years behind John C. Calhoun, but two of his brothers had been in Calhoun's class and one, John, had also been in Phi

Beta Kappa with Calhoun. Yale was the favorite college of the fire-eating South Carolinians of the time, and it is believed that their later states' rights and secessionist convictions were, to a certain extent, gained in New Haven from President Timothy Dwight and other extreme Federalists who were believed to have favored secession from the Union at the Hartford Convention of 1814. After graduation, Gadsden served in the Army during the War of 1812 and later with Andrew Jackson during the Florida campaign of 1817–1818. He became quite a political pet of Old Hickory's, although he never was able to win an elective office. However, he was quite successful in business and became president of the South Carolina Railroad Company.

Gadsden, as minister of the United States, went to Mexico, and in December, 1853, succeeded in purchasing the needed territory, which is now marked on historical maps as the Gadsden Purchase, from the Santa Anna administration, for ten million dollars. Of this sum, the slippery Mexican president took a *mordida*, or bite, of seven hundred thousand dollars for alleged damages done to his own personal property by American troops during the late war, which damages were probably in the fertile imagination of the self-styled "Napoleon of the West." Another favorable result of Gadsden's negotiations was the abrogation by the Mexicans of an article in the peace treaty whereby the United States had agreed to restrain the Indians from raiding into Mexico, a manifest impossibility to enforce with a force of only eight thousand soldiers, in 1852, in all the huge territory acquired from Mexico in 1848. The Gadsden Purchase was ratified in June, 1854, and now, at long last, the decks were completely cleared for a satisfactory and final survey of the boundary. And Major William H. Emory was just the man to accomplish this.

In August, 1854, Emory received his orders to survey this new acquisition and to complete the gaps in the old survey, and he proceeded to do these with promptness and efficiency. Emory was accompanied by the usual bevy of scientists and artists, the latter being Arthur Schott, John Weiss (or Weyss), and A. de Vaudricourt, and these three men also doubled as scientists and surveyors when needed. With their help, Emory turned in an interesting and well-illustrated report.[1] This commission stuck strictly to business along the line of survey and there were no wild junkets over the hills and far away.

Emory had been thoroughly disgusted with the careless administration of his predecessor, and the consequent chaotic conditions and low morale of Bartlett's commission. He reported that he had found things in a frightful mess when he arrived in El Paso to succeed Gray and Colonel Graham. Bartlett had spent about five hundred thousand dollars on a commission which was cluttered with idle, useless people, and at the time when Emory appeared many of the men were unpaid and in a state of semimutiny, while Commissioner Bartlett was off visiting Chihuahua, Sonora, and the geysers of California. Everybody was feuding with everybody else; the commission was in debt; and not one cent of funds was available. Of the five hundred thousand already spent by Bartlett, Emory estimated that not more than a hundred thousand had gone into actual surveying work. The rest had been frittered away on a useless multitude of officers, quartermasters, commissaries, paymasters, agents, secretaries, subsecretaries and whatnots, who knew nothing about science or surveying, and spent their time squabbling in a swelter of red tape and bad temper. This, of course, was the other side of the story not mentioned by Bartlett in his book; and the odds are that Emory was right.

[1] *Report on the United States and Mexican Boundary Survey*, 3 Vols. in 2 (Washington 1857).

In a little more than a month after his appointment, Emory had not only assembled another surveying party, including his brain trust of scientists and artists, but also had landed them at Indianola, Texas, after a hurricane which nearly wrecked the party at that port. His military escort of one company of the 7th Infantry was commanded by Captain E. Kirby Smith, a native of Florida, whose family had come from Litchfield, Connecticut. Kirby Smith was a West Pointer, class of 1845, who had made a splendid record in the Mexican War and later went on to become a full general in the Confederate Army in command of Texas and all Confederate territory west of the Mississippi River, which was called "Kirby-Smithdom" because of his absolute rule. He also acted as a botanist on Emory's expedition and a report of his observations was published by the Smithsonian Institution. By the end of that year, in three months, Emory had completed the gaps in the survey of the Rio Grande (or Rio Bravo as he called it).

Emory met the same troubles and tribulations which had beset Bartlett — diseases and Indians — but he came through it all with the loss of only two men, and no losses whatever of livestock by thievery or stampedes. His attitude toward the Indians was the direct opposite of Bartlett's, for he was a believer in General Phil Sheridan's later dictum: "The only good Indian is a dead Indian." Emory was interested only in surveying, and gave orders that no Indians with a hostile record were to be allowed in his camps and to shoot any found hanging around. A harsh order but the result spoke for itself. The accompanying Mexican commission, with the usual easy-going attitude toward the Indians, was robbed repeatedly. He wrote that "civilization must consent to halt when in view of the Indian camp, or the wild Indians must be exterminated." He believed kindness was wasted on these savages, for the Catholic priests had tried everything in that line for centuries and had failed completely. His opinion of the lawless border Mexican *pelaos* or peons of the lower class was equally dim, and he blamed Mexican miscegenation for the constant turmoils in that country, saying that the cross between Spanish men and Indian women, because of the "absence of the women of the cleaner colored race," had resulted in "a very inferior and syphilitic race"; and that the resulting children of all colors produced suspicion in the male which led to resentful adultery by his wife; but that where the pure Spanish blood was preserved the integrity and character of the people were very good. Emory was no ethnologist but he certainly knew how to survey.

The most difficult part in the survey of the Rio Grande had been the course of the river through a part of the Big Bend where it makes a giant turn to the north and, narrowing its channel from three hundred to twenty-five feet, rushed in rapids "foaming and tumbling in a furious manner" through deep canyons and gorges over a bed filled with huge rocks and boulders. At that time nobody had ever navigated these rapids, and the surrounding country was so rough and wild that no white man had ever crossed it. After a flatboat had been sunk in one of the unnavigable rapids, the survey was finally made along the summits of the enclosing walls of the canyons. Today this area is the Big Bend National Park and its highest peak bears the name of Mount Emory. The far-sighted Emory rightly predicted there would be much future trouble, in spots, from the constantly changing course of the river, which had not been provided for in the treaty; but he sensibly decided that was not the commissioners' worry and got on with the job as the river then flowed.

Having completed the work on the Rio Grande, Emory moved his men to El Paso to work on the boundary line of the recent

Gadsden Purchase. The new Mexican boundary commissioner was Señor José Salazar who had been the official surveyor under General Condé. He and Emory got on very well, so well that when Salazar was forced to drop out, he asked Emory to continue the line to the west. This Emory did until he met the American and Mexican parties, at the 111th meridian, who were working eastward from the Colorado River. There was excellent co-operation between the two commissions at all times and markers were placed at intervals through this arid country which, once and for all, showed the permanent boundary line between the two countries.

Lieutenant Nathaniel Michler, another topographical engineer, commanded the surveying party coming from the west. He had gone to San Diego from Washington, D. C., via Panama, and had then come overland to Fort Yuma, where he arrived in early December, 1854. Before leaving San Diego, he took a long look at the local Indian squaws and wrote: "The women are beautifully developed, and superbly formed, their bodies as straight as an arrow," but after this complimentary opening he must have raised his eyes and approached nearer, for he concluded that "their features, however, are coarse and uninviting, their persons filthy, and their actions still more disgusting." [2] He described the notorious miseries of the blast-furnace climate of Fort Yuma and mentioned as being there Major George H. Thomas, the Virginian who became a Union general during the Civil War, and was called the "Rock of Chickamauga."

The Mexican surveying party arrived at Fort Yuma and accepted an initial point, under the terms of the Gadsden Purchase, which Michler had established about twenty-eight miles below the junction of the Gila and Colorado Rivers (instead of the old

---

[2] Emory, *Report on the United States and Mexican Boundary Survey*, 3 Vols. in 2 (Washington 1857), I, p. 107.

point at the junction). The two parties worked harmoniously eastward together, although Michler commented that "Imagination cannot picture a more dreary, sterile country. . . ." They kept meeting disappointed people returning from California, one defeated group of a woman and three men on foot, with a pack horse carrying their all. The three men had given up in the desert and had lain down to die from thirst, but the undaunted woman climbed a mountain to a spring and saved them all. The joint survey parties found the going so rough and their provisions so low that they gave up the work and went east to meet Emory.

Then Lieutenant Michler turned back and ran the survey west from what is now Nogales, Arizona, to where he had been forced to stop previously. They met the famous local Gila monster, known to the Mexicans as *el scorpion*, which Michler described as "a large, slothful lizard, in shape a miniature alligator, marked with red, black, and white belts — a hideous-looking animal," and they were plagued with other reptiles, for "The glare of our fires attracted a large number of rattlesnakes; the whole place seemed infested with them." Some had "tiger-colored skins and were exceedingly fierce and venomous"; others had horns, or small protuberances above their eyes. At night they followed the old Mexican custom of circling their beds with horsehair *reatas* (ropes), for the snakes were said to have a perfect repugnance to being pricked by the coarse hairs and would not cross them, a practice which desert campers still observe against the scoffings of modern scientists.

Despite the heat, thirst, and repulsive reptiles, the complete survey was finished in August, 1855, and it has stood the test of time to this day, except for changes in the course of the Rio Grande which have caused serious problems and disputes, as Emory predicted. All the reports of the scientists of both the

Bartlett and Emory expeditions were included in Emory's official report, which ran to two fat volumes and covered the geology, paleontology and zoology of the region, with many subdivisions such as ornithology, ichthyology, and others; so that about a half of the text appears to be in Latin. Some of the members of the commissions were immortalized by having their names given to new botanical specimens, such as *Daubentonia Thurberi*, *Dalea Emoryi*, and *Dalea Schotti*. It was all most impressive and pretty much set the tone for later reports of government exploring expeditions.

The artists turned in an excellent job as well, especially Arthur Schott, who also served as a surveyor with Emory. The one mystery is the fate of the many sketches, drawings, and paintings made by Henry Cheeves Pratt, the Bostonian artist who accompanied Bartlett and whose work was repeatedly mentioned in the latter's book. This book was commercially published but it was illustrated almost entirely by Bartlett's own drawings, with the exception of a few by Pratt. Emory's report contains no Pratt drawings. These missing pictures were, of course, government property, but there seems to be nothing known about them today in the National Archives, the Library of Congress, or the Smithsonian Institution, in one of which they certainly should be. There is information that Bartlett turned over several portfolios of what he claimed were Pratt's sketches to the Department of the Interior in June, 1854, to be delivered to General R. B. Campbell, his successor for a short time as boundary commissioner; but Emory and Campbell refused to accept these as unworthy, unfinished, and incomplete. What then happened to these and to others which Emory seemed sure Bartlett was withholding appears unknown.[3]

---

[3] William H. Emory Papers in possession of Edward Eberstadt and Sons, New York City. Correspondence of April, May, and June 1854.

CHAPTER VIII

Probing for Roads

BEFORE the acquisition by conquest of about one half of the area of the Republic of Mexico, the Oregon Trail, running from Wesport, Missouri, up the Platte and North Platte Rivers, through South Pass into present northeastern Utah, and then approximately following the Snake and Columbia Rivers to the Pacific coast, was well established as the main line for American emigrants to the Far West. This trail was usable by wagons, and was in United States territory until the Oregon country was reached, which, before the settlement of 1846 with Great Britain, was a huge mass of land west of the watershed of the Rocky Mountains, running well north into present Canada and including our present states of Oregon, Washington and Idaho, a great chunk of Montana, and a part of Wyoming. This Oregon country was a condominium held in joint occupancy with Great Britain, until it was divided in 1846 along the present boundary lines.

South of this, a rough and dangerous way turned off the Oregon Trail toward California at Fort Hall and followed the course of Mary's River (later named the Humboldt by John C. Frémont) to the Sierras, which were only crossed with the greatest difficulty, but there was only a trickle of emigration along this way until the discovery of gold in California. Still farther south

the Santa Fe Trail, starting also from Westport, ran as far as the
old capital of the Mexican territory of New Mexico. From there
what was called the Spanish Trail ran in a northward arc through
what is now southern Utah to descend from there southward to
Los Angeles. The Mormons, after 1846, extended a branch trail
down from Salt Lake City to join this as it curved away to California. But the Spanish Trail was not practicable for wagons.
Below this, Philip St. George Cooke's route could be used by
wagons and soon became filled with emigrants to California,
after 1848, as Bartlett had noted when he stemmed this tide from
the west.

But these few wagon roads to the Pacific coast were not
enough to drain the mounting flood of eager gold seekers and
emigrants after the Mexican War. Except for California, which
became a state in 1850 all this land, through which the emigrants
passed west of Missouri, Arkansas, and Texas, was Federal territory, and so it was the responsibility of the government in Washington to explore and survey the possible roads across it.

Various expeditions, notably two under Captain (later General) Randolph Barnes Marcy, one of the really great frontiersmen, pushed through and surveyed new routes for wagon roads
which were later developed at government expense. Other exploring parties sought for artesian wells along some of these
roads to supply water in the arid regions of the Southwest. Congress even appropriated a hundred thousand dollars in 1857 for
Captain John G. Pope, another topographical engineer, to sink
wells in west Texas and eastern New Mexico along the trail to
El Paso. But these wells, even with shafts sunk to thirteen hundred feet, mostly turned out dry holes. Camels were brought
from Africa and the Near East and proved rather successful, in
this desert country, on a trial trip to California under the command of a naval lieutenant, Edward F. Beale, another famous

trail breaker. But the Indian menace in the Southwest mounted instead of abating, so that, on the whole, the Oregon Trail, and its branches to California, despite its closure in the winter, probably served the majority of the emigrants. It was exceedingly tough going in wagons by any way, and the obvious solution was the building of a transcontinental railroad.

There had been considerable agitation for a railroad to the Pacific, even before the Mexican War. Asa Whitney, a native of Connecticut, had been bombarding Congress for years with petitions for Federal aid to build a railroad from Lake Superior to a point on the Pacific coast in Oregon, although that latter territory was then held in joint occupancy with Great Britain. In the East, railroads were booming after the mid-century mark, for their mileage rose from 8800 miles in 1850 to 21,300 miles in 1854. But sectional feeling had blocked Whitney's project, for the Southerners foresaw what an advantage to the free states a far-northern route like this would be. After the acquisition of the huge area from Mexico, however, the field was thrown wide open for a transcontinental railroad and an intense rivalry naturally ensued.

Most of the topographical engineers favored a far-southern route, along the Mexican border, which would have the best year-around climatic conditions, would be the shortest, and would also serve to keep the rampaging border Indians under control. But, of course, this was not palatable to the Northerners, who wanted Whitney's suggested route or one along the Oregon Trail between the other two. The arguments were long and bitter, pro and con, and finally Secretary of War Jefferson Davis was authorized in 1853 to make four railroad surveys from the Mississippi River to the Pacific coast under the general supervision of the Topographical Engineers. The Oregon Trail was not included as this was well known and taken for granted as being suitable for a railroad. So well done were these assignments that four transcontinental railroads of today follow the surveys made, and the Union Pacific, the first railroad to be completed (1869), follows the old Oregon Trail.

The largest and most costly expedition of the four — it was twice as large and cost twice as much as any other — surveyed the northernmost route, following part of the way of Lewis and Clark in 1805–1806, and is today largely used by the Northern Pacific, and in spots by the Great Northern Railway. Probably Jefferson Davis, who naturally favored a southern route, leaned over backwards to prevent charges of favoritism, for he gave this expedition the best of everything in supplies, instruments, and equipment, and a picked personnel of scientists and artists to collect, classify, and sketch the natural wonders of this route. It was under the command of a Yankee of Yankees, Isaac Ingalls Stevens, originally from North Andover, Massachusetts, a West Pointer, class of 1839, who had served with distinction in the Mexican War. He had resigned from the army in 1852, when appointed governor of the new Washington Territory, and he took charge of this expedition on his way to his duties. This survey, of course, was the only one not in any territory acquired from Mexico.

Among the large ménage of scientists and artists along was an outstanding artist, John Mix Stanley, a grandfather of Mrs. Dean Acheson, the wife of our former secretary of state. He was a native New Yorker, then about forty years old, who had previously traveled widely in the West and had accompanied General Stephen Kearny on his dash to the coast in 1846; and Stanley's sketches of this march were used to illustrate Major William H. Emory's official report. He was a painter of Indians as well as of scenery, and Seth Eastman, that rare combination of an army officer and artist, believed that his portraits were better than those of George Catlin, who is generally considered the great painter of Indians. In 1852, Stanley put on exhibition two hundred of his paintings of forty-three different Indian tribes, which represented ten years' work, in the Smithsonian Institution, where later all but five were destroyed by fire in 1865. He also afterwards exhibited in Washington, in September, 1854, a panorama, *Scenes and Incidents of Stanley's Western Wilds*, which was reported to have been shipped from there to Boston and London for exhibit but which has disappeared. It would be priceless today.

Stevens sent Captain George B. McClellan, a topographical engineer later in command of the Army of the Potomac during the Civil War, by water to the coast of Oregon with orders to work eastward, exploring the mountain passes in the winter to see what difficulties the snow would make for a railroad. McClellan reported that the snows were too heavy in several passes, which annoyed Stevens, who was fanatical in his desire to prove this northern route practical. Perhaps McClellan was supercautious, a trait which he certainly displayed later in the Civil War, or perhaps he was right in those days before rotary snowplows.

The main party worked rapidly west from St. Paul under Stevens's dynamic drive and avoided any hostile encounters with the warlike Sioux or Blackfeet Indians because of the leader's eternal vigilance and strict discipline. The most interesting meeting was a friendly one with a large party of half-breed French Canadians at the Red River of the North. Some fifteen hundred of these, including their families in wagons, were on a buffalo hunt, and they hailed the Americans with pleasure and gave them much valuable information about the limitless prairies to the west. After meeting McClellan, coming from the west, and receiving all the reports from various exploring parties which he had fanned out in different directions to inspect all the possible mountain passes, Stevens sent Stanley back to Washington via the Isthmus of Panama with his report, illustrated by the artist's excellent drawings. Stanley remained in the East until his death in 1872. Stevens was later killed as a Union major general at the battle of Chantilly in September, 1862.

Down to the south, below the Oregon Trail, another survey was made near the 38th parallel of latitude which is now approximately followed by the Denver and Rio Grande Western Railroad, the "Main Line Thru the Rockies"; and through the very heart of the Rockies it goes in Colorado, through the Royal Gorge, hugging the Arkansas River nearly to its source, and on to the great watershed, where it picks up the course of the Colorado River to the west, the most mountainous and scenic route of all. Captain John W. Gunnison from New Hampshire, a West Pointer and topographical engineer, assisted by Lieutenant E. G. Beckwith of the artillery, had charge of this survey, which had a terrible ending. Gunnison had been in Utah in 1849-1850, on an exploration and survey of the Great Salt Lake, under the command of Captain Howard Stansbury,[1] still another topographical engineer, and had written a good book, *The Mormons, or Latter Day Saints in the Valley of the Great Salt Lake*, published in 1852.

After he and Beckwith had worked their way through the roughest sort of country to the western slope of the Rockies, just as they had finished the hard, tough work, the Pah-Utah (Paiute) Indians ambushed and killed Gunnison, his artist, Richard H. Kern, the naturalist Creutzfeldt, and five soldiers of his escort.

---

[1] See Captain Howard Stansbury, *Exploration and Survey of the Great Salt Lake of Utah* (Philadelphia 1852), for a report of this interesting expedition.

Beckwith was luckily absent and later officially reported this ghastly massacre as follows:

Captain Gunnison had encamped early in the afternoon, while the wind and storm were yet fresh, and doubtless feeling the security which men come to indulge after passing long periods of time surrounded by savages without actually encountering them. The abundant grass and fuel of a little nook in the river bottom, sheltered by the high second bank of the river on one side, and thick willows, distant scarcely thirty yards, on two of the others, with the river in front, offered a tempting place of comfort and utility, which was perhaps accepted without even a thought of danger. It was known to the party that a band of Indians was near them, for we had seen their fires daily since entering the valley; but an unusual feeling of security against them was felt, as Captain Gunnison had learned that a recent quarrel, resulting in several deaths, which they had had with emigrants, had terminated . . .

The usual precaution of a camp guard had been taken, each of the party (including the commander) in turn having performed that duty during the night. At the break of day all arose and at once engaged in the usual duties of a camp preparatory to an early start. . . . The sun had not yet risen, most of the party being at breakfast, when the surrounding quietness and silence of this vast plain was broken by the discharge of a volley of rifles and a shower of arrows through that devoted camp, mingled with the savage yells of a large band of Pah-Utah ·[Paiute] Indians almost in the midst of the camp; for, under cover of the thick bushes, they had approached undiscovered to within twenty-five yards of the camp-fires. The surprise was complete. . . . All was confusion. Captain Gunnison, stepping from his tent, called to his savage murderers that he was their friend; but this had no effect. They rushed into camp, and only those escaped who succeeded in mounting on horseback, and even they were pursued for many miles.[2]

[2] *Pacific Railroad Surveys*, Vol. II (Washington 1855), pp. 73-74. See next footnote for full official title of these surveys.

Gunnison himself fell pierced by fifteen arrows.

Some believed that the Mormons had instigated this massacre, for that sect was still naturally bitter about the maltreatment which it had received from the "Gentiles" back in Missouri and at Nauvoo, Illinois, and did not want a stream of unbelievers pouring into their new sanctuary by any kind of road. But Lieutenant Beckwith did not believe this accusation to be true and he should have known the circumstances. After Gunnison's murder, Beckwith went on to explore the vicinity of Salt Lake City and then turned westward, along the 42nd parallel to Fort Reading (now Redding), California. The murdered Captain Gunnison was deservedly immortalized by his name being given to the Gunnison River in Colorado and to a national park through which this river flows in the awesome depths of its famous Black Canyon.

Far to the south, almost on the Mexican border, Captain John G. Pope and Lieutenant J. G. Parke explored the later route of the Southern Pacific Railroad and the Texas Pacific Railroad along the 32nd parallel. Both these officers later became Union major generals in the Civil War, and Pope commanded at the disastrous defeat at the Second Manassas. These two topographical engineers divided up the route, Parke leaving San Diego in January, 1854, and working through the new Gadsden Purchase (which incidentally had not yet been officially ratified or its boundary surveyed), and reaching Fort Fillmore, just north of El Paso, Texas, the following year. Pope, who drilled for water in this area afterwards, left the Rio Grande in February, 1854, and cut eastward across the Staked Plains of Texas to Big Spring, thence northeast by way of Fort Belknap and Gainesville to Preston on the Red River.

The fourth survey was made by our old friend Lieutenant Amiel W. Whipple, the steady and sure wheelhorse of Bartlett's and Emory's boundary commissions. He marked the present route of the Santa Fe Railroad west of Albuquerque, New Mexico. Starting from Fort Smith, Arkansas, on the Arkansas River, he worked along the 35th parallel to Albuquerque, and from there to Los Angeles, on an expedition which was second only to Isaac Ingalls Stevens's in extent and importance. He had two assistants who were noteworthy: Lieutenant J. C. Ives, who later explored the Colorado River, and Heinrich Baldwin Möllhausen, a German artist, whose later writings about his experiences in the American West gained him the title of "the German Fenimore Cooper." Many of the artists and scientists on these scientific-surveying expeditions were Germans, who seem to have had a wanderlust and love of the exotic which drew them to the American frontier.

The reports of all four surveys, and a fifth made by Lieutenant R. S. Williamson for connecting passes through the Pacific coastal ranges, ran to twelve volumes, which are fascinating in their narratives, the thoroughness of their scientific reports, and colorful in the many illustrations by a galaxy of artists; and these are still useful for a basic description of the animals, Indians, geology, and flora and fauna of our West of a century ago.[3]

Secretary of War Jefferson Davis mulled over these voluminous reports and then recommended the southernmost route for a railroad, along the 32nd parallel near the Mexican border, across which John Russell Bartlett had so often passed, as the least costly, the shortest, and in the most clement climate. The protests from the partisans of a northern route were clamorous and indignant, but Davis was probably fair and right in his decision. Twice as much money had been expended on Stevens's

[3] *Reports Of Explorations And Surveys, To Ascertain The Most Practicable And Economical Route For A Railroad From The Mississippi River To The Pacific Ocean*, 12 Vols. in 13 (Washington 1855–1860). Often referred to as simply *Pacific Railroad Surveys*.

northern route but numerous surveys and explorations upheld Davis's judgment. The sectional opposition, however, was so fanatical and bitter that it caused a deadlock in Congress, and no further action was taken on a transcontinental railroad until after the Civil War, when the Union Pacific was completed, along the old Oregon Trail, in 1869.

CHAPTER IX

Death in the Mountains

BEFORE following one of the railroad surveys — that led by Lieutenant Whipple — it seems in order to turn to the best known of all Western explorers, John Charles Frémont, "the Pathfinder," another topographical engineer who was un-usual because he was not a West Pointer, which unquestion-ably prejudiced some of his fellow officers who also believed that his rapid advance was greatly helped by his influential father-in-law, Senator Thomas Hart Benton of Missouri. Frémont ac-tually, as Mr. Allan Nevins so well points out in his biography,[1] was more of a "Pathmarker" than a "Pathfinder"; for almost all of the paths he trod on the Great Plains, over the Rockies, across the Great Basin, and through the coastal Sierras had earlier been discovered and used by the Indians, Spanish conquistadores and priests, or by the mountain men in their restless and ceaseless search for new trapping grounds. What Frémont did, however, was to map and describe those regions systematically and note their flora, fauna, and possible natural resources. And for these diligent and intelligent observations he deserved all the fame which came to him, because the earlier casual word-of-mouth descriptions of these areas were so vague and often contradic-

[1] *Frémont, Pathmarker of the West* (New York 1939).

tory as to be practically worthless for the oncoming emigrants to the Pacific Coast.

Frémont was, like Charles Lindbergh, a symbol of romantic, youthful daring in his time. Also in some ways he resembled George Armstrong Custer. Both were fearless and brilliant but both just missed ultimate success and both, when their names were under a cloud, took reckless chances to re-establish themselves by winning honor at the cannon's mouth or in the face of the hostile elements — Custer to fail completely and lose the lives of all his men and himself, Frémont to fail and lose the lives of part of his men but save his own, which probably was the worse fate. Both had attractive and intelligent wives who wrote well and often, and would, at the drop of the hat, take up the cudgels to defend their husbands and attack any and all who in any way questioned their heroic and glorious accomplishments; so that it became a very touchy thing indeed to write impartially about these histrionic officers during the lifetime of their stanch wives.

Frémont's deserved reputation was made before the end of the Mexican War in 1848, previous to the period of this book, during which time he led three expeditions into and beyond the Rocky Mountains. The last of these was the most significant and eventful. With a well-armed force of about sixty men, which included that greatest of scouts, Kit Carson, and the talented and exuberant young artist Edward M. Kern of Philadelphia, Frémont suddenly appeared at Sutter's Fort in northern California in December, 1845. This was too large and well equipped a band for the exploring mission which was ostensibly its purpose, and the suspicion is strong that the powers in Washington, especially Frémont's father-in-law, Thomas Hart Benton, had a strong premonition of the coming outbreak of war with Mexico and planted this force as a cadre for future hostilities. In all events, Frémont and his men played a vital part in the subsequent conquest of California, which was one of the primary objectives of our government.

But Frémont found himself in serious difficulties before the treaty of peace. It was a question of divided authority, of whether he should obey the orders of a superior army or navy officer, in the persons of Brigadier General Stephen Kearny and Commodore Robert F. Stockton. Frémont decided to obey Stockton, possibly because the latter offered him a better reward as civil governor of California, but it was a rather stupid mistake because as an army officer himself he should have known it was wiser to obey a superior of his own branch of the service. It was all a very confusing and controversial question and Frémont cannot be too severely blamed for his decision. But the final result was that Kearny preferred charges against him, one of them being for mutiny. The following court-martial was held in Washington and was a sensation, a *cause célèbre* of the times; and a court of regular army officers found Frémont guilty on all counts and sentenced him to dismissal from the service. Popular opinion, however, believing him to be a victim of a regular army cabal, was overwhelmingly on his side, and President James Polk, while approving the sentence, canceled the punishment and ordered: "Lieutenant-Colonel Frémont will accordingly be released from arrest, will resume his sword, and report for duty." As life in the regular army, after this contradiction, would probably have been difficult, the high-spirited explorer resigned his commission at once and at the age of thirty-four became a civilian without a career but with a burning desire to confound his enemies by further achievements on the frontier. And a chance to do this soon arose.

The talk of one or more railroads to the Pacific coast rose in intensity after the end of the Mexican War, as we have seen, and one of the leading exponents was Senator Benton, who favored a middle way, running west from St. Louis across what is now Kansas and Colorado, and then on through the Rocky Mountains between the 38th and 39th parallels of latitude. Money was raised, from private sources, with the help of Benton's prestige, to run a survey along this route and Frémont was chosen to lead the expedition. As the main question was whether the snow in the high mountains would prove an impassable obstacle, Frémont chose midwinter to cross this area, which was the roughest and most mountainous of all the proposed ways. To him it was a chance to silence all his critics by achievement and he picked the most difficult and hazardous route at the worst possible time of year. It was a direct challenge to the fates; the odds were unfavorable, the stakes were high — and the result was disaster.

In the party were two brother artists from Philadelphia, Edward M. Kern, who had been with him in California, and Richard H. Kern; and another brother, Benjamin J. Kern, a physician, who lost his life in an aftermath to this ill-fated expedition. Others along included an adventurous English soldier, Captain A. Cathcart of the 11th Prince Albert Hussars, three businessmen from St. Louis who had given financial backing, F. Creutzfeldt, a German botanist (later to die with Captain John Gunnison), and various experienced Indians, guides, and mountain men, and later on Old Bill Williams, one of the most colorful and famous of all that breed. A new recruit to the West was young Micajah McGehee from Mississippi, who kept a diary in which the later horrors of the trip were described.[2] In all there were thirty-three men well armed and amply furnished with horses, mules, and all the usual equipment.

[2] Micajah McGehee, "Rough Times in Rough Places. A Personal Narrative of the Terrible Experiences of Frémont's Fourth Expedition," *The Century Illustrated Monthly Magazine*, March 1891, pp. 771–780.

The party set out from Westport on October 21, 1848, and reached Bent's Fort on the Arkansas River by the middle of November. Here the snow was already a foot deep and the local weather prophets shook their heads ominously toward the western mountains and gloomily forecast an unusually severe winter in their heights. Frémont had not been able to secure his old standby Kit Carson as a guide, and a little farther on, at the hamlet of Pueblo, he hired the famous mountain man Old Bill Williams.

Old Bill was then sixty-two years old and his years of hardships had begun to tell although he was still made of steel and gutta-percha. He was one of the real characters of the frontier, full of oddities, but had been the most successful of all the trappers in the mountains and probably knew the Indians and their ways better than any other mountain man from his years spent among them and from his numerous and constantly renewed line of squaws; for when Old Bill tired of one he would swap her off for a horse or two and buy himself another. He was a lone wolf in his trapping, marked and scarred with wounds from his many fights, in which he was a terror and had always emerged victorious. McGehee wrote that he could not hold a rifle steady and shot with a "double wobble" but when his sights crossed the mark the bullet always went dead home. Old Bill was a tireless walker but staggered erratically in his gait from side to side and his seat while riding was as strange and misleading. He had started life as a sort of missionary to the Osage Indians but had gradually become the epitome of all the reckless and excitement-loving mountain trappers who only lived to spend their year's earnings from the most dangerous calling in the country on a big spree — and then broke and usually in debt turned back into the incredible dangers and hardships of trapping beavers in the high mountain streams, often in the midst of hostile Indians. Old Bill once had come into Taos with six thousand dollars (a real fortune in that place in those days) and had left before many days completely cleaned out and in debt. The money had all gone for gambling and liquor, and for occasions of exuberant generosity when he would buy whole bolts of costly calico and taking hold of one end of a bolt would throw the other end as far as he could across the plaza and yell to all the bystanding Mexican women to scramble for it. G. F. Ruxton, a famous early English traveler through the West, described him as follows:

Williams always rode ahead, his body bent over his saddle-horn, across which rested a long heavy rifle, his keen gray eyes peering from under the slouched brim of a flexible felt-hat, black and shining with grease. His buckskin hunting shirt, bedaubed until it had the appearance of polished leather, hung in folds over his bony carcass; his nether extremities being clothed in pantaloons of the same material. . . . The old coon's face was sharp and thin, a long nose and chin hob-nobbing each other; and his head was always bent forward giving him the appearance of being hump-backed. He *appeared* to look neither to the right nor left, but, in fact, his little twinkling eye was everywhere. He looked at no one he was addressing, always seeming to be thinking of something else than the subject of his discourse, speaking in a whining, thin, cracked voice. . . . His character was well known. Acquainted with every inch of the Far West, and with all the Indian tribes who inhabited it, he never failed to outwit his Red enemies, and generally made his appearance at the rendezvous, from his solitary expeditions, with galore of beaver when numerous bands of trappers dropped in on foot, having been despoiled of their packs and animals by the very Indians through the midst of whom old Williams had contrived to pass unseen and unmolested. On occasions when he had been in company with others, and attacked by Indians, Bill invariably fought manfully — but always "on his own hook." [3]

[3] George Frederick Ruxton, *Life in the Far West*, edited by Leroy R. Hafen (Norman, Oklahoma, 1951), pp. 113–115.

Old Bill had his misgivings about the deep snows, which were daily increasing, but thought he could guide Frémont's party through the mountains though with considerable suffering. Nearly all the experienced Indians and mountain men in Pueblo warned against the trip but Frémont was determined to try and the expedition plunged into the mountain defiles before November ended. Young McGehee took one last look from a foothill back over the prairies and wrote that "the sight was beautiful, the snow-covered plain far beneath us, stretching eastward as far as the eye could reach, while on the opposite side frowned the almost perpendicular wall of high mountains."

The heavy snows and the extreme cold (the mercury plummeted to the bulb of the thermometer and stayed there) made the going extremely difficult from the start, and each day, as they struggled upward, conditions became worse, with terrific sleet storms freezing men and mules. Soon the animals, one by one, began to drop and die and the hoofs of those surviving became so packed and balled with snow that they could move but a short distance at a time. They finally crossed the first mountain range, the Sangre de Cristo Mountains, and descended into the Rio Grande Valley but found it deeply covered with snow with no forage for the animals, who subsisted only on a daily pint of corn apiece which was packed on their backs. In a temperature of 17° below zero they crossed the frozen river, not without some of the mules breaking through the ice and nearly perishing, and stumbled on toward the main chain of the Rockies, which rose on the western side of the valley.

Here Frémont and Old Bill Williams had an ominous disagreement. Old Bill sensed that it was impossible to get through the way they were going and wanted to turn north to the well-known Cochetopa Pass or else head south and skirt the mountains along the comparatively level ground which now lies along the Colorado–New Mexico boundary. But Frémont was adamant about continuing straight on westward along the 38th parallel. He replaced Old Bill as guide with a younger and comparatively inexperienced man in this region named Alexis Godey; although he afterwards blamed Old Bill for all the ensuing horrors.

Then, figuratively lowering his head and trying to carry the ball straight through center, Frémont stubbornly and doggedly bulled on to lose the game, and the lives of a third of his men, in the most disastrous of all the exploration trips in the West.

As they struggled on they often broke through the ice of the mountain streams, becoming soaked and freezing, and poor Old Bill Williams once nearly froze to death. As Micajah McGehee wrote, "He dropped down upon his mule in a stupor and was nearly senseless when they got into camp." The hands, feet, and faces of all became frozen to painful degrees. The corn was exhausted and no forage was available, so the ravenous animals ate each other's tails and manes and even tried to devour their bridles and pack saddles or any loose article about the nightly camp, and died in increasing numbers. Finally they came to a dead stop about the middle of December at an elevation of twelve thousand feet in a raging blizzard. It was the end of human and animal endurance and now the vital question became how to get out of this cul-de-sac.

The realization of failure must have been a bitter dose to Frémont, who had counted so much on a startling success over these huge obstacles to dispel the shadows of his court-martial, and his leadership and behavior in defeat was not up to the high standards of his earlier successes when he had won the respect and devotion of his followers. He finally ordered that all the instruments and baggage should be packed back to the Rio Grande by the men on foot, leaving the surviving mules where they were, which, as Dr. Kern noted, meant the sacrifice of much "good provisions" which might later have saved human lives. It took the exhausted and frozen men about a week to move these supplies a distance of two miles, time which could have been far better spent in getting his weakening men along on the way to Taos and the Mexican settlements farther down the river. Later in the spring the baggage could have been recovered and every minute wasted sapped the ebbing powers of his followers.

On Christmas Day, while this moving was going on, Frémont sent a small party of four men down the Rio Grande for supplies. He picked, for this duty, Old Bill Williams, the German botanist Creutzfeldt, and two other men. Just why he wanted to bring in provisions to the party instead of taking the party to provisions and much needed medical attention can only be explained by his obstinate desire to get over the mountains the way he had started. After the relief party had left, Frémont still kept the rest of his men busy carrying the baggage and equipment on their backs, but they hardly made a mile a day through the deep snow and became weaker by the minute. The food was practically gone and they were forced to eat rawhide and their parfleches, which had been boiled to softness. The first man to give out lay down and froze to death beside the trail and nobody had the strength to bury him. Young McGehee found shelter from the almost ceaseless storm for two days in a cave, where he and a companion found some rawhide snow-shoe strings which they boiled up with a few dry bones found in a nearby wolf's den, and on this they managed to keep alive. Finally the party finished this foolish moving early in January, but when they finally camped on the Rio Grande they found all the game had left for the south because of the unusually deep snow. It was truly a desperate situation.

Eighteen days had passed since Old Bill and his companions

had left for relief and this was beyond the allotted time for their return. Frémont then set out with five men to track down the relief party and to plow through to the nearest Mexican village for help. Time was now of the essence and so precious much had been wasted in moving the heavy baggage, which now had to be cached and abandoned. The men were so starved and weakened by this time that within the next seventeen days ten more were to give out and die along the way south down the Rio Grande. Frémont, at long last, had apparently given up his determination of getting over the mountains, for he told the remaining twenty-odd men to follow after him and to be quick about it as he was going on to California by a southern route. As can be imagined, this cavalier treatment of his dying men did not endear him to some who finally struggled through alive. The glamorous Path-finder seemed more and more like a fair-weather explorer each day of misery and suffering.

Frémont and his four companions left on January 11 and made good time down the river until they met a Ute Indian who took them to his village, where they procured horses and food. Con-tinuing on, they found Williams, Creutzfeldt, and one man, Thomas Breckenridge, who were in pitiful shape. Old Bill's years had told on him and even his experience was useless when there was just no food available. One of the men had given out and died and the other three had struggled on for another day before Creutzfeldt reached his limit and Williams and Brecken-ridge stopped for him to die. Suddenly Breckenridge spotted a small herd of deer a short distance off and shot one. That saved them. He first tore out the liver and devoured it raw and then staggered back to his two companions with a haunch. Old Bill tore off great mouthfuls of the raw flesh with his teeth like a wild animal and Creutzfeldt was revived by the smell of the meat and returned to life to eat his share. Thus Frémont found them feasting on venison and later wrote his wife that he mounted them on horses and brought them to the settlements. Breckenridge, however, denied this and said that Frémont remained with them only long enough to eat some of their venison before pushing on with his men, leaving the three of them to crawl on the ice and snow for ten days to cover the remaining forty miles to a settlement.[4]

Behind these two advance parties seeking relief came the main body, who soon disintegrated into a sort of panic stumble with small groups of the desperate men fending for themselves, group by group. One lot consisted of the three Kern brothers, the English officer Captain Cathcart, young McGehee, and three others; and these were the most intelligent of the party. They manfully agreed not to leave each other and seldom have men gone through such hardships and lived to tell of it. They dug for roots and bugs in their frozen agony and snow blindness and could only stagger ahead a few steps at a time. Finally, as they had abandoned any hope, the relief came dramatically.

Frémont and Godey had reached Taos, where Frémont remained like an Achilles in his tent but Godey gathered supplies and animals and with four Mexicans started back to aid his companions. The survivors of the Kern brothers' group had reached the end of their strength and huddled around a fire to await their fates. Occasionally someone would fire a gun hoping that a relief party would hear it. On the morning of the third day of this huddling in despair they heard a shout, and shortly afterwards Godey and a Mexican rode among them. The other straggling survivors were picked up and all brought into Taos on muleback. When the final roll was called eleven men were missing. Frémont went so far as to intimate that the responsibility

[4] "The Story of a Famous Expedition," as told by Thomas E. Breckenridge to J. W. Freeman and Charles W. Watson, *The Cosmopolitan*, August 1896, pp. 400–408.

for this disaster rested on Old Bill Williams, whom he strongly hinted had deliberately led the party astray so they would lose their baggage and he could come back the next spring to claim it. He also hinted that Old Bill had practiced cannibalism in his extremity, which was an unmanly charge with absolutely no evidence to support it.

Some of Frémont's formerly devoted followers left him in disgust in Taos. Among these were the English officer Captain Cathcart and the three Kern brothers, who had served on the expedition without pay and had started as his enthusiastic supporters. One of these, Edward M. Kern, had been Frémont's trusted assistant on his third expedition when he entered California just before the outbreak of the Mexican War in the spring of 1846. This Kern had served with great credit in the campaign and had commanded at Fort Sutter. Later, Kern River, Kern County, and Kern Lake in California were named in his honor. He had gone back from California to Washington, carrying Frémont's private papers, and had assisted him in the court-martial. But his old leader's behavior in adversity was not to his liking and he quit him in Taos saying that "twas best to part before coming to a rupture with him, which certainly would have been the case had we continued together." [5]

The three Kern brothers were definitely noteworthy; two of them, Richard and Edward, were able artists, and two of them, Richard the artist and Benjamin the physician, were afterwards killed by the Indians. Before Richard died, however, he and his brother Edward were to make Santa Fe their headquarters, from which place they worked out as artists on various government exploration trips. Both accompanied Lieutenant James H. Simpson on his journey to the Navajo country in 1849, and Richard

[5] Alpheus H. Favour, *Old Bill Williams, Mountain Man* (Chapel Hill 1936), p. 176. Quoted from letter of Edward M. Kern to Mary, February 1849, in Huntington Library.

was with Captain Lorenzo Sitgreaves on his expedition from the Zuni pueblo westward to the Colorado River in the summer and fall of 1851, and then was murdered by the Indians, along with the ill-fated Captain Gunnison and several of his men in 1853, while on one of the railway surveys.

Edward Kern afterwards turned from land to sea and accompanied the eccentric Commander Cadwalader Ringgold on his naval expedition to Australia and China by way of the Cape of Good Hope in 1853–1854. At Hong Kong, Commodore Matthew C. Perry, who had been opening the Japanese door to the Western world, relieved Ringgold of his command, after a board of naval physicians had found him unfit for duty, and replaced him by Lieutenant John Rodgers, who then visited Japan, Kamchatka, and the lands about the Bering Straits. From there they touched San Francisco, the Hawaiian Islands, and Tahiti before rounding Cape Horn to return to New York. Edward Kern had charge of the photographic apparatus on board but also made many sketches and water colors, of which a goodly number are today in the Museum of Fine Arts in Boston. In 1858 he accompanied another official naval expedition which sailed from San Francisco to China and Japan, remaining for a pleasant six months in the latter country. He returned home on a Japanese war steamer, the first vessel of that country to visit the United States, reaching San Francisco in March, 1860. He served for a while as a Union officer in the Civil War and died in 1863 when only forty; but he had lived a useful and extremely adventurous life.[6]

But Dr. Benjamin Kern's number was about to come up soon after the arrival of the three brothers at Taos. They had been forced to leave a collection of birds and many other specimens

[6] An excellent summary of this unusual artist's career is: William Joseph Heffernan, *Edward M. Kern, Artist-Explorer* (Kern County Historical Society, Bakersfield, California, 1953).

of natural history, also instruments and valuable papers, in a cache when all the baggage was left in the mountains. Less than a month after their safe arrival in Taos, Dr. Benjamin Kern and Old Bill Williams, with a pack outfit and a few Mexican helpers, started back up the upper Rio Grande to regain this property. Unluckily for them there had been an outbreak of fighting with the Utes. A detachment of dragoons had given these Indians a real whipping and the fleeing and resentful survivors stumbled on the camp of Old Bill and Dr. Kern at Frémont's cache, where they had recovered and packed all the property for the return to Taos. The Indians were evidently burning to revenge their defeat on any white men, as was their custom, and, after being well received by Kern and Williams, they, without warning, shot down both men in cold blood but spared the Mexicans. Thus died Old Bill, before he had a chance to answer the slanderous accusations which Frémont was to make later against him, in which the blame for the disastrous expedition was neatly placed on a dead man's shoulders, all of which had the purpose of helping Frémont as the Republican candidate in the presidential campaign of 1856.

The two remaining Kern brothers tried for years to regain their papers and other property, which the Utes had evidently taken along with them after the murders. Many years later in an unknown and mysterious way these papers suddenly came to light and are now in the Huntington Library at San Marino, California. They have been edited and published under the name *Fort Sutter Papers* [7] and contain most interesting information about the conquest of California and about this disastrous expedition. As can be guessed, they are not complimentary about the

---

[7] Seymour Dunbar, *The Fort Sutter Papers with Historical and Critical Commentaries*, published by Edward Eberstadt, n.d.

Pathfinder's behavior in this tragic debacle in the snowbound Rockies during the winter of 1848–1849.

But, in all fair play, it should be said that Frémont had his stanch defenders as well, notably Kit Carson, who remained his firm friend and admirer through all his mercurial ups and downs, and it was Carson who took him into his house in Taos and nursed him back to health. Soon afterwards Frémont, taking those survivors of the original party who volunteered, went on to California, following generally the route of Philip St. George Cooke south of the Gila River. This journey was made in safety and without unusual hardships.

CHAPTER X

The First Photographer

ABOUT five years later Frémont came back again for another go at this route through the Rockies. In the meantime he had struck it rich on his property in California, the famous Mariposa ranch, on which large gold deposits were discovered, and he had been elected a United States senator from California. Seldom has the wheel of fortune turned so quickly and so favorably for a man. But probably there lurked in his spirit the desire to cross the same mountains which had proved his downfall, at the same time of year.

His influential father-in-law, Senator Thomas Hart Benton, was as anxious as before to prove the feasibility of a central route to the Pacific, for he believed the Southern interests had stacked the cards to defeat all proposed routes except the one hugging the Mexican border, despite the four impartial official railroad surveys along the various routes from north to south which were then under way. Earlier that same year, in the spring of 1853, he had been instrumental in sending along this central route an exploring party under the leadership of Lieutenant Edward F. Beale, a naval officer, accompanied by another active young man, Gwinn Harris Heap, both from Chester, Pennsylvania. These two had gotten through without any troubles, except for threats and near-hostilities from the truculent Utes. We shall meet both of these men later in unusual circumstances. Right behind this first group came the official government party surveying a railroad route along or near the 38th parallel under the command of the ill-fated Captain John Williams Gunnison, who also safely passed through the mountains before his murder by the Indians in October.

In the autumn of that year of 1853, Frémont again appeared on the scene of his debacle of five years before. He had probably hoped that he would be appointed to lead one of the government surveys for railroad routes, but the military powers that were had small use for him after his court-martial and he finally organized an expedition on his own and probably footed most of the expenses, which he could well afford for he was now a multimillionaire — for the time being. The way through the mountains, near the 38th parallel, had, of course, just been successfully blazed by Beale and Gunnison, but these two had gone through during the summer and Frémont had purposely waited until the first snowfall so that he could again buck the elements at their worst and erase the stain of his previous failure. He led a party of twenty-two on this expedition, ten of these being Delaware Indians, the reliable wheelhorses of western explorations, and two being Mexicans. Also along was a German artist-topographer named F. W. Egloffstein who was later to accompany Lieutenant Joseph Christmas Ives on his exploration of the Colorado River in 1857–1858.

Also in this party was the owner of a daguerreotype studio in Baltimore, Solomon N. Carvalho, a native American of Portuguese descent, who went along as artist-photographer. He was a thirty-nine-year-old tenderfoot who had spent all his life at sedentary and indoor work and had never even saddled a horse before. He had joined the expedition, at Frémont's invitation, on the spur of the moment without even consulting his family, and Mrs. Carvalho's probable reactions to her middle-aged husband's impulsive decision can be imagined. He was the first official photographer to accompany a Western expedition and his difficulties in the intricate chemical processes of developing daguerreotype plates while standing up to his waist in snow were almost unbelievable. But Carvalho accomplished these near-miracles and also produced a book, *Incidents of Travel and Adventure in the Far West* (New York 1859), which is an exciting and vivid account of a trip which finally ended successfully but just missed being another disaster.

Carvalho was an ardent admirer of Frémont and never once in his book did he deviate from the key of hero worship; possibly because he wrote it before the presidential election of 1856, in which the Pathfinder was the Republican nominee, and a close association with a possible President was something to be cherished by an enterprising photographer. Anyway, the inexperienced but adventuresome Carvalho began his book by writing: "I know of no other man to whom I would have trusted my life, under similar circumstances." But it was only by the grace of God that the plucky city-bred daguerreotypist came through the snowbound mountains alive.

The party left Bent's Fort in early December, following up the courses of the Arkansas River and its tributary Huerfano (Orphan) Creek to the foothills of the Rockies. At this point, Carvalho wrote enthusiastically: "If ever a railroad is built through this valley, I suggest that an equestrian statue of Col. J. C. Frémont be placed on the summit of the Huerfano Butte; his right hand pointing to California, the land he conquered." This rather fulsome proposal may have been appropriate during a presidential campaign but it has never been adopted; possibly the memory of the eleven men previously lost still lingered in that area.

They crossed the upper valley of the Rio Grande, following the wagon tracks of Gunnison and Beale, and this time Frémont veered to the northwest to Cochetopa Pass instead of butting dead ahead into the impassable mountains which had been his downfall in his reckless attempt to cross them five years before. But, at best, a trip through the Rockies in the dead of winter smacked of the foolhardy and the party soon found themselves in difficulties as they struggled on, leaving their predecessors' trails, through virgin country in the usual winter blizzards and howling gales of sleet and snow and bitter, biting cold.

Carvalho had his difficulties with the cumbersome photographic equipment of the time. The mule packers did not take kindly to all the clumsy paraphernalia with which he had appeared at Westport, Missouri, the starting place, and the baskets in which it was all packed were soon quickly destroyed by careless packing, mostly by intent, Carvalho believed, to rid the muleteers of all this unusual bother. The determined photographer, however, was not to be denied the satisfactions of a pioneer in his art in the Rocky Mountains, and much to the disgust of the muleteers he managed to purchase some substantial wooden boxes, just before leaving the last settlements, to replace the baskets. Even then the difficulties continued, and as he wrote:

Twice I picked up on the road the tin case containing my buff, etc., which had slipped off the mules, from careless packing — done purposely; for if they had not been fortunately found by me, the rest of the apparatus would have been useless. On one occasion, the keg containing alcohol was missing; Col. Frémont sent back after it, and it was found half emptied on the road.

But Carvalho's persistence had its rewards when he later took views of the great Rockies. He needed one to two hours to make a daguerreotype picture, most of which time he spent in unpacking and reloading the equipment on the mules. After exposure, the polished silver plate was held over iodine vapor, and then developed by subjecting it to fumes of mercury which had been heated in a plate by a small hand-lamp — and this all had to be done in the complete darkness of a temporary tent, often erected in waist-deep snow. While crossing the continental divide at Cochetopa Pass, Carvalho climbed a "rugged mountain, barren of trees, and thickly covered with snow" which "reared its lofty head high in the blue vault above us. The approach to it was inaccessible by even our surefooted mules." Carvalho and Frémont, with two men assisting, struggled for three hours up to the top of this peak, carrying the equipment, and there the pioneer photographer stood in snow up to his waist until he had made "a panorama of the continuous ranges around us." That any pictures at all resulted speaks highly for the skill and determination of Solomon Carvalho, who with justified pride later wrote to the editor of the *Photographic Art Journal:*

> Notwithstanding the earnest prognostications of yourself and my professional friends, both in New York and Philadelphia, that under the difficulties I was likely to encounter on the snow-capped mountains, I would fail, I am happy to state that I found no such word in my vocabulary, although I had not much youthful, or physical strength to bring into the scale.[1]

The pity of it is that all the infinite patience, toil, and pluck of this pioneer photographer went for naught when the daguerreotypes and paper prints made from them were consumed by a fire which destroyed many of the possessions of the Frémonts. Professor Taft of the University of Kansas, by far and away the leading authority on the artists of the West,[2] believes,

[1] From Robert Taft, *Photography and the American Scene* (New York 1938), p. 265.
[2] His book *Artists and Illustrators of the Old West* (New York 1953) is a veritable gold mine of information.

however, that some paper prints made of Carvalho's pictures by M. B. Brady, later to achieve great renown as a photographer during the Civil War, may still exist.

The party reached the Grand (Colorado) River and crossed without too much trouble, although poor Carvalho was in the icy water for a quarter of an hour while swimming his horse across and was nearly drowned. He emerged on the farther bank and his clothes quickly froze stiff in the wind, but the Delaware Indians had built a large fire at which he soon dried out. At this point in his book he tossed off another encomium for Frémont, writing of the latter's part in the conquest of California:

> With the flag of his country in one hand and the genius of Liberty resting on his brow, he penetrated through an enemy's country, converting all hearts as he journeyed, conquering a country of greater extent than Caesar's whole empire. . . . Frémont's name and deeds will become as imperishable as Caesar's.

Continuing westward, the party soon had to begin killing its "brave horses for food." Frémont took the occasion to make a little speech to his assembled followers in which he pointed out the extremities to which they had come, and Carvalho reported him as saying that "a detachment of men whom he had sent for succor on a former expedition, had been guilty of eating one of their own number." He then threatened to shoot any man who even hinted at such a repulsive deed; and all, "white men, Indians, and Mexicans, on a snowy mountain, at night, some with bare head and clasped hands," made a solemn compact to banish the horrid idea of cannibalism.

As there were still plenty of horses and mules to eat, it seems like one of Frémont's little histrionic acts which he was prone to stage with the proper dramatic background. And the slur on Old Bill Williams's eating habits was unjustified. There was no proof whatsoever that Old Bill had practiced cannibalism and, in fact, the evidence was strongly against this slanderous hearsay rumor. But looking back at it all, a century later, and considering the Pathfinder's later checkered career, one can wonder if it would not have been a good thing if Old Bill had eaten Colonel Frémont.

They crossed the Green River with their hunger and sufferings increasing in the continual snowstorms and Carvalho thought of his mother and noted:

I thought of the remark my good old mother made on a less inclement night, when I was a boy, and wanted to go the play [sic]. "I would not let allow [sic] a cat to go out in such weather, much less my son."
Dear soul! how her heart would have ached for me, if she had known a hundredth part of my sufferings.

A while later they even ate a coyote but the photographer, although he had fasted for twenty-four hours, could not partake of this uncleanly balanced diet. More and more the whole trip seemed unnecessarily foolhardy but Frémont was determined to get through at all costs. He finally decided to cache all the superfluous baggage, including Carvalho's heavy daguerreotype equipment, and to mount the men, who had been slogging along on foot, on the animals which had been packing the supplies. The lesson of his previous disaster, when he had sacrificed men for baggage, showed that it was high time for this action.

They reached the Wasatch Mountains, beyond which lay the Mormon settlements and safety; but the snow was piled up so deep in the unknown passes that the remaining animals sank in the drifts over their heads. It was a desperate time and for a while it looked as if all the horrors of Frémont's last expedition might be repeated. But fortunately he made some stellar observations which located their position as only about forty miles east of the town of Parowan, and with this encouragement, the men made superhuman efforts and climbed the last barriers to descend into a sheltered valley where grass was found for the animals and a deer shot for the men. None had any shoes left, and some limped into this haven with rawhides bound round their feet while others were half shod with worn-out moccasins and stockings. One man, Oliver Fuller, the assistant engineer, gave out and died on this final drive, but he had been in torture from frozen and gangrenous feet for some time and his companions marveled that he had come so far.

From this valley they soon reached Parowan, where the Mormon settlers received them with the greatest kindness and were especially considerate of poor Carvalho, who was but a wraith of the once well-fed proprietor of a photographic studio in Baltimore; he had lost forty-four pounds on the trip and was about at the end of his physical strength when he tottered into this frontier village. The men had been living on horse and mule meat (except for the one treat of coyote) for fifty days and never again did Mr. Carvalho look a horse squarely in the eye. As he described himself upon arrival:

My hair was long, and had not known a comb for a month, my face was unwashed, and ground in with the collected dirt of a similar period. Emaciated to a degree, my eyes sunken, and clothes all torn into tatters from hunting our animals through the brush. My hands were in a dreadful state; my fingers were frost-bitten, and split at every joint; and suffering from diarrhoea, and symptoms of scurvy, which broke out on me at Salt Lake City afterwards. I was in a situation truly to be pitied, and I do not wonder that the sympathies of the Mormons were excited in our favor, for my personal appearance being but a reflection of the whole party, we were indeed legitimate subjects for the exercise of the finer feelings of nature. When I entered Mr. Heap's [his Mormon host in Parowan] house I saw three beautiful children. I covered my eyes and wept for joy to think I might yet be restored to embrace my own.

About two weeks later, Frémont, leaving the emaciated and exhausted artists Carvalho and Egloffstein behind in Parowan, pushed on westward with the rest of the party and successfully crossed the deserts of present-day Utah and Nevada, sticking doggedly along the 37th parallel of latitude until he reached the Sierras of California, when he turned south to cross these at a favorable pass. Frémont crossed the Sierras into the setting sun and it was, in a sense, symbolic, for this marked the end of his career of exploration, at which, all things considered, he had made a deservedly fine name for himself.

From then on his life was to be one of violent ups and downs: he became the first, but unsuccessful, Republican candidate for President in 1856; he made a huge fortune on paper from the gold deposits on his California land, only to be gulled out of it all by the chicanery of supposed friends and by his own lack of business acumen. Then, during the Civil War, he became a military problem child to President Abraham Lincoln when, for political reasons, he was made commanding general of the Union forces in Missouri, a position for which he had had neither training nor previous experience in the handling of large bodies of men, and where his flair for the dramatic caused him to elevate himself into an Olympian aloofness, surrounded by a gorgeously uniformed bodyguard of exotic Hungarian, French, and Italian soldiers of fortune. This Olympian isolation, combined with his inefficiency of command and the charges of corruption against some of his aides, quite naturally irked the loyal but staid German burghers of St. Louis and the serious Union sympathizers of the state. When Frémont went so far as to issue, without any authority, a sort of emancipation proclamation of his own, long before the time was politically ripe for any freeing of slaves, Lincoln was forced to remove him from command. Later the President gave him another chance when he assigned him to head the Mountain Department, which covered western Virginia, eastern Kentucky, and a slice of eastern Tennessee. Soon afterwards, Stonewall Jackson made a complete monkey out of Frémont and another political general, Nathaniel P. Banks of Massachusetts, and Frémont returned to civil life. By degrees he lost all his California assets and interests and turned to a career of Western railroading in the dog-eat-dog business world of the 1870's. The result was that he, quite innocently, became involved in some shady promotions which ended in catastrophe with a consequent blemish upon his name. He died a poor and broken man in 1890. Perhaps, after all, Old Bill Williams had the better end.

But to return to the artists Carvalho and Egloffstein, left behind to recuperate in the Mormon village of Parowan. Both were evidently made of resilient stuff, for they were soon able to make the three-hundred-mile journey north to Salt Lake City, where they arrived on March 1, 1854. There Egloffstein, who, Carvalho noted, had recovered so far from his exhaustion that "there were no clothes in the city of Salt Lake to fit him; he had grown so fat and corpulent," joined the party of Lieutenant E. G. Beckwith, who was leading the remnant of the massacred Captain Gunnison's surveying expedition on to California, as a replacement artist for the murdered Richard H. Kern; and early in May this group left the city and arrived safely, the following July, 1855, at what is now Redding, California. Egloffstein was an artist of considerable skill, a native Prussian, thirty years of age when he joined Lieutenant Beckwith. During the Civil War, he was mustered into the Union Army as the colonel of the 103rd New York Infantry and was later brevetted a brigadier general for gallant and meritorious services.[3]

Carvalho remained, however, for a while in Salt Lake City and became quite the social butterfly and the fashionable portrait painter to the Mormon elite. He had politely called on Brigham Young shortly after his arrival, and was received "with marked attention" by the Mormon leader. Evidently he made a very favorable impression, for he was soon showered with invitations to all the smart social occasions and appeared at a grand ball where Governor Young gave him a general introduction: "A larger collection of fairer and more beautiful women I never saw in one room." He went on to note:

> Polkas and waltzing were not danced; country dances, cotillions, quadrilles, etc., were permitted.
> At the invitation of Gov. Young, I opened the ball with one of his wives. The Governor, with a beautiful partner, stood *vis-à-vis*. An old fashioned cotillion was danced with much grace by the ladies, and the Governor acquitted himself very well on the "light fantastic toe."

This grand ball gave Carvalho an entree into the best society of the city and he attended all the social functions of the season; also, he painted portrait after portrait of the Mormon dignitaries and their good-looking wives which must be family heirlooms in Salt Lake City today. Certainly it was pleasanter than eating horseflesh in the high Rockies, and the affable little artist soon put back the forty-four pounds he had lost with Frémont and gained another seventeen for good measure. He liked the hospitable Mormons and wrote sympathetically of them, and this feeling was evidently reciprocated, as shown by his social whirl

[3] Robert Taft, *Artists and Illustrators of the Old West* (New York 1953), p. 264.

and his commissions for many portraits, and also by his being invited to join a party going to California consisting of twenty-three Mormon missionaries headed for the Sandwich (Hawaiian) Isles.

Brigham Young himself accompanied this group as far as Parowan and made things comfortable for Carvalho, who wrote that when they entered that town, "I was affectionately greeted by those persons who administered to my sufferings some weeks before. I had changed so much, and grown so fat, that not one of them knew me." And as a sort of farewell acknowledgment to these kindly friends, he noted of them: "Certainly, a more joyous, happy, free-from-care, and good-hearted people, I never sojourned among."

From Parowan to California the going was comparatively easy with such an experienced and well-prepared group of travelers, and Carvalho arrived safe and sound, with probably no appreciable loss of weight, in Los Angeles and San Francisco, in both of which places he painted several portraits of prominent citizens. His account of his travels ends at that point. It is pleasant to write that he returned safely to the East, where he won considerable recognition for his paintings of Rocky Mountain scenes, and one in particular, "Grand Canyon of the Colorado," became quite famous in his day. He died in New York City in 1899.[4]

[4] Robert Taft, *Photography and the American Scene* (New York 1938), p. 490.

CHAPTER XI

The German Fenimore Cooper

O N a day of horror and terror in Berlin in April, 1945, the Staatliches Museum fur Volkerkunde (the State Museum for Folklore) was in flames from Russian artillery fire or American bombing raids. The building housed, among other irreplaceable treasures, the original portfolio of Heinrich Baldwin Möllhausen's pencil sketches and water colors, about a hundred and thirty in all, made on his excursions to the American Far West, mostly while on Lieutenant Whipple's survey for a railroad and on a later trip with Lieutenant Joseph Christmas Ives up the Colorado River. Only six of his paintings were saved, and if the fire was set by American bombings it was a cruel twist of fate for the works of an enthusiast for an earlier America.[1]

Nearly a century before this holocaust, on a hot July evening in 1853 in the little frontier town of Fort Smith, Arkansas, a group of men sat around a table drinking beer and singing with *Gemütlichkeit* and great enjoyment *In einem kühlen Grunde, Ich weiss nicht was soll es bedeuten*, and other German songs. The surrounding crowd of Americans applauded with enthusiasm, for the Germans were a hearty and jovial group in the

[1] Robert Taft, "The Pictorial Record of the Old West. VI. Heinrich Baldwin Möllhausen," *The Kansas Historical Quarterly*, August 1948. This article afterwards appeared as a chapter in Professor Taft's *Artists and Illustrators of the Old West* (New York 1953).

Dighton Rock, etched by Seth Eastman from a daguerreotype. From
Schoolcraft, *Indian Tribes.*

Military Plaza at San Antonio, Texas, by Arthur Schott. From
Emory's *Report.*

Crossing the Pecos River, by I. Rabuski. From Bartlett's *Narrative*.

Fort Yuma on the Colorado River, by Carl Schuchard. From
A. B. Gray's *Report*.

The Mission of San Diego, by Henry C. Pratt.

Camp of Red River Hunters, by J. M. Stanley. From *Pacific Railroad Surveys.*

A Section of Inscription Rock, by R. H. and E. M. Kern. From
Simpson's *Report.*

Buffalo Dance of the Zuni Indians, by R. H. Kern. From Sitgreaves's
Report.

Navajo Indians, by Baldwin Möllhausen. From Ives's *Report.*

Yampais Indians, by R. H. Kern. From Sitgreaves's *Report.*

Mohave Indians, by Baldwin Möllhausen. From Ives's *Report.*

Co-Co-Pas Indians, by Arthur Schott. From Emory's *Report.*

The *Explorer* Steaming up the Colorado River, by Baldwin
Möllhausen. From Ives's *Report.*

The Hualpais Indians, whom Ives called "squalid, wretched-looking
creatures," and one of whom Möllhausen wanted to preserve in alcohol as a zoological specimen. By Baldwin Möllhausen, from Ives's
Report.

The Grand Canyon, by F. W. Egloffstein. From Ives's *Report*.

Crossing the Rocky Mountains in Winter, by A. R. Waud. From
Marcy's *Thirty Years of Army Life on the Border.*

Utah Indian Prisoners, by A. Fay. From Stansbury's *Report.*

Midshipman Beale, from Frémont's
Memoirs.

George Horatio Derby, from a photograph
of about 1846. From George R. Stewart,

Wrestling Camel from Asia Minor, by G. H. Heap.

Sidewinder Rattlesnake. Drawn by J. H. Richard. From Emory's *Report.*

"Char," Rio Blanco, Texas, by Dr. C. B. Kennerly. From *Pacific Railroad Surveys.*

Prairie Dog, by J. H. Richard. From *Pacific Railroad Surveys.*

Little Crane, unsigned. From *Pacific Railroad Surveys.*

These four drawings are samples of the hundreds made by the naturalists and artists on the government expeditions.

about-to-set-forth exploring expedition in charge of Lieutenant Amiel W. Whipple. Especially popular with the Americans, among these genial and musical Teutons, was "the Dutchman," the stocky and bearded Heinrich Baldwin Möllhausen, official artist and naturalist of the party, who, although still in his twenties, was an old hand on the frontier. He had first come to America in 1849, and, after two years of wandering about the Middle West, he had accompanied the famous Duke Paul William of Würtemberg on a trip to the Rocky Mountains in 1849–1851. They had reached Fort Laramie, on the Oregon Trail, after some narrow squeaks from the Indians. On the return trip to St. Louis, in the dead of winter, they lost most of their horses and drew lots to see which man would push on for help. Möllhausen's luck destined him to remain and he nearly perished from the extreme cold in a flimsy hut and his diet of frozen wolf meat. He killed an attacking Indian and wounded others, and was finally rescued by some friendly Otos who brought him to their village and took such a liking to him that they wanted to adopt him into the tribe and give him two of their medicine man's daughters as squaws. He finally reached St. Louis, dressed as an Indian, and worked his way back to Germany as the keeper of a consignment of wild animals for the Berlin Zoo. Möllhausen then became a protégé and intimate friend of the famous German scientist Alexander von Humboldt, and later married his foster daughter.

But the lure of the American West was in the young German's blood and he had come back to America in the spring of 1853, to find immediate employment in the Whipple expedition. About three years later he returned to America for the third time to join Lieutenant Joseph Christmas Ives on a government exploration up the Colorado River and into the Grand Canyon. His pictures illustrated both the Whipple and Ives official reports.

In after years he wrote at least forty-five books in German, mostly about the American frontier, which were immensely popular in Europe and won him the title of "the German Fenimore Cooper." It is because of Möllhausen's literary talents in supplementing Whipple's official report (which was in the usual technical tone) by a book written in German in a personal and entertaining style [2] that this expedition is chosen to be described in fuller detail than the four other official surveys made under the direction of Secretary of War Jefferson Davis.

About the middle of July, Whipple and his party set forth from Fort Smith on their way to the Pacific. The party seemed to be an unusually congenial one and all turned with good will to their various tasks, the scientists collecting their specimens, the surveyors and chain men following their compass directions, and the military escort, under Lieutenant John M. Jones,[3] carefully guarding them, night and day, from Indian attack. The party was largely mounted on mules, those temperamental but foolproof beasts who could stand unbelievable hardships but had to be tended by experienced Mexican *arrieros*, or mule skinners.

They marched west to the reservation of the Choctaw Indians, one of the so-called civilized tribes who had been moved there from their homes east of the Mississippi River. Möllhausen described the game of lacrosse, as played by these Indians, in which hundreds of players, tribe against tribe, competed against each other, from sunrise to sunset, in what was a sort of mass mayhem with nothing barred except the wearing of shoes or moccasins. Next they came to the villages of the Creeks, Shawnees, and

[2] *Diary of a Journey from the Mississippi to the Coasts of the Pacific*, 2 Vols., translated from the German by Mrs. Percy Sinnett (London 1858). All quotations are from this book.

[3] Jones was called Johns in the English translation. Either Möllhausen or his translator garbled the proper names of various United States Army officers connected with the narrative.

Cherokees, other "civilized" Indians also moved from the East. Here they fortunately found an interpreter, a young Mexican lad named Vincente who had the gift of tongues and, as Möllhausen described him, "a very artful expression of countenance." He had been a captive of the Shawnees, who had bought him from the wild Comanches, who were called "uncivilized" because of their roving, and warlike ways farther to the west, beyond the control of the American authorities. The Comanches had kidnaped Vincente at the age of four from his native Mexican village and as Möllhausen wrote had "placed him among a troop of Indian children, and from this school of savages the boy issued, wholly ruined for a tranquil civilized life." The Comanches constantly kidnaped women and children to be adopted into the tribe, and these grafted Indians often turned out more savage than their kidnapers.

Going on, they next came to the lands of the Delaware Indians, another Eastern tribe who had once lived in Pennsylvania, New Jersey, and Delaware. This tribe was friendly and also "civilized," and traditionally furnished many of the hunters and scouts to the white men's expeditions beyond the frontiers, for the Delaware braves were natural explorers and wanderers who knew every nook and cranny of the Far West. But Whipple was unable to persuade any of this tribe to guide his party through the country of the savage Comanches and Kiowas, lying just beyond. Up to this point the going had been easy, for they had followed the trail blazed by the extraordinary frontiersman Captain Randolph Barnes Marcy, his soldiers, and a large company of California emigrants in 1849.

Whipple's party then marched on into the Great Plains, where they soon met the usual huge herds of buffaloes and passed through enormous prairie-dog towns, which Möllhausen described colorfully and in great detail for his German readers, and came to the hunting grounds of the Comanches and their allies the Kiowas, two of the most warlike tribes of the Great Plains. The Comanches for years had been raiding down their famous war trail, which ran from the Staked Plains of what is now west Texas southward through the Big Bend of the Rio Grande into the Mexican states of Chihuahua and Coahuila, often pushing as far south as Durango, as John Russell Bartlett had noted. Mounted on half-wild horses, riding stirrupless on pads of buffalo hides, carrying lances, bows and arrows, and shields of buffalo bull hides, these unexcelled horsemen of the plains would ride south along this well-marked trail in the light of the full September moon to desolate the Mexican settlements and return with many stolen horses and captured women and children to be taken into the tribe. Later their hostilities turned against the Americans, but when Whipple arrived among them they were still nominally friendly and his well-armed party passed through without trouble.

From there, following up the Canadian River, they reached a camp of the Kiowas where the chief advanced toward them and asked in broken Spanish for the *capitano* of the party. Whipple happened to be in the rear and one of the young Americans pointed out Dr. John M. Bigelow, the elderly botanist and physician of the party, whom Möllhausen described as a "graybeard" and who had been on Bartlett's boundary commission. Möllhausen described this meeting. The tall and fierce-looking warrior

after contemplating attentively the mild-looking, little old gentleman, mounted on a small mule, and without any kind of warlike decoration, seemed to have some suspicion that he was hoaxed, and inquired of the by-standers whether that was really the Capitano. He was assured that the doctor was not only a chief, but a most powerful medicine man; and thereupon the Indian advanced to perform his salutations in due form. He threw back his blanket, opened his arms wide, stepped before the doctor, and embraced him in the most affectionate manner, rubbing his painted cheeks against the other's whiskered ones, according to a custom that seems to have been transplanted from Mexico. The worthy doctor was quite affected by these demonstrations, and leaned tenderly towards the savage from Billy's back, patting him on the head and the bronze-colored shoulders, and exclaiming repeatedly, "Good old fellow!"

The Kiowas tried a major shakedown of Whipple for presents but his party was too large and well armed for any such blackmail, and the lieutenant compromised by giving them a cow, which the savages, mounting their horses, goaded into madness with their lances, and then, pursuing her like a wild buffalo, filled her with arrows until she fell.

When the Americans left, four Mexican traders who had been held under duress by the Kiowas attached themselves to the expedition, and a little later a small group of Pueblo Indians from the Rio Grande joined it. The weather was perfect and the going good and one night by spontaneous combustion all broke out into a grand fandango on the plains. An American wagoner perched himself on the highest point of the luggage with an old battered fiddle, and at the first cracked notes a crowd gathered below him as he sawed away on the jangling strings to produce Negro melodies alternating with "Hail Columbia" and "Yankee Doodle." Logs of wood were thrown on the fire for more light and Americans, Mexicans, and half-naked Pueblos, all armed to the teeth, "began to foot it as if possessed."

Möllhausen wrote:

Here two long Americans seized each other, and jumped and whirled round together in mad circles; there a Mexican was seen waltzing with an Indian; on one side were two Kentucky men performing an energetic jig, and a little way off two Irishmen, in the

4
4 THE GREAT RECONNAISSANCE

uniform of the United States infantry, were working away enthusiastically at a national dance, and shouting "Ould Ireland for ever!"
and, "Oh if we had but plenty of whisky!"

The party crossed a corner of the Llano Estacado, the Staked
Plains of west Texas, a then mysterious and largely unknown
tableland rising abruptly from the plains, which was a bailiwick
for the marauding Comanches; then on into New Mexico by
the Tucumcari Mountains to the isolated and sleepy little hamlet of Anton Chico, on the Pecos River, the first settlement they
had seen since leaving the villages of the civilized Indians. The
usual dun, one-story adobe houses, baking in the sun, looked
uncommonly like a collection of brickkilns grouped around a
church and a fandango saloon.

The Mexican population rushed to their flat roofs, or into
the streets, to welcome the incoming cavalcade. The alcalde, or
mayor, was a stately man, condescending to his constituents, but
theatrically gracious, with the air of a Spanish grandee, to the
gentlemen of this important party. Nothing could be a better
excuse for a fandango, and the invitations were issued on the
spot and joyfully accepted by the socially starved explorers. All
fell to at once to make themselves presentable; needles plied furiously to mend rents and tears, shirt collars and dickeys were
made from Möllhausen's stiff drawing paper, long whiskers were
trimmed or shaved off, and the river was full of bathers. The
final results were comical as, summoned by the church bells,
which rang impartially for divine services and fandangos, all set
out in demicostumes. Those who had coats wore leggings and
boots, and those who had trousers wore rough flannel shirts.
But few were formally dressed from neck to feet although one
guest actually produced a pair of white kid gloves. The wearing of arms was expressly forbidden at the ball as was the usual
and sensible custom.

The fandango was a good party. The American men and the Mexican *señoritas* mostly couldn't understand each other, but that was a minor handicap and "the tongues went merrily" aided by an authoritative whisky punch, and the lift of an orchestra of two guitars and a violin. The black-eyed *señoritas* rolled delicate cigarettes which they licked, lighted, and gracefully offered to their beguiled partners. The dancing started seriously and deliberately but soon picked up speed, "and the wildest excitement gleamed from the bearded visages of the Americans, who took part in every dance in defiance of all rules of art and fashion." The laughing *señoritas* did not seem to mind and at every pause rolled more little *cigaritos* for the enchanted Americans, "who could only accept them with a 'Thank You,' and 'Ah, if I did but know a little Spanish!' " They "danced and sang, and laughed, and drank and did not go home till morning." There were no arguments, no fights, and everybody had a good time, which was remarkable, as all the mule skinners, wagoners, and soldiers attended "with unsteady feet and cloudy brains." It was a testimonial to the inherent tact of Mexican women.

The next day, "The cocks crowed in the little town, and the mules neighed in the distant ravines, but their tones struck no other ear than those of the sentinels, who, leaning on their muskets, were doubtless making sorrowful reflections on the hard fate that had debarred them from sharing in the delights of the last night's festivity."

The party rested that day and then went on to Albuquerque in two detachments by two different routes. Whipple and Möllhausen, en route, inspected the Indian pueblo of Santo Domingo, one of the progenitors of the modern set-back skyscrapers. They were fascinated, as all Americans were, by the architectural novelty of these buildings, and climbed up and down the ladders connecting the different levels. The Pueblo Indians were a gentle, peaceful lot and good-naturedly showed the visitors their strange town from top to bottom.

Coming into Albuquerque, smaller then than Santa Fe, the party passed long buildings whose doors and windows were filled with curious men in the uniform of the United States Dragoons, light cavalrymen of the time who played a valiant part in exploring and subduing the Wild West. These were commanded by an officer whom Möllhausen called "Old Fitzwater," [4] and described as one of the great curiosities of the frontier. He was reputed to have had every bone in his body shot or hacked through by the Indians or Mexicans with his left leg kept stiff by an iron rod, so that he had to mount his horse on the right side. "Old Fitz" was the blood enemy of the Apache Indians, who were constantly trailing him in the hope of catching him off his guard but so far without success.

The dragoons took Whipple's party in hand and showed them the town, which seemed quite a place to men who had seen practically nothing of civilization for three months, and they learned "the names of the streets . . . and above all of every handsome senorita," where to buy the best wine and to enjoy the pleasures of the fandango. The *Amigo del Pais*, a weekly newspaper, published a glowing report of the expedition's accomplishment in surveying a proposed railroad route and pronounced the first half of the survey to the Pacific a great success.

Whipple's party remained in Albuquerque for about a month, repairing equipment and writing reports during the daytime. At night most of the men relaxed in the pleasanter exercise of the fandango, to which they were summoned by the ringing of the church bell, and "might be seen streaming towards the spacious

[4] Again Möllhausen was wrong on his name. There was no officer named Fitzwater. Probably it was Brevet Major Edward H. Fitzgerald of the 1st Dragoons.

hall where smiling and dance-loving Mexican fair ones were awaiting . . ."

Shortly before their departure, another young topographical engineer, with a festive name, arrived to join the expedition — Lieutenant Joseph Christmas Ives, fresh out of West Point in the class of 1852, who was a native New Yorker but had been appointed to the Military Academy from Connecticut. Ives was quite a fellow and his later report of an exploring trip up the Colorado River stood out, for interest and literary style among the rather flat and monotone technical efforts of his contemporary army officers, like a diamond on a coal pile. Ives later threw in his lot with the Confederacy during the Civil War; he was, by no means, the only Northerner to do this. (But more about him later, when we shall follow him up the great Colorado River as the first white man since the Spaniards to reconnoiter the Grand Canyon.)

Before leaving Albuquerque, the gentlemen of Whipple's expedition gave a big party to pay off all their social obligations, as Möllhausen put it, "to all the good folks of Albuquerque whom we could regard as at all educated and presentable." The country was combed for miles around for delicacies of food and drink, and canned oysters from the Atlantic Coast and French champagne were lavishly served. It was a fete not often seen in that dusty little Mexican town, and the youth and beauty and all the dignitaries flocked to the party. Among the guests was Brigadier General John Garland, who happened to be there on an inspection trip, and he "mingled in the dance with as much frolicksome activity as the youngest lieutenant." The aftermath of pleasurable retrospection of this superfandango later often buoyed the weary spirits of the party while toiling through the desert wastes or the snow regions of the high country to the west.

CHAPTER XII

High Country and Low Comedy

IN Albuquerque, Lieutenant Whipple was fortunate enough to obtain the services of Antoine Leroux as a guide for the rest of the survey to California. Leroux, as we have seen, had been with Captain Lorenzo Sitgreaves, a topographical engineer, on his pioneer reconnaissance (not a survey) to the Colorado River from Albuquerque in 1851. Sitgreaves's *Report of an Expedition down the Zuni and Colorado Rivers* was printed in Washington the next year, in 1854, and illustrated by R. H. Kern, but the data was available to Whipple for his survey as far as the Colorado River. Leroux, as will be remembered, had gone on to San Diego after this expedition and had then guided Commissioner Bartlett back from that place to El Paso. He had also helped Captain J. W. Gunnison through the Rocky Mountains before the latter's tragic death in the massacre at Sevier Lake, Utah. One of the most celebrated and able of the old mountain men, Leroux was a distinct asset to the party.

Whipple's expedition left Albuquerque in early November, driving a large flock of sheep for rations en route, and with more than two hundred mules for packing, riding, and drawing sixteen heavy wagons. Including an additional military escort of twenty-five men from Fort Defiance who soon joined them, their strength was nearly a hundred and twenty.

After some days they arrived at the famous Inscription Rock, or El Morro as the Spaniards called it, which rises steeply to two hundred feet from the floor of the surrounding valley. This remarkable rock is now a national monument and was made famous over a century ago by a report about it by Lieutenant J. H. Simpson,[1] still another topographical engineer, which was illustrated by ten drawings by the ubiquitous artists the Kern brothers, Edward and Richard, both of whom we have met on Frémont's disastrous expedition in 1848–1849. On the rock today one can read, *Lt. J. H. Simpson, U.S.A. and R. H. Kern, artist, visited and copied these inscriptions, September 17, 1849.*

The old Spanish conquistadores, way back in the seventeenth century, had first run across this lonely pinnacle and had started the custom of carving their names and the dates upon it, the earliest apparently being in the year 1606. Ever afterwards most travelers along this way stopped to cut their names and dates into this historical register of old New Mexico. Möllhausen and his companions were greatly impressed by the old Spanish inscriptions, and he wrote:

There is a strange and even solemn feeling in standing before these mouldering and half-illegible, but still venerable, relics of past times. . . . But the impression was more powerful, and we were more immediately carried back in imagination to those long-departed generations, when we stood face to face with these newly-discovered tokens of the presence of the mail-clad Spaniards who also once stood here laboriously carving those inscriptions . . .

Möllhausen was right. Even today the writings of the old Spaniards of two and three centuries ago are partly legible and it is impressive to read that on the *28th day of September, of the year 1737, came past this place Batchelor Don Juan Ignacio de Arrasain;* or that *on the 29th of July, of the year 1620* the gov-

[1] James H. Simpson, A.M., *Journal of a Military Reconnaissance from Santa Fe, New Mexico, to the Navajo Country* (Philadelphia 1852).

ernor and captain-general of the province of New Mexico came by here after placing the Pueblo of Zuni under the protection of the King of Spain — and this, far out in the wilds, before the Pilgrims had set forth in the *Mayflower*.

From there, they moved on to the famous Zuni Pueblo, built in the same terraced style as the others with from three to seven stories, each set back from the one beneath. Smallpox, that fatal curse of the Indians, was ravaging the town, so that only a short stop was made to allow Whipple and a few others to confer with the local chiefs and to ascend to the top of the pueblo. The lieutenant noticed the usual tamed eagles, which all the Pueblo Indians possessed as pets, and mentioned in his report the presence of light-skinned members of the tribe which, with certain words similar to their English equivalent, he thought might be the reason for the revival of the old legend, so prevalent at the time all over the West, that some early Welsh explorers had merged with various Indian tribes.

Möllhausen had been much struck by the fine large garnets which the Zunis wore in their ears as ornaments, and when the party moved on westward from the Zuni Pueblo they came to a collection of hillocks, made by large ants, which contained many precious stones excavated by the industrious inhabitants. The jovial artist reported that the members of the party picked up garnets, emeralds, and rubies out of these heaps — none, however, larger than a pea; but alas, this treasure trove has been lost to posterity. Possibly, except for the garnets, it was described for the benefit of the good Möllhausen's German readers. But a short distance farther on, they did enter a real wonderland, the great petrified forest, now a national monument in eastern Arizona; and Möllhausen properly expressed his wonder at the beautiful colorings of the thousands of trees turned to stone which lay in fragments for miles around.

Beyond the petrified forest they skirted the country of the Moquis (now called Hopis) but saw none of these Indians, for the smallpox was raging amongst them as well; and they crossed the range of the Navajos, the warlike and dreaded tribe who had stampeded Commissioner Bartlett's livestock at the Santa Rita copper mines. The party's whole herd of mules took off in a mass panic flight one night and these marauding Indians were blamed at first, but later the true culprits were found to be the encircling packs of wolves and coyotes who had crept in amidst the herd during the darkness. Fortunately the errant mules were finally rounded up and returned to the camp but the journey was delayed for a few days during the search.

While the party was impatiently waiting for the roundup of its animals, there was again a stir and excitement in the camp, but this time an agreeable one as Lieutenant John C. Tidball (whom Möllhausen or his female English translator insisted on calling Fitzball) arrived from Fort Defiance [2] with a reinforcement to the military escort whom Möllhausen described as "five-and-twenty wild daring-looking fellows, whose physiognomies, and entire bearing, were strongly indicative of their having been long in remote, uncivilized territories." They were provided with pack and enough saddle mules so that half of them could be mounted, and proved a mobile and efficient guard to the expedition. Within half an hour the enlisted men were "making merry round our blazing fires and roaring jovial songs" which raised the confidence and morale of the whole party, then about to enter into really hostile Indian country which, except for Captain Sitgreaves's reports, was almost unknown to Americans.

Ascending into the high plateau country, "The waggons rolled along easily over the frozen ground, the hoar frost spar-

[2] Colonel Edwin Vose Sumner established this lonely post, in the summer of 1851, in the heart of the Navajo country to maintain order in that turbulent tribe. It is just within the eastern boundary of the present-day Arizona.

kled and glittered in the sunbeams . . . further and further westward we journeyed, mile after mile was passed, and at last the snowy mountains of San Francisco could be distinctly seen . . ."

On the way several cases of smallpox, presumably caught from the Zuni Indians, developed, but Möllhausen mentioned these in a casual way as not hindering the progress of the party, and noted that all nine cases recovered although the victims were rather uncomfortable from the jolting of the wagons and the cold and snow. It seems incredible that a government expedition could set forth without the simple precaution of vaccination, which was then well enough known, but perhaps this casual procedure was worth the lack of the usual red tape.

Christmas was spent on the southern side of these mountains, about where the town of Flagstaff now lies, and Christmas Eve was observed by a mammoth celebration. The poor draft animals were showing the effects of the scantiness of fodder and the labor of pulling the wagons through this rough, volcanic country and it was decided to lighten drastically all the loads. "Various dainties that had been hitherto carried in closed cases were brought forth to be eaten up at once"; and a chest of eggs, and all the carefully guarded private stocks of rum and wine were produced to make a gigantic bowl of eggnog under the supervision of Lieutenant Jones. There was also a large surplus of gunpowder and this was given to the Mexican muleteers to use as they wished for fireworks and displays. The eggnog party quickly developed into the hilarious stage and as Möllhausen wrote, "toasts and jokes followed one another rapidly, hearts became lighter, the blood ran more swiftly in the veins, and all present joined in such a lively chorus as echoed far and wide through the ravines, and must have sadly interfered with the night's rest of the sleeping [wild] turkeys."

Nor were the Mexican *arrieros* remiss in their celebrations. The free gunpowder was expended in shot after shot, then salvo after salvo, which shook down the snow from the branches of the surrounding pines and cedars, all accompanied by whoops and songs of Old Mexico. Finally they decided on a gigantic bonfire and set alight the resinous trees themselves, which lit up the country for hundreds of yards around. The fun became fast and furious, with the Mexicans howling their native songs, punctuated by the continuous firing of pistols, while the Americans bellowed forth their favorite Negro melodies. As the whole camp had been without liquor for a long time, the effect of the spirits consumed was considerable, and this was increased by the tremendous heat of the gigantic bonfires on one side and the frigid temperature of 16° Fahrenheit in the rear. The next phase was an Indian war dance by some of the Mexicans who had been held prisoners by the Navajos and the applause was thunderous by the wildly enthusiastic audience. The only man who was worried during this riotous gaiety, which was reaching a perilous pitch, was Antoine Leroux, the guide, who quite sanely observed, "What a splendid opportunity it would be for the Indians to surprise us tonight." But fortunately nothing went wrong and the celebrators gradually wore themselves out and staggered off to bed.

The next day, Christmas, must have been blanketed by as general a hangover as Arizona has ever seen. Möllhausen tactfully wrote of it: "The 25th of December was passed in perfect quiet, in thinking over past times and our distant homes, where the church bells were now summoning all to the religious celebration of the season," which certainly was a euphemistic description of the crapulous hush of a mass morning-after. The party rested in this favorable place for three days before resuming its westward trek.

From this spot on, Whipple's surveying difficulties multiplied. The problem was how to find a gradual descent from this high plateau country, about seven thousand feet above the Colorado River, which would be necessary for the downward grade of a railroad to that river. Whipple decided to follow the southerly course of what he called the Bill Williams Fork, which flowed into the Colorado River to the southwest, instead of keeping along Sitgreaves's route, westward to the river. The only trouble was that this fork was farther to the west than Sitgreaves had reported it and Whipple spent much futile time searching and probing for it too far to the east. As a matter of fact, the Atlantic and Pacific Railroad (later the Santa Fe), when eventually built, did not follow Whipple's route down the Bill Williams Fork but pushed straight on to the west, as Sitgreaves had, to cross the Colorado River at Needles, California.

Incidentally, the river, a mountain, and the town where one now branches off, to the north, to the Grand Canyon from the main line of the Santa Fe railroad and from the highway, were named for Old Bill Williams, whom we met as Frémont's guide on his disastrous fourth expedition.

After much reconnoitering and searching, during which the scouting parties saw many Indian signs, the main party reached what Möllhausen and Whipple called the Bill Williams Fork, or the Williams River, but which is now known as the Big Sandy River, which flows south into the present Williams River. On the way, two skulking Indians were enticed into the camp, after a parley with a couple of the Mexican muleteers during which one of the savages was described by Whipple as facetious because he converted, without ceremony, the white towel used by the Mexicans as a flag of truce, into a breechclout, and transferred one of the Mexicans' hats to his own head. Möllhausen wrote of these Yampais Indians that "more repulsive-looking physiognomies and figures than those of our two prisoners could hardly be imagined." These Yampais led the party to a hidden spring and after this good deed departed in peace, laden with presents.

The expedition turned due south down the shallow Little Sandy and Big Sandy, with Lieutenant Whipple and a few men keeping a day or so in advance of the main party. They had been forced to abandon several of the wagons and to leave behind or shoot many of the exhausted mules. The flock of sheep, which had been driven along for food, had diminished rapidly, for the hundred and sixteen men in the party depended on this source for their daily meat rations, and it began to look as if some of the remaining mules would have to be used for food, for game was almost entirely lacking in this country. They reached the junction of the Santa Maria, coming from the east, to form the present Bill Williams River, which flows westward into the Colorado, and on February 20, 1854, the party beheld the broad flood of that long sought for river, which sight "the Mexicans saluted with shots and the Americans with a hearty hurrah."

There were many Indian signs at the junction of the two rivers (where the Parker Dam today impounds their floods to furnish a water supply to Los Angeles and southern California) and it was not long before various friendly Indians swarmed into the camp to stare, barter, and fraternize. A crossing at this spot was impractical as a steep, rocky chain of hills rose abruptly from the western bank, so the expedition turned northward up the river to find a crossing near the mouth of the Mohave River, which was believed to flow into the Colorado from the west. Two large wagons had survived the rough trip, which proved the possibility of wheeled transportation to the Colorado, but these were now abandoned and their loads distributed on the pack mules. One light carriage, however, which carried the delicate surveying instruments and some of the scientific specimens, was taken along.

As they trudged northward beside the river, more and more Indians appeared, and these were Mohaves, a fine-looking lot in marked contrast to the skulking and degenerate natives of the high country to the east. The jovial Möllhausen was enchanted by the affability of these fine physical specimens who wandered freely about the camp, and wrote:

The herculean forms of the men, with their hair dressed with white, blue, red, and yellow paint, and hanging down to their feet, their brilliant eyes flashing like diamonds — looked even taller than they were from the plumes of swans', vultures', or woodpeckers' feathers that adorned their heads.

The women, however, did not seem up to the male standard and Möllhausen described them as "being short, thickset, and so fat as to border on the comic." This ridiculous impression seems to have been reciprocal, for Möllhausen said:

. . . and our copious beards, which had now had the benefit of nearly a year's undisturbed growth, and with most of us reached down to the breast, seemed particularly to amuse the ladies. . . . Whenever one of us bearded fellows rode past them, the women burst into a fit of laughter, and put their hands before their mouths, as if the sight of us rather tended to make them sick.

These Mohaves had previously had a skirmish with Captain Sitgreaves's expedition, a few years before, but these hostilities with the white men seemed forgotten, with "the perpetual good-humor that seemed to prevail among them, their playing and romping with each other, and the shouts of laugher that followed their reciprocal jokes, the whole day long." Nothing was ever stolen from the expedition's camp by the visitors and in their turn the Americans scrupulously respected the Mohaves' cultivated fields of corn and other vegetables and paid for all unavoidable damages caused by the passage of the pack train.

After much genial palavering, trading, and the ceremonial exchanges of courtesies with the Mohave chieftains, Whipple and his men prepared to cross the river. This was a tough job, for the Colorado River ran deep, wide, and swift, and without the aid of the helpful Mohaves, who were expert swimmers, it might have been a costly operation. Lieutenant Ives had brought along an inflatable canvas boat and this was pumped full of air to serve as a ferry. The light carriage with the instruments was placed on this and successfully hauled across by a rope to an island in midstream. The canvas boat shuttled back and forth carrying the loads of a hundred pack mules with only a few capsizing mishaps. The Mohaves were entranced by the procedure and:

> Every time the boat came in or went off, the Indians hailed the event with wild yells of glee. By degrees they learned the simple mechanism in use, and placed themselves in a row to pull at the rope, making the empty boat fly back like lightning over the water. . . .

From the island the same process was repeated to the west bank with the only near-serious mishap being the accidental firing of a musket in the boat, which just missed taking off the leg of old Doctor Bigelow, the botanist. The animals were then driven across and the Indians made a field day of this, harrying the mules and sheep into the water by howls and yells, and much waving of arms to head off would-be stampeders in the wrong direction. As Möllhausen said, "They had never had such a jubilee apparently . . . But not an animal was stolen in the hurly-burly and only two or three of the sheep drowned, which was amazing, considering the love of Indians for meat and its dearth in that area."

Before leaving the villages of this affable tribe on the west bank of the Colorado, Möllhausen and Lieutenant Tidball put on an act which had their Indian audience gasping in amazement. Möllhausen remembered some of the conjuring tricks of his boyhood "and performed them with great success, and to the exulting delight and astonishment of our guests." But Lieutenant Tidball made the smash hit of the occasion when he opened his mouth and showed the entranced audience one of his front teeth, which was a false one held in place by a spring. He then closed his mouth, swallowed several times with heavings and shudderings, and then again opened wide to show an empty space, at which the Indians gazed in wonder. As the grand finale, he laid one hand over his mouth and massaged his stomach and throat upward with the other in a paroxysm of regurgitation. Again an opening of the mouth to display a full set of teeth. The surprise of the Indians at such supernatural powers almost amounted to terror, and their shouts of wonder drew all the Indians within hearing distance to witness several encores of this incredible feat. Alas, Lieutenant Tidball probably overdid this miracle and an anticlimax came when one sagacious old warrior came up to him and requested him to perform the feat with one of his other teeth. The faith of the Indians in the lieutenant's magical power was evidently much shaken by his refusal to do this.

Guided by two of the friendly Mohaves, the party set out westward, roughly following the dry bed of the Mohave River, whose current evidently flowed underground in its lower reaches, if at all, a fact which had not been realized by the armchair map makers who had planned this survey route. The consequence was an almost complete lack of water, and the party would have experienced the greatest hardships, if not destruc-

tion, in crossing this region – now called the Mohave Desert –
if it had not been for their Indian guides, who knew the location
of various well-concealed water holes. Some of the water holes
were so inadequate that the expedition was broken up into three
divisions, each spaced about a day apart, so that the tiny springs,
in this rocky and sun-drenched country, would have time to
refill each hole before the arrival of the next detachment. Whipple and his men realized how vital the services of their guides
had been across this desert and to show their gratitude all plied
them with gifts of spare apparel, and "their fine muscular forms
. . . were hidden under such a heap of clothes and coverings,
that they were scarcely recognizable . . . so that they looked
like wandering bundles of old clothes."

They entered the country of the "evil-disposed Pah-Utahs,"
who were said to live "in the caves and holes in the rocks on
both side of the Mohave." The river itself now contained water,
and a false confidence that all dangers were past imbued the men,
despite the warnings of the experienced Antoine Leroux about
relaxing their vigilance against the invisible Pah-Utahs, who, he
felt sure, were watching and trailing the party, waiting for a
favorable chance to strike. This careless confidence brought its
punishment when a straggling Mexican and three mules were
reported missing. A search party found one of the mules, shot
dead with arrows, and the tracks of the others leading into the
mountains. Following this trail they reached a hastily abandoned
Indian camp which Möllhausen described as "a true picture of
a detestable murder hole." The embers of a small fire still glowed
and "The heads and the limbs of the mules which had been
gnawed by the savages lay scattered about and completed the
disgusting character of the scene." Nearby lay the cap and
trousers of the Mexican, the trousers "covered with blood and
pierced in many places with arrows," and there was no doubt

about the fate of the poor fellow "who had left a wife and five young children in New Mexico, to wait in vain for the return of their husband and father." The Americans caught never a glimpse of the murderous Indians, who had disappeared into the background, but they destroyed or burned all the weapons and utensils which had been left behind in the hasty flight. Incidentally, many of the Southwestern Indians had a strong predilection for mule meat, the rarer the better, and the Apaches had the inhumane habit of often carving out a steak from a mule, literally on the hoof, without bothering to kill the animal first, and eating the meat raw. But this habit was only in line with the inherent and unbelievable cruelty of that tribe, whom General George Crook later called "the tigers of the human species."

The sad fate of the poor Mexican, the only casualty of the whole march from Fort Smith, Arkansas, naturally depressed the party for a while, but the nearness of the San Bernardino Mountains and the promise of their journey's end beyond those ramparts soon dissipated any vain regrets. The two Mohave guides, their services no longer needed, turned back towards their home, heavily laden with rich gifts for their valuable services. Lieutenant Whipple tried to present them with two mules to ride back to their homes, but the Indians refused these because they would have to return through the country of the ferocious Pah-Utahs by concealed mountain paths which no mule could travel.

Shortly after the departure of the faithful guides, the expedition struck the much-traveled Emigrant or Mormon Road (part of which was also called the Spanish Trail and led to Santa Fe), which ran from the Mormon settlements in the San Bernardino Valley to Salt Lake City. This was the home stretch and on March 14, 1854, the party met for the first time since leaving the Rio Grande mounted white men, who happened to be "four Mormons, stout energetic looking fellows who, trusting to their good fortune and their good weapons, were making their way towards a distant goal — the great Mormon city on the Salt Lake." Soon after this, the party passed through Cajon Pass and the paradise of the California coast unfolded before them, with neat ranches and farms dotting the lush landscape to give the perfect background for a return to civilization.

The party rode into Los Angeles, where it disbanded. Möllhausen went by water to San Francisco and from there sailed to New York by way of the Isthmus of Panama. About three years later he returned again to the American West to accompany his friend Lieutenant Joseph Christmas Ives in an exploration by boat up the Colorado River to the lower reaches of the Grand Canyon, and then beyond, into the canyon itself.

CHAPTER XIII

The River of Mystery

BESIDES all their explorations and surveys on land, the
Topographical Engineers had an amphibious side as well
and occasionally turned to water in their activities. Two young
engineers of this picked corps, Lieutenants Derby and Ives, who
commanded floating exploring expeditions, also happened to be
about the most colorful and entertaining officers of their times.
Derby was a humorist whose fame still lingers, and Ives wrote
the most readable of all the official reports of government exploring expeditions; so that their experiences afloat on the Colorado
River are more interesting than the reports of most of the usual
expeditions on land.

To go back to the beginning, the early Spaniards in our Southwest had a way there (as elsewhere) of slapping an appropriate
stock name on certain natural features of the countryside, and
this might be repeated over and over again at geographic intervals. Their alternative choice was the name of a saint or some
religious term. For example, Saint James being the patron saint
of Spain, they named innumerable towns San Diego or Santiago,
and Santa Fe (Holy Faith) was another favorite. And when one
of the early wandering conquistadores ran across a river whose
muddy waters had a reddish tinge (and many of them did in the
mountain and desert country), he would usually call it the Rio
Colorado — Red River. The number of Rio Colorados in Span-

ish America was legion, but there was only one great Rio Colorado (the name that finally stuck after several other false starts),
the turbulent and unique river which carved out the Grand
Canyon on its way to the Gulf of California from the high
Rockies. This was the River of Mystery because for centuries
after the discovery of its mouth in the Gulf of California,
nothing was definitely known of its rugged course through
deserts and awesome canyons, except for a few rare glimpses of
its upper channel by wandering explorers.

The present-day pampered tourist who stays in comfort at the
modern hotels and tourist camps on the brim of this canyon, or,
if he be a daring soul, rides on reliable muleback down to its
bottom on the Bright Angel Trail (a veritable boulevard by
comparison with the earlier paths) may catch an inkling of the
old mystery and wonder which this river and its terrible canyons
created in the minds of the Indians and the early white explorers.

Some years after the stout Cortez had completed his conquest
of the heart of Mexico (in the wildest adventure story of all
time), he turned his attention to its distant frontiers in the hopes
of finding another treasure to equal that seized from the Aztecs
with which he might bolster his waning prestige at the court of
Spain. Stories had come in of the seven golden cities of Cibola,
far to the north, and in 1536, Cortez sent three ships out from
Acapulco, under the command of Francisco de Ulloa, to sail
northward up the Sea of Cortez, as the Gulf of California was
then called, to an approximate point from which these fabulous
cities could be reached by land. Ulloa faithfully sailed on until
he found he was at the head of a gulf instead of in an open sea
which had been believed to separate California, as an island,
from the mainland. His three little clumsy caravels ran into the
great tidal bore at the mouth of the Colorado River, which he
described as a wall of water running with "a great rage into the

land" and which still today makes navigation there an extremely ticklish undertaking. Ulloa found a tidal rise of thirty-six feet, and how he ever pulled those flimsy craft through the treacherous mud flats of the river's delta was a miracle. Anyway, he must have reached a point considerably above the present mouth of the river, which has steadily encroached southward into the gulf from the constant deposits of silt through the centuries since. Ulloa dispatched one ship back to Acapulco with news of his discovery, and rounding the tip of Lower California with the other two, he disappeared without a trace of his fate.

Four years later, Antonio de Mendoza, who because the first viceroy of New Spain (Mexico), sent another seaborne expedition, under the command of Hernando de Alarcon, to the same place, which was supposed to aid and supplement the famous expedition by land of Francisco Vasquez de Coronado, both heading into the unknown north by parallel routes to find those same fabulous golden cities of Cibola. Alarcon found again the treacherous mud flats and shoals at the mouth of the river and the ever dangerous tidal bore, but somehow passed through these perils, and with the help of the native Cocopah Indians, who hauled his ships with ropes from the banks against the current for fifteen days, he reached about the location of present-day Yuma. Probably only one of those fabulous conquistadores of that miracle century of Spain could have persuaded the easy-going natives to do this for the simple rewards of little crosses made of sticks and paper. But then, Alarcon had convinced the Indians that he was a son of the sun, which orb they worshiped, and these gewgaws must have seemed like holy talismans to them. The original Spanish conquistadores could almost always accomplish the unbelievable. Alarcon waited around for some time for word from Coronado, but finally was forced to return south without ever establishing a contact.

In the meanwhile, the much more famous Coronado expedition had marched north by land to find that the mystical cities of Cibola were nothing more than the adobe houses of the Pueblo Indians, with no gold and no treasure whatever. After this shattering disappointment, Coronado led his men on east, to the plains of Kansas, in the vain hope of somewhere finding some kind of treasure to bring back to Mexico, but all in vain, and his quest proved one of the pricked balloons of Spain's glorious century and ended in an inglorious retreat to Mexico by the survivors.

But as Coronado had approached the rumored golden cities he had sent out one of his most daring men, Lopez de Cardenas, at the head of a small band to investigate reports of a great river to the north, and this soldier made the most spectacular discovery of that luckless wandering expedition when his Indian guides led him to the brink of the Grand Canyon. This must have been a far more impressive sight than any other Spaniards had ever faced, and Cardenas and his awestruck men even held the idea that they might possibly have stumbled upon a part of hell itself. However, that breed were afraid of nothing, including the devil, and soon recovering from that truly fearsome view, his strongest followers attempted to climb down to the river itself, which from the brim looked about three feet across. They tried to descend the precipitous sides for three days but were not able to reach more than a third of the distance down, at which point they reported that pinnacles which had seemed the height of a man from the brim were in reality taller than the spires of the great cathedral of Seville. Cardenas finally gave up the attempt to reach the bottom and returned to join the ill-fated main body of the expedition.

For over three centuries after that the Grand Canyon remained a sort of gigantic legend on the horizon and no white man is known to have reached its depths. There was the possibility that one of the early American trappers might have done so because those mountain men wandered into far and fearsome places, but if anyone did, he never reported it. It became the lot of Lieutenant Joseph Christmas Ives and the German artist Baldwin Möllhausen, and a few companions, to be officially the first white men to set their feet on the bottom of that stupendous chasm.

Although the Spanish conquistadores were almost always accompanied by priests and were truthfully said to conquer with the sword in one hand and the cross in the other, the better type of padres did not return to the region of the lower Colorado River until about a century and a half after Coronado's fiasco. Then the Jesuits, that picked body of disciplined padres, came to establish missions along the long, narrow peninsula of Lower California and in what is now southern Arizona. But in 1767 that remarkable order was expelled and replaced by the Franciscans, who allowed the established missions in the long desert peninsula to crumble, but founded a new chain along the beautiful coast of upper California, from San Diego to San Francisco.

It was to establish and reach these missions that the Franciscans again pushed into the desert country above the mouth of the Colorado River. The Spaniards did not like to travel by sea and would go many times farther by land to reach an objective, preferring the heat and lack of water of the desert to the chances of seasickness, scurvy, and shipwreck. The trip to upper California from Mexico by sea would have seemed infinitely easier to the English, but the Spaniards of the eighteenth century shunned water with a catlike aversion. Possibly this was largely because of the prevalence of scurvy, which the Spaniards had not learned how to prevent by lime juice and the scouring of their water kegs. An example of this prejudice was their discovery of San Francisco Bay, not from the Pacific Ocean but by an expedition marching overland. Also, the Spaniards seemed to be claustrophobes of a sort and liked the arid wide-open spaces, which resembled the barren high plateaus of their own Castile. They often carried this feeling against being shut in to the extent of cutting down trees (except immediately around the mission or hacienda) for miles around so as to have a sense of space to the horizon, a spiritual satisfaction which usually caused the erosion of the countryside. But they were, without question, as much superior to the English in the exploration of dry desert country as the latter race was to them on the waterways of the world. And so to reach California the Spaniards would march up from Mexico through the blazing deserts of northern Sonora and Arizona, and then up over the high Sierras; and the waters of the Gulf of California remained unexplored and uncharted.

Quite naturally enough, it was an Englishman who again sailed to the mouth of the Colorado River to explore and chart this almost forgotten estuary. In 1826, about five years after Mexico had won its independence from Spain, Lieutenant R. W. H. Hardy, an inactive officer of the Royal Navy on half pay, sailed up the Gulf of California to investigate the old pearl fisheries along its coasts for a London syndicate and later told of his experiences in a very rare book in American libraries, *Travels in the Interior of Mexico, in 1825, 1826, 1827, and 1828*, which was published in London in 1829. Hardy had the usual difficulties with the politicians of the new republic but finally obtained the necessary concessions and, after an uncomfortable trip on muleback from Mexico City to the port of Guaymas on the Pacific Coast, he sailed forth in a twenty-five-ton schooner named the *Bruja* (Witch) to explore the old fisheries of the gulf. He found these to have been either worked out or much overrated, and he obtained part of this information firsthand by learning to dive himself to the depths, carrying a short stick pointed on both ends which could be thrust vertically into the open jaws of a threatening shark, thus preventing the shark from snapping off a hunk of the diver. His crew was a lazy lot of mixed nationalities, but Hardy managed them and the boat well and made the first noteworthy survey of these waters since the time of Ulloa and Alarcon, both of which early navigators he does not mention in his book and probably had not heard of.

He visited and made friends with the hostile Ceres Indians on the island of Tiburon and wrote the description of how they poisoned their arrowheads which Boundary Commissioner John Russell Bartlett quoted.[1] From there he worked north to the mouth of the Colorado, apparently being under the impression that he was the first to enter these uncharted waters, and in this belief he was meticulous about his soundings and observations. As he crept carefully along, he scattered good English names right and left on points, islands, and channels. The earlier Spaniards had plastered these same features with most of the saints' names in the calendar and quite naturally most of these older and holier names stuck, but a few of Hardy's brain children supplanted the saints, notably Gore and Montagu Islands, and Hardy's Channel at or near the mouth of the river.

Hardy described the peculiar tidal bore of the Colorado River estuary as he encountered it in July, not a month for high flood tides, by writing: "But in the Rio Colorado *there is no such thing as slack water*. Before the ebb had finished running, the flood commences, boiling up full eighteen inches above the surface and roaring like the rapids of Canada . . ."

His ship went aground at intervals during the month he spent in the river; he was tormented by the mosquitoes and a particularly vicious and aggressive type of local horsefly; and he was

[1] See page 57.

continually apprehensive about the overwhelming numbers of the Cocopah Indians who swarmed on the banks of the river and congregated about the boat whenever it anchored or went aground.

Hardy explored a little upriver in a rowboat, and along the nearby banks, where he was once roundly cursed by a drunken old squaw of whom he reported: "She must have been exceedingly old. Her skin was as shrivelled as a bit of boiled tripe; and her sharp bones protruded, not unlike a sackfull of pans and kettles!" He was visited on shipboard by a stream of Indian women, old and young, the old behaving badly by pigging all the food in sight and the young shocking him by their lack of attire and their generally indelicate behavior. One young girl of about sixteen even swam to the *Bruja* and boarded it completely naked, and Hardy was forced to cover her charms with a sheet. As he put it, he was not less astonished "at the beauty of the damsel than by the singularity of her unadornments . . ." But he resisted all temptations, possibly helped by his repulsion at the Indians' practice of plastering their heads to kill off the lice, or as he explained it ". . . this practice of ornamenting their heads with this terrestrial pomatum, when it is recollected that the number of animals which they carry about with them in their hair is inconceivably great; and they may thus be prevented from biting, or even moving, the instant the mud becomes dry and stiff."

Once two of the young women sat on the bank and Hardy wrote:

The young ladies began immediately to assist each other in the offices of the toilet, and in arranging their hair. I saw one of them making a meal of the colonists about the other's pericranium, with the avidity of children despatching sugar-plums! It was a disgusting spectacle, and I would not allow one of the party to visit us.

Finally the tides allowed him to sail down and out of this disturbing river, and such was the joy and relief of all that he marked his exit by firing a salute of his two heavy guns and all of the small arms on board, and as he wrote:

I gave a bottle of brandy to be distributed amongst our almost worn-out crew; and as they had not been suffered to taste this, their favorite nectar, since the first day we entered the river, they felt their spirits revive in due proportion to their long abstinence from its use.

Twenty-four years went by after Lieutenant Hardy's departure before another survey was made of the delta of the river, this time by an American, the first to appear on the scene. Why Nicholas Trist, the American commissioner who signed the treaty of peace with a hapless Mexico in 1848, did not include the mouth of the Colorado (or for that matter Lower California, and what was later gained by the Gadsden Purchase) in the territory ceded to the United States is just one of those things. He probably could have if he had raised the amount of the indemnity paid that unfortunate country by a few hundred thousand dollars. But he didn't nor was there any real effort later to include these areas in the Gadsden Purchase, which would probably have been much more difficult against the opposition of both Mexico and the free states of the North. But the possession of the Colorado's mouth would have obviated a lot of later trouble.

After the discovery of gold in the newly acquired California, a horde of forty-niners poured along the southern way to that promised land, generally following the route pioneered by Philip St. George Cooke, as we have seen. To protect these emigrants against the hostile Apache and Yuma Indians, the government established the military post of Fort Yuma, on the Cali-

fornia side of the Colorado River, a bit downstream from where
the Gila River joins that stream from the east, opposite and a
little below where the town of Yuma, Arizona, now stands. This
post was considered a veritable hellhole from the frightful heat of
its interminable summers, but it was most useful for the safety
of the westering wagon trains. The great difficulty in maintain-
ing this fort was in logistics; for to bring equipment and supplies
by land over the mountains and deserts from California was
difficult, slow, and costly. The apparent solution was to ship
these supplies from California by water to the mouth of the Colorado River, where they could be transhipped into shallow draft
boats and brought up the river to the fort. So, in 1850, a survey
of the Colorado's delta was made by a young army officer, a
topographical engineer, Lieutenant George Horatio Derby.

Derby was an even rarer type of military bird than Seth Eastman,[2] the soldier-artist, for he was a soldier-wit and humorist
who afterwards achieved national prominence under the pen
names of John Phoenix and Squibob, but, as may be guessed, his
flair for flippancy and his light touch with the pen often did him
no special good in military circles. Born in Massachusetts, he had
graduated from West Point in 1846 and had served with distinction as a topographical engineer in the Mexican War, where
he was severely wounded at the battle of Cerro Gordo. After the
war he was soon "exiled" to California, for (as rumor had it)
seriously disturbing the equilibrium of the Secretary of War by

[2] Seth Eastman, from Maine, graduated from West Point in 1828, and
served for many years as an infantry officer on the frontier, mostly in the Northwest around Fort Snelling (now Minneapolis), but his only frontier activity
within the period of this book was a tour of duty in Texas in 1848–1849. After
that he served in Washington, D. C., where he illustrated several books about
Indians by his talented wife, Mary Henderson Eastman, and Henry R. Schoolcraft's monumental six-volume work on the Indian tribes of the United States.
Also he produced several large paintings of Indian and frontier subjects which
hang in the national capital today. He was a talented and important artist of
the West but his works nearly all belong to the years before the Mexican War.

the flippancy of one of his reports.[3] In San Diego, he edited a
newspaper, in the absence of its regular editor, in addition to his
regular army duties, and created local pandemonium by reversing
all the political principles of its absent mentor. He became famous
for his hilariously funny articles in which he set the pace for
early Western American humor, and his style of varying under-
statement and exaggeration later markedly influenced the writings of Mark Twain. An example of this was a burlesque he
wrote of the usually stuffy and heavy railroad survey reports
which was titled, "Official Report of Professor John Phoenix,
A.M. of a Military Survey and Reconnoisance [*sic*] of the route
from San Francisco to the mission of Dolores, made with a view
to ascertaining the practicability of connecting those points by
a Railroad"

The distance between "those points" was a little over two
miles, but Professor Phoenix filled it up with all the usual accounts of hardships and Indian dangers and with the scientific
jargon, completely garbled, of a transcontinental survey; all
reported by a ponderous staff, most of whom had the last name
of Phoenix, and were working in a fog of nepotism for the good
professor.[4]

There was a fabulous story told of an encounter between
young Lieutenant Derby and the superflorid General Winfield
Scott, upon whose staff the young lieutenant worked as a topographical engineer during the Mexican War. Derby was much
irked by Scott's habit of anglicizing his name into Darby, and
the story goes that the general rode up to this young engineer,

    [3] George R. Stewart, in his book *John Phoenix, Esq., The Veritable Squibob*
(New York 1937), demolishes this rumor and says: "California was hardly a
place for exile in the ordinary sense; if so, almost every officer who later became prominent in the Civil War, Union or Confederate, was sent into exile
in the next few years." (P. 56.)
    [4] John Phoenix, *Phoenixiana or Sketches and Burlesques*, with an intro-
duction by John Kendrick Bangs (New York 1903), pp. 3–5.

who had been wounded at the battle of Cerro Gordo and was resting on the ground:

GENERAL SCOTT: My god, *Darby*, you're wounded!

DERBY: Yes, General *Scatt*.

GENERAL SCOTT (bristling): My name is *Scott*, not *Scatt!*

DERBY: And my name is *Derby*, not *Darby*.[5]

Derby died in 1861, but his original sense of humor and practical jokes became legendary in the army and in California.

This young officer arrived at the firth of the Colorado in September, 1850, at which time of year the fearsome tides of that place were at their least troublesome stage. The powers in Washington had evidently not read Lieutenant Hardy's book, for they dispatched for Derby's use a hundred-and-twenty-ton "United States transport," a ship which was five times larger than the *Bruja* in which Hardy had explored. Perhaps the unwieldiness of this ship and its consequent perils dampened the effervescence of the young lieutenant, or perhaps his recent **depressing** experience with a humorless Secretary of War had temporarily stilled his muse, for his final report disappointingly followed the usual heavy, official style.

Fortunately Derby had read Hardy's book and profited therefrom as much as he could in handling such a cumbersome ark. He found the Cocopah Indians as helpful as had Alarcon, centuries before, and had none of Hardy's tremors and apprehensions about their warriors or tempting women. He managed to float the clumsy transport upriver on flood tides to about where the English lieutenant had reached; from there he proceeded upstream in a rowboat until he met Major Samuel Peter Heintzel-

[5] George R. Stewart, *John Phoenix, Esq., The Veritable Squibob* (New York 1937), p. 4.

man and a small party coming down from Fort Yuma. After a month's surveying and sounding, he reported that navigation between the gulf and Fort Yuma would be possible "at any season of the year by a steamboat of eighteen or twenty feet beam, drawing from two-and-a-half to three feet water," and recommended that the best type of vessel would be "a small stern-wheel boat, with a powerful engine and a thick bottom," to combat the strong current in an often narrow channel "somewhat obstructed by small snags and sawyers."

Derby's recommendations were adopted and the next year (1851) saw the beginning of a regular freighter service up and down the river. George A. Johnson, a flatboat freighter, was the pioneer skipper in this service and, after losing a couple of experimental flat-bottomed stern-wheelers, he finally established a reasonably regular schedule to Fort Yuma, and even above that point. All of which was most satisfactory, but, as usual, the armchair officers in Washington wanted to expand a success and had visions of extending the service far up the river, possibly into Utah and Colorado. And so, in 1857, Lieutenant Joseph Christmas Ives was ordered to explore by boat up the river to the last inch of its navigable depth.

CHAPTER XIV

Lieutenant Ives Goes Up the Great Colorado River

AS soon as Lieutenant Ives received this assignment, he ordered a fifty-foot shallow-draft steel steamboat to be built to his specifications by a Philadelphia firm. Now, just why he went to all this trouble and expense (or was allowed to) is an enigma. There were already specially designed boats in operation on the lower Colorado River, manned by experienced rivermen, and certainly the logical thing to have done would have been to charter one of these craft for his exploration up the river. He explained this seeming extravagance by writing in his report: "The company employed in carrying freight from the head of the Gulf to Fort Yuma were unable to spare a boat for the use of the expedition, excepting for a compensation beyond the limits of the appropriation." [1] If so, the company must have asked a staggering price to make it higher than the cost of building a brand-new steamboat, disassembling it, transporting the parts by water to Panama, across that isthmus by the new Panama Railroad Company, reloading them on a Pacific steamer to San Francisco,

---

[1] Lieutenant Joseph Christmas Ives, *Report Upon the Colorado River of the West* . . . , House Exec. Doc. No. 90, 36 Cong. 1st Sess. (Washington 1861). This is the most readable and entertaining narrative of all the official reports by topographical engineers on Western explorations. Ives had a real gift for colorful and humorous descriptions of the scenery and the native Indians.

transshipping them from there on the deck of a coastal schooner, and then finally landing the parts at the mouth of the Colorado River to be reassembled at that miserable place under the most unfavorable conditions, which is exactly what was done.

Certainly Ives's explanation doesn't seem to hold much water, and Mr. Lewis R. Freeman in his excellent book *The Colorado River* has a plausible theory for this seeming imposition on the taxpayers: "The truth may well have been that some keen theorist in the War Department — or possibly Ives himself — had conceived and designed the steel steamer and so went to considerable lengths in railroading it through to a trial."

Anyway, the steamboat, which was named *Explorer*, was satisfactorily tested on the Delaware River in August, 1857, and then shipped as described in charge of a Philadelphia engineer named A. J. Carroll.

In the meantime, Ives was gathering together the usual brain trust of artists and scientists to accompany the expedition, and in this there can be no criticism of his choices. Dr. J. S. Newberry was appointed physician and naturalist and he later became a man of considerable note. Born in Ohio, he had graduated from Western Reserve University in 1846, and had then obtained an M.D. degree and later studied geology in Paris. He had also been associated with the Smithsonian Institution and had taught geology at Columbian (now George Washington) University. He had had field experience in the expedition of Lieutenant R. S. Williamson, another topographical engineer, who had simultaneously explored north and south along the Sierras in California for passes through which the oncoming surveys from the East for railroad routes could go, and his report was included with the four other surveys for railways to the Pacific. In 1859, Newberry accompanied Captain J. N. Macomb (still another topographical engineer) on an exploration from Santa Fe to the

junction of the Grand and Green Rivers where they formed the
Colorado River, and wrote a geological report which formed the
greater part of Macomb's official account of this trip.[2] Afterwards he went to the Columbia School of Mines, and Yale, published many scientific articles and books, and finally died in New
Haven in 1892. Ives's topographer and map maker was F. W.
Egloffstein, a native German who had been on the exploring expedition with John C. Frémont in 1853, and, later that same year,
had gone with Lieutenant Beckwith from Salt Lake City to
California. The "artist and collector of natural history" was none
other than our jovial friend Baldwin Möllhausen, who had returned all the way from Germany to accompany his friend Ives.

Lieutenant Ives and the rather beat-up parts and machinery of
the *Explorer* arrived at the mouth of the Colorado River, on a
small schooner, in November, 1857, and his troubles really began.
They were unable to moor the schooner against the soft mud
banks of the river, which were constantly caving in, and so
warped it into one of the side drainage gullies at an unusually
high tide; this left the ship stranded high and dry until another
equally high flood tide floated her off two weeks later, during
which interim her skipper nearly had a nervous breakdown.

The *Explorer* was assembled on makeshift ways, dug by hand
out of the sides of this gulch and lined with driftwood. The digging was most laborious, for, as Ives wrote, "The wet, wavy,
and tough clay adheres to the spades like glue, and nearly every
spadeful has to be scraped off with the hand." When the hull
was uncrated, it was found badly bent and had to be pounded
back into shape with hammers and strengthened by bolting four
scantlings lengthwise along its bottom, which later caused much
trouble because of the increased draft and resistance. Nearly

[2] See Captain J. N. Macomb, *Report of the Exploring Expedition from
Santa Fé, New Mexico to the Junction of the Grand and Green Rivers of the
Great Colorado of the West, in 1859* . . . (Washington 1876).

sixty holes had to be drilled manually to fasten these scantlings, and to top this herculean task the three-ton boiler had to be gently lowered into place. Finally it was all accomplished, largely thanks to the competent engineer Carroll, who had practically slept with the *Explorer* since she left Philadelphia.

While all this back-breaking toil was going on, Lieutenant Ives was following Carvalho's pioneer experiment in photography with Frémont. This pristine art was still in its diapers and he wrote:

There being a little photographic apparatus along . . . and having constructed out of an india-rubber tarpaulin a tent that entirely excluded the light, have made repeated efforts to obtain a view of camp and the river. The attempt has not met with distinguished success. The chemicals seem to have deteriorated, and apart from this the light is so glaring, and the agitation of the atmosphere near the surface of the ground so great, that it is doubtful whether, under any circumstances, a clear and perfect picture could be secured.

Two of the regular river steamboats arrived from Fort Yuma, before the launching of the *Explorer*, to pick up the cargo of the schooner, which fortunately had been floated again. These brought a load of curious Indians from the upriver villages and Ives was quite favorably impressed:

Several of the men had good figures. The women were rather too much inclined to embonpoint, with the exception of the young girls, some of whom were by no means ill-favored. Bright eyes, white teeth, and musical voices, they all possessed. In point of apparel they were about as deficient as the men, a very short petticoat, their only garment, taking the place of the strip of cotton.

These Cocopahs, from their comfortable positions on the decks of the two floating steamboats, thought the strenuous labors of Ives's men a great joke:

One or two long-legged fellows, the wits of the party, were fore-most in facetious criticism. They seemed to be pointing out to their female companions our makeshifts and deficiency in numbers, and were, no doubt, very funny at our expense, for their sallies were re-ceived by the young belles with great favor and constant bursts of merriment.

Finally all was in place and on Christmas Day the boiler was filled and steam got up. "The engine ran beautifully – a great triumph to Mr. Carroll after the trouble he has had with it." Mr. Robinson, the river pilot, arrived from Fort Yuma and all was ready for the launching. In the brilliant moonlight of December 30, 1857, at full tide, the *Explorer* backed out of the ways under her own steam, and "few boats have ever been surveyed by their builders with as much admiration and complacency."

Ives was delighted and wrote:

She is fifty-four feet long from the extremity of the bow to the outer rim of the stern wheel. Amidships, the hull is left open, like a skiff, the boiler occupying a third of the vacant space. At the bow is a little deck, on which stands the armament – a four-pound howitzer. In front of the wheel another deck, large enough to accommodate the pilot and a few of the surveying party, forms the roof of a cabin eight-feet by-seven.

The next night they started up the river with the *Explorer* almost loaded down to the gunwales (she had only six inches freeboard), with two heavily loaded skiffs lashed alongside, and towing a sloop astern. With this unwieldy combination, Ives started up through the rips and eddies of the lower channel, un-der the caving river banks, groping along by moonlight, and it was a wonder the expedition didn't end then and there with the foundering of the boat and considerable loss of life. It was a close thing:

As the wind freshened, waves began to rise, and the water to dash into the boat. The prospect was somewhat alarming, for even throwing overboard the cargo would not have saved the open boat from swamping had the breeze continued long enough to have raised a sea, and though near the land, the strongest swimmer would have stood little chance in such a current, with nothing to cling to but a steep bank of slippery clay. We shipped so much water that we were on the point of commencing to lighten the boat, and I think if the wind had held fifteen minutes longer the Colorado expedition would have come to a disastrous issue; but the breeze died away as suddenly as it had sprung up; the water again became smooth, and in a couple of hours all danger from winds and waves was over; the low banks on the opposite side came in sight, and the broad and hazardous sheet of water narrowed into a moderately sized and shallow stream.

At night the party put into shore to eat and sleep on land and slowly they pushed up the current, averaging about twelve miles a day, which was considerably less than a man could walk, but they were delayed by the winding channel, the necessity of stopping to chop firewood, and the frequent grounding on shoals and sand bars. Ives was impatient to reach Fort Yuma before the departure of the next outgoing overland mail and decided to proceed by land. He rowed up the river one evening to the ranch of a settler, hoping to borrow a horse and ride on to the fort, and that night he shared the couch of one of the ranch hands, "between the dirtiest pair of blankets . . . with the dirtiest looking man I ever saw in my life."

The next morning he borrowed a stallion which he was warned was "of great spirit and value" and might be dangerous to ride. Ives mounted this steed with caution, but:

I soon found that my charger was not likely to volunteer a faster gait than a leisurely walk, and, with a half dread of arousing some slumbering fires, touched him with the spur. This producing no effect, I dug the spur into his side a little harder, and at last, with the help of a stout cudgel, broken from a tree, urged him into a trot.

By spurring and beating his mount, Ives made slow but steady progress toward the fort until he met an ox wagon with a white man lying on his back on top of the load, who roused up as Ives passed and inquired with a muddled air and thick utterance what he was doing on that horse. The lieutenant quickly inferred that this was the ranch owner, "somewhat intoxicated," and explained the circumstances. But the man indignantly declared the stallion was worth at least five hundred dollars and demanded that he be returned at once. Ives argued, but the man persisted with drunken obstinacy that he should not be ridden a step further. As for Ives:

I was revolving the probability of being able, by a sudden violent attack of whip and spur, to excite the cherished beast into a trot, and thus escape from his guardian, when the latter all at once changed his mind and told me that every horse he had in the world and all that his friends had were at my disposal as long as I wanted, and after an affectionate squeeze of the hand, gave me a benign smile, and falling upon his back called to the driver to go on.

The lieutenant arrived at Fort Yuma and enjoyed a pleasant interlude in meeting old army friends and greeting the artists and scientists who had come overland from California to join the expedition there. While awaiting him, Dr. Newberry and Baldwin Möllhausen had been busy collecting specimens, while Egloffstein had begun a series of topographical sketches of the countryside.

Two days later the *Explorer* chugged up to a landing amidst a welcoming throng of soldiers and Yuma Indians. As Ives wrote: "Fort Yuma is not a place to inspire one with regret at leaving. The barrenness of the surrounding region, the intense heat of its summer climate, and its loneliness and isolation have caused it to be regarded as the Botany Bay of military stations." But it had been useful in subduing the fierce Yumas, "who had been a scourge to their neighbors and to California emigrants."

Shortly before, rumors had arrived that the Mormons were inciting the upriver Indians to some kind of trouble, and a detachment of soldiers had been dispatched upstream on one of the other steamboats to investigate. It must have annoyed Ives to learn that he must follow in the wake of another boat in his exploration, but he made no comment and humorously remarked on the *Explorer* going solidly aground within sight of the fort, just after she had left amidst pomp and ceremony for the long haul upriver: "The delay would have been less annoying if it had occurred a little higher up. We were in plain sight of the fort, and knew that this sudden check to our progress was affording an evening of great entertainment to those in and out of the garrison."

The *Explorer* slowly bucked her way over shoals and bars, and it became a dingdong grind from morning till night for her harassed crew and passengers, who spent a great part of the time overboard in the water shoving and pulling, or else manfully hauling by ropes the bottom-bumping *Explorer* up rushing rapids. The Indians, from miles around, soon learned of the expedition's constant difficulties and gathered in hordes on the banks to watch the fun. They even picked their spots in advance, and a hilarious group on the shore was a sure sign of shallows ahead, so that the engineer would slow down and run cautiously whenever he spotted a group of awaiting Indians.

Two Yuma Indians came along as nominal guides and interpreters, and "when we make a landing to take in wood they instantly disappear, and refresh themselves with the absence of civilization until the whistle signals that it is time to start. . . ." A few days up the river these two asked permission to spend a day or two with their friends, which Ives granted as they could easily have taken off anyway at will, but they returned promptly, one of them bringing back

an urchin whom he introduced as his son, and requested me to furnish with some cotton. As to the first part of his statement, I concluded, from the boy's features and complexion, that either Mariano was trying to impose on me, or had himself been grossly imposen upon; but the white cotton, or "manta," as the Indians call it, was provided, to the great satisfaction of the young gentleman in question.

The party reached the country of the Chemehuevis, who seldom went to Fort Yuma and consequently had rarely seen steamboats, but:

If we had anticipated inspiring them with awe or admiration, we should be sadly disappointed, for I am sure they regard our method of ascending the river with unaffected contempt. . . . They can foot it on the shore, or pole along a raft upon the river without interruption; and that we should spend days in doing what they can accomplish in half as many hours, strikes them as unaccountably stupid. The gleeful consciousness of superiority at all events keeps them in an excellent humor.

The Chemehuevis made a field day, at first, out of the troubles of the pathetic, hard-puffing *Explorer*, but were finally moved to compassion and would run ahead of the boat to point out the passages over a sand bar. But on one occasion the boat was loaded with the curses of an Indian witch as an additional burden:

An old woman, among others, endeavored to help the captain along, but as we approached the place she indicated his knowledge of the river showed him that it would not do, and he sheered off without making the trial. The benevolence of the old hag was at once converted into rage, and with clenched fists and flaming eyes she followed along the bank, screaming at the captain, as long as he was in hearing, a volley of maledictions.

They reached the mouth of the Bill Williams River, down which Ives and Möllhausen had traveled with Lieutenant Whipple at the same time of year, February, four years before. But now that stream was practically dried up to a mere trickle because of the drought which had prevailed for three years, and the Colorado was about as low proportionately as its tributary. In fact, the Ives expedition couldn't have picked a more unfavorable season in which to steam up the river and things worsened as they ascended. As Ives wrote on January 31:

One bar would scarcely be passed before another would be encountered, and we were three days in accomplishing a distance of nine miles. A boat drawing six inches less water, and without any timbers attached to the bottom, could have probably made the same distance in three hours.

Straining and puffing, the *Explorer* reached the cluster of slender and prominent pinnacles which Whipple had named "The Needles," where the Santa Fe Railroad now crosses the river, and these marked the beginning of the lands of the Mohave Indians, with whom the Whipple expedition had been on such friendly terms. Before leaving the Chemehuevis, however, Ives reported:

Mr. Möllhausen has enlisted the services of the children to procure zoological specimens, and has obtained, at the cost of a few strings of beads, several varieties of pouched mice and lizards. They think he eats them, and are delighted that his eccentric appetite can be gratified with so much ease and profit to themselves.

They met the other steamboat, which had preceeded them up the river from Fort Yuma, returning downstream, and Ives sent back Lieutenant Tipton to bring up a pack train by land. This means that the other boat may have reached as far north as the mouth of the Virgin River, considerably beyond the eventual stopping point of the *Explorer;* and, if so, this must have been galling to Ives on his expensive, specially built craft, but he says nothing about it and continues on his colorful description of his own adventures.

Ives had done some vivid word-painting about the scenery they had passed through and Freeman in *The Colorado River* comments on this: "Indeed . . . Ives, having exhausted the stuff in his heavy artillery lockers upon the rather insignificant gorges of the Mohave and Bill Williams, found himself without adequate ammunition when he came up against the real thing at Black Canyon and the still more stupendous Grand. But this Dorésque vision of Mohave Canyon, like a Whistler nocturne, is worthwhile for itself alone, however little it suggests the original inspiration."

Ives's description of Mohave Canyon was as follows:

A low purple gateway and a splendid corridor, with massive red walls, formed the entrance to the Canyon. At the head of this avenue frowning mountains, piled one above the other, seemed to block the way. An abrupt turn at the base of the apparent barrier revealed a cavern-like approach to the profound chasm beyond. A scene of such imposing grandeur as that which now presented itself I have never before witnessed. On either side majestic cliffs, hundreds of feet in height, rose perpendicularly from the water. As the river wound through the narrow enclosure every turn developed some sublime effect or startling novelty in the view. Brilliant tints of purple, green, brown, red, and white illuminated the stupendous surfaces and relieved their somber monotony. Far above, clear and distinct upon the narrow strip of sky, turrets, spires, jagged statue-like peaks and grotesque pinnacles overlooked the deep abyss.

The waning day found us still threading the windings of this wonderful defile, and the approach of twilight enhanced the wild romance of the scenery. The bright colors faded and blended into a uniform dark gray. The rocks assumed dim and exaggerated shapes, and seemed to flit like giant spectres in pursuit and retreat along the shadowy vista. A solemn stillness reigned in the darkening avenue, broken only by the plash of the paddles or the cry of a solitary heron,

startled by our approach from his perch on the brink of some over-
hanging cliff.

What a contrast to the usual military report! One wonders
how Ives ever got through West Point.

The expedition came out of this canyon into the beautiful
Mohave Valley at a time "before the burning heat has withered
the freshness and beauty of the early vegetation"; and:

It may be that the eye, weary of the monotonous sterility of the
country below, is disposed to exaggerate its charms, but as we first
saw it, clothed in spring attire, and bathed in all the splendor of a
brilliant morning's sunlight, the scene was so lovely that there was a
universal expression of admiration and delight.

The Mohave Indians in this idyllic valley welcomed the explorers and Ives noted:

The men, as a general rule, have noble figures, and the stature of
some is gigantic. Having no clothing but a strip of cotton, their
fine proportions are displayed to the greatest advantage. Most of
them have intelligent countenances and an agreeable expression. The
women, over the age of eighteen or twenty, are almost invariably
short and stout, with fat, good-natured faces. Their only article of
dress is a short petticoat, made of strips of bark, and sticking out
about eight inches behind. Some of the younger girls are very pretty
and have slender, graceful figures. The children wear only the apparel
in which they were born, and have a precocious, impish look. Their
delight today has been to mimic the man at the bow who takes the
soundings, every call being echoed from the bank with amusing
fidelity of tone and accent. . . . [The babies] . . . are . . . carried
upon the projecting petticoat, where they sit astraddle, with their
legs clasping their mother's waist and their little fists tightly clutched
in her fat sides.

Lieutenant Ives made an address to the Indians, who flocked
in for trade and sight-seeing, "which differed from any speech

ever yet made to a band of Indians since the formation of our government — inasmuch as it contained nothing about the 'Great Father at Washington.' " This had to be relayed through three interpreters, one who translated it from English to Spanish, another from Spanish to Yuma, and finally from that tongue into Mohave; and Ives said: "What changes my remarks have undergone during these different stages, I shall never know; but I observe that they are sometimes received by the Mojaves with an astonishment and bewilderment that the original sense does not at all warrant."

Anyway, things went well enough and the Mohaves were disposed to be friendly, and these relations became even more cordial when two old friends of Ives and Möllhausen appeared, the two braves who had guided Whipple's expedition across the Mohave Desert, about four years before. One of these, named Cairook, was an important chief who arrived with the pomp and ceremony of a large retinue to greet his old friends and to inquire "for Lieutenant Whipple, for whom he had conceived an exalted opinion." Incidentally, many of the tribe remembered Lieutenant Tidball and his magic dentures and "they were inquisitive to learn something of the man who could carry his teeth in his hand." The other guide, Ireteba, also turned up and was delighted at the cordial greeting he received, and agreed to act again as a guide, this time up the river. Ives invited Cairook and his wife to ride on the steamboat for a day or so when the expedition continued northward upstream:

. . . and they sat in dignified state [upon the exclusive upper deck], and enjoyed the admiring gaze of their neighbors, who were assembled in crowds along the banks. From the airs that were put on by Madam Cairook in consequence of being the only female thus distinguished, I am afraid that the trip turned her head, and that she must have been quite unbearable to her friends after she left us.

Ives and his companions left this agreeable and superior tribe with regrets. The Mohaves unquestionably considered the white men as being a little bit peculiar and rather to be pitied; and were not at all impressed by most of their inventions and equipment. For example, Ives gave them a concert by a few musicians in the party, but they were rather bored and promptly brought forth "two or three of their own musicians to show ours how the thing ought to be done. These artists performed a kind of chant, in a discordant, monotonous tone, and after making some of the most unearthly noises that I ever listened to, regarded us with an air of satisfied triumph." Incidentally, this tribe was a living example of the rewards of vegetarianism, for "They subsist almost exclusively upon beans and corn, with occasional watermelons and pumpkins, and are probably as fine a race, physically, as there is in existence."

CHAPTER XV

On to the Grand Canyon

THE *Explorer* had comparatively easy going up through the rest of the level Mohave Valley, but renewed troubles began as soon as they came anew to the mountains and entered more canyons. Again the steamboat had to be shoved and hauled by manpower over swift and shallow rapids studded by dangerous rocks, and upon one occasion:

The boat was lightened and, after several hours of hard labor, had been brought to the crest of the rapid, when the line broke and the *Explorer* drifted down, bumping upon the rocks, and was in imminent danger of having her hull stove. The day's work was undone in an instant, and we were glad that it was no worse. When she finally brought up, it was upon some rocks, where she was wedged so fast that it occupied half of the next day to extricate her.

To cap this disheartening setback, the next night " the fiercest norther sprang up that has yet been experienced, and continued throughout the following day. We ate, drank, breathed, and saw little but sand for twenty-four hours, and the *Explorer* was dragged from her anchorage and driven upon the rocks."

The timbers, or scantlings, bolted to the outside of the *Explorer's* hull made all kinds of trouble. They increased the boat's draft by four or five inches and this was just enough, in the unusually low waters of the river, for the boat to scrape bottom constantly and often become wedged in the rocks, from which it was extremely difficult to extricate her. With six inches less draft, the *Explorer* could probably have gone far above her final stopping place.

It took the party five days to pass over a dozen rapids in the last twenty miles to the mouth of Black Canyon, just below the modern Hoover Dam. Here they began to see the real thing in canyons and to realize how picayune, by comparison, were the previous gorges they had floundered through. But their equipment was in bad shape to challenge these superchasms, for "the lines have become almost worn out by hard service; the skiff is badly battered and scarcely able to float, and all the oars are broken."

The final stop to the *Explorer* came like a thunderbolt, just as they entered the mouth of this huge, lowering canyon:

. . . we were shooting swiftly past the entrance, eagerly gazing into the mysterious depths beyond, when the *Explorer*, with a stunning crash, brought up abruptly and instantaneously against a sunken rock. For a second the impression was that the Cañon had fallen in. The concussion was so violent that the men near the bow were thrown overboard; the doctor, Mr. Möllhausen, and myself, having been seated in front of the upper deck, were precipitated head foremost into the bottom of the boat; the fireman, who was pitching a log into the fire, went half-way in with it; the boiler was thrown out of place; the steam pipe doubled up; the wheel-house torn away; and it was expected that the boat would fill and sink instantly by all but Mr. Carroll, who was looking for an explosion from the injured steam pipes.

It took three days to repair the damages but, after this disaster, Ives decided to reconnoiter up Black Canyon in the skiff to see what other dangers lurked in the dark chasms above. He and two other men then shoved off to row upstream, leaving the others to await Lieutenant Tipton's pack train, which was daily expected to arrive from Fort Yuma. Signs of the hostile Pai-Utes had been seen and all were warned to keep on the alert against that invisibly dangerous tribe.

For two days the rowers struggled upstream against the three-miles-an-hour current, threading "the mazes of a cañon, far exceeding in vastness any that had been yet traversed. The walls were perpendicular, and more than double the height of those in the Mojave mountains, rising, in many places, sheer from the water, for over a thousand feet." They met frequent rapids over which they had to haul the skiff, and it became apparent that the larger *Explorer* would have exceedingly tough going in this pinched-in abyss. Ives wrote:

No description can convey an idea of the varied and majestic grandeur of this peerless waterway. . . . Stately façades, august cathedrals, ampitheatres, rotundas, castellated walls, and rows of time-stained ruins, surmounted by every form of tower, minaret, dome, and spire, have been molded from the cyclopean masses of rock that form the mighty defile. The solitude, the stillness, the subdued light, and the vastness of every surrounding object, produce an impression of awe that ultimately becomes almost painful.

They suddenly emerged from a "narrow passage, between two mammoth peaks, that seemed to be nodding to each other across the stream, and unexpectedly found, at the upper end, the termination of the Black Cañon." They rowed further up the river, the next day, to the mouth of a shallow, brackish creek which Ives supposed to be the Virgin River, flowing in from the north, but which was actually Las Vegas Wash. The outlook for further navigation was unfavorable and:

. . . we had seen drift-wood lodged in clefts fifty feet above the river, betokening a condition of things during the summer freshet that would render navigation more hazardous at that season than now [March 12]. It appeared, therefore, that the foot of the Black Cañon should be considered the practical head of navigation.

The three weary men embarked in their skiff and enjoyed an easy and pleasant trip downstream, shooting the rapids "with exhilarating velocity," and made the thirty-mile trip back to their companions in between six and seven hours. The next day, a Mohave messenger arrived from Fort Yuma with the news that he had passed Lieutenant Tipton's pack train just below the Bill Williams River. The *Explorer* was headed downstream, and, helped by a rise in the river, it reeled off a record-making day's run of thirty miles.

While they were encamped that evening, a white man hailed them from the opposite bank and was brought over in the skiff. He was one of a party of four who claimed to be emigrants on their way to Los Angeles, but one of Ives's men who had been in Utah recognized the visitor as a Mormon bishop. This was a bit disturbing, for, as Ives must have known, the Mormons were in a state of semirebellion against the United States Government, a state of affairs which had caused the government to send an army punitive expedition, the previous autumn, against that defiant sect. Ives's apprehension was that the Mormons were stirring up the surrounding Indians against his party and he noted a marked change for the worse in the attitude of the Mohaves, who suddenly became shy and shunned the camp. He believed the Mormons were spreading the canard that his men were scouting out the country for later occupation by white settlers. The Mormons were indefatigable missionaries among the Indians and had some success in their proselyting, although Ives reported: "Ireteba [his trusty Mohave guide] told me, with a grin, that Cairook was among the number, and that the big chief was greatly disgusted when they tried to duck his head in the river."

Lieutenant Tipton's pack train clattered in, after a rough trip over difficult mountain trails and across arid, grassless deserts, bringing long-needed supplies, especially coffee and salt. The combined parties then proceeded southward together by land and water until they reached the agreeable bottom lands of the Mohave Valley. There Ives met Chief Cairook and was able to dispel the suspicions which the Mormons had implanted in the tribe. Good feeling was restored and Ives then divided his party with confidence. He, with Dr. Newberry, the artists Egloffstein and Möllhausen, and an assorted lot of Mexican packers and laborers, guarded by an escort of twenty soldiers under Lieutenant Tipton, and guided by the faithful Ireteba, turned east by land through the pass used by Captain Sitgreaves. The rest of the expedition continued on downstream in the *Explorer* to Fort Yuma.

Ives's party labored through the mountain passes to the country of the Hualpais Indians, a singularly unattractive lot, whom he described as "squalid, wretched-looking creatures, with splay feet, large joints, and diminutive figures," and "one of them had features like a toad's, and the most villainous countenance I ever saw on a human being. Mr. Möllhausen suggested that we should take him and preserve him in alcohol as a zoological specimen. . . ." After prolonged negotiations, of which Ives remarked: "The sententiousness belonging to Mr. Cooper's and other story-book Indians is not a gift of the tribes that one encounters in travelling," two Hualpais agreed to guide the party through their lands.

Continuing on northeast, they plunged into a narrow and precipitous ravine through which Diamond Creek flowed roughly northward into the Grand Canyon itself. Descending along this, guided by the Hualpais, through a maze of side defiles

. . . the increasing magnitude of the colossal piles that blocked the end of the vista, and the corresponding depth and gloom of the gaping chasms into which we were plunging, imparted an unearthly character to a way that might have resembled the portals of the infernal regions. Harsh screams issuing from aerial recesses in the cañon sides, and apparitions of goblin-like figures perched in the rifts and hollows of the impending cliffs, gave an odd reality to this impression.

They passed scattered huts of the Hualpais in this subterranean retreat and:

Our party being, in all probability, the first company of whites that had even been seen by them, we had anticipated producing a great effect, and were a little chagrined when the old woman [Ives called her "a hideous old squaw"], and two or three others of both sexes that we met, went by without taking the slightest notice of us. If pack-trains had been in the habit of passing twenty times a day they could not have manifested a more complete indifference.

After camping that night on a clear stream in an "oasis of verdure," Ives, the next morning, walked a short distance to where the creek flowed into the Colorado River at the bottom of the Grand Canyon itself. Ives had probably shot all his bolts of purple prose in describing the lesser canyons he had seen, or else he was literally left wordless by the indescribably titanic scene, for the best he could do was to mumble that it was "on a larger scale and thus far unrivalled in grandeur." Not so his artists. Egloffstein and Möllhausen had been gradually working into high gear along the way and, when they saw the grand-daddy of all earthly canyons, these two talented Germans pulled out all their artistic stops and produced some drawings which Mr. Freeman, aptly quoting from Samuel Taylor Coleridge's "Kubla Khan," says look like:

Where Alph, the sacred river, ran,
Through caverns measureless to man,
Down to a sunless sea.

And he continues: "With the shrouded figures of Dante and Virgil mooning on a pinnacle above the gloomy depths it would get away unchallenged with some such title as 'Source of the River Styx.' "

Their sketches are unquestionably Dorésque, but then, they were to illustrate Ives's Dantesque descriptions; and, after all, they were the first white men of record to set foot on the bottom of that stupendous chasm, so that full allowances should be made the artistic temperament for Gothic extravagances at such an exciting time and place.

The expedition retraced its steps back up Diamond Creek till it came to a place where the sides of the enclosing canyon could be ascended and the march resumed to the eastward, skirting, on the south, the heads of the arroyos and canyons which sharply declined northwards toward the Grand Canyon. The faithful Mohave guide, Ireteba, left them at this point, and Ives commemorated him by saying, "He is the best Indian that I have ever known." This left the party under the guidance of the Hualpais, of whom Ives disgustedly remarked: ". . . their intelligence is of so low an order that it is impossible to glean information from them, and their filthiness makes them objectionable." But the Hualpais soon relieved the situation by deserting, which Ives philosophically accepted as a temporary inconvenience but, on the whole, a good riddance.

For a while they groped on, guideless, without water until a heavy blizzard covered the ground with snow, which, however, was a mixed blessing, for it also covered the grass and chilled the mules and men so recently arrived from the hot lower Colorado valley. After this, they again struck an arid section, and finding a well-marked Indian trail leading down a ravine toward the Grand Canyon to the north, they followed it to find water, for which they were again in acute need. The trail pinched down to a narrow ledge along the side of a cliff over a sheer gulf of a thousand feet, and Ives wrote:

. . . on the other side, nearly touching my knee, was an almost vertical wall rising to an enormous altitude. The sight made my head swim, and I dismounted, and got ahead of the mule, a difficult and delicate operation, which I was thankful to have safely performed. A part of the men became so giddy that they were obliged to creep upon their hands and knees, being unable to walk or stand. In some places there was barely room to walk, and a slight deviation in a step would have precipitated one into the frightful abyss. I was a good deal alarmed lest some obstacle should be encountered that would make it impossible to go ahead, for it was impracticable to return. After an interval of uncomfortable suspense the face of the rock made an angle, and just beyond the turn was a projection from the main wall with a surface fifteen or twenty yards square that would afford a foothold. The continuation of the wall was perfectly vertical, so that the trail could no longer follow it, and we found the path descended the steep face of the cliff to the bottom of the cañon. It was a desperate road to traverse, but located with a good deal of skill — zigzagging down the precipice, and taking advantage of every crevice and fissure that could afford a foothold. It did not take long to discover that no mule could accomplish this descent, and nothing remained but to turn back. We were glad to have even this privilege in our power.

The mules had been two days without water and "with glassy eyes and protruding tongues" were in truly bad shape. Ives ordered the Mexican muleteers to drive them up out of the canyon and back along the trail to the last water holes, almost thirty miles distant. It was the only chance to save most of them, although "somewhat dangerous to detach them thus far from the main party, but there was no help for it."

After the mules had left, Ives led a picked exploring party, including Lieutenant Tipton and Mr. Egloffstein, again down the trail to try and reach the bottom on foot. They descended the precipice without serious difficulty and continued lower and lower along the floor of the canyon below, until halted by a sheer drop of forty feet over which fell a little cascade of water from a nearby spring. Mr. Egloffstein spied "a crazy-looking ladder, made of rough sticks bound together with thongs of bark," standing beneath the falls and immediately essayed a descent upon it. The rotted rungs collapsed beneath him and he made a precipitate trip to the bottom in a general crash, but was fortunately unhurt, although cut off. He went on down the lower canyon, following a pretty stream, fringed with cottonwoods and willows, until he reached "a narrow belt of bottom land, on which were fields of corn and a few scattered huts." Beyond this he was really stopped by another cascade, but he saw he was very near to where the stream flowed into the Colorado River in one of the deepest parts of the Grand Canyon. He had stumbled into what is now called Cataract Canyon and was the second white man to reach the settlement of the Havasupai Indians, celebrated now for their isolated self-sufficiency. The first had been a zealous priest, Father Francisco Garces, who had wandered, in his missionary zeal, into Cataract Canyon in 1776.

Mr. Egloffstein was hauled up by a line made of the leather slings on the soldiers' muskets, but the party was unable to get out of the canyon before dark and all spent an uncomfortably cold and sleepless night, in their light walking clothes, on the hard rocks and boulders. They finally arrived back at their camp, completely exhausted from their strenuous climbings and from lack of food or rest for twenty-four hours. The mules returned and the reunited party, having more than had their fill of canyons, turned south to skirt the heads of all the subsidiary defiles, ravines, and canyons running northward into the great canyon which blocked their way to the east. Ives probably expressed the consensus of opinion of all the weary members of the expedition, but in doing so, proved them and himself poor prophets indeed. He wrote:

The region last explored is, of course, altogether valueless. It can be approached only from the south and after entering it there is nothing to do but to leave. Ours had been the first, and will doubtless be the last, party of whites to visit this profitless locality. It seems intended by nature that the Colorado river, along the greater portion of its lonely and majestic way, shall be forever unvisited and undisturbed.

If he but could have foreseen the present-day hordes of sightseers at the Grand Canyon!

The expedition headed south, the mules being in wretched shape; ". . . the weakened brutes staggered under their packs as though they were drunk, and their dismal moaning portended a speedy solution of their troubles should water not soon be found"; but luckily a pool of clear, delicious water was discovered, and: "The crazy beasts, crowding and huddling upon one another, plunged into the pond and drank till they were ready to burst." They reached the fertile northern slopes of Bill Williams's mountain, where men and mules rested and recuperated for a few days in a comparative paradise. From there they rode on eastward, but by that time the animals, who had just buffeted a roaring gale of snow and sleet in their weakened condition, were really on their last legs and looked and moved "like slightly animated skeletons." Also the equipment was nearly worn out and the provisions almost gone. Ives then sent Lieutenant Tipton, probably accompanied by Möllhausen, and the main train directly on to Zuni and Fort Defiance, while he, with Dr. Newberry, Mr. Egloffstein, and ten men, using the least exhausted mules, turned north to visit the Moqui (Hopi) towns, about which he wrote: "The impassable cañons west of the territory of these Indians have thrown them out of the line of travel and exploration, and there has been no record concerning them since the accounts of the early Spanish missionaries. . . ." This statement was not literally true, but most probably no official American expedition had visited that tribe and certainly it was an interesting ending to an unusual exploration.

So, in early May, 1858, after crossing the Little Colorado River (which Ives called the Flax), in a collapsible boat, which he had designed and lugged all this way on muleback (probably the same model he had supplied Whipple's expedition to cross the Colorado River), he led his small band off in a direction a little east of north. Möllhausen must have gone on with Tipton's party, for he disappears from Ives's narrative and all the drawings of the Moquis and their country were made by Egloffstein. Again in desert country Ives wrote: "As the sun declined and a pleasanter atmosphere succeeded to the oppressive heat, scorpions, spiders and centipedes emerged from their retreats to enjoy the evening air. A collector in that department of natural history could have reaped a harvest of these reptiles in almost any part of our campground."

On the fifth evening, after fairly hard going, Ives sighted two of the Moqui towns through his spyglass across a wide valley. The next day they were vociferously greeted by two outriders of the tribe, mounted on crowbait ponies, but the men were remarkable for their cleanliness and neatness, qualities not usually considered by the Indians as a part of the most elaborate toilet. Others came running out on foot to shake hands with the lieutenant and each member of the party. All were clean and nice-looking but dressed in no particular tribal costume. "Large flocks of sheep were passed; all but one or two were jet black. . . ." (Probably the results of inbreeding). And the visitors' mules were hospitably led to water and to a grazing ground which, however, seemed woefully bare and explained the puniness of the local ponies.

The Moquis are now called by their original name of Hopis, and are best known today for their famous annual snake dance, which has been much publicized and is attended by hundreds of tourists and sightseers, now that the distant pueblos can be easily reached by automobiles. But when Ives's party arrived, they were truly almost isolated, as he said. He spent some time climbing up and down one of their impregnable pueblos (of which they had seven, perched on high mesas), and found them a pleasant and rather attractive tribe, with light complexions, and he noticed: "Many have an Italian physiognomy." Their towns were proof against attacks by other Indians, but the Navajos and Apaches often descended upon them and ran off their livestock in the open fields below.

Ives must have had a recurrence of Grand Canyon fever at that point, for he made a futile effort to reach it again from the Moqui towns, even after he was advised against it by the tribal chiefs and could not secure any guides. After riding north for some distance and seeing nothing ahead but a barren, waterless desert, he sensibly decided to give it up as a bad job, and turned again east toward Fort Defiance, that lonely army outpost in the heart of the Navajo country.

The cavalcade was joined by some Moquis and two Navajos who had been visiting among them. Ives wondered at the boldness of the latter pair in going to the Moqui pueblos so soon after a recent cattle-stealing foray, and described them as "merry, impudent-looking knaves" who ate, smoked, and laughed among the Americans and "finally asked for a glass of liquor as independently as though they were in a tavern. It was impossible to put them down; favors or rebuffs made the same or rather no impression; they received all with a grinning indifference that would have been good-natured, had it not been so impertinent."

The cavalcade was swelled by more Moquis and Navajos falling into line as it proceeded into the country of the latter tribe. The Navajos wondered at the Americans coming from the west, which had never happened before, and one chief impudently suggested that they must be friends of the Apaches, "who had lately stolen the Moquis's horses, of which act the Navajos had been wrongfully accused." The grins of his fellow tribesmen at this harangue showed that it was intended for Moqui consumption but, wrote Ives, "I perceived, however, that the Moquis were as unconvinced as ourselves by the plausible reasoning."

Ives gave the Navajos credit for "one trait of character which I had never seen exhibited by Indians." Being so near his destination, he had given all his remaining trade goods and trinkets to the surrounding Navajo throng. "The women were highly delighted, and not long after some of the men, whom I supposed to be their husbands, brought into camp a quantity of cheese and joints of mutton — enough to have lasted our company a week. I offered to pay for what we required, but they insisted upon my accepting all as a gift."

The little band clattered on into Fort Defiance, the end of the line. And none too soon, for a fortnight later fighting broke out between the United States troops and the Navajos. If Ives had not turned back when he did from his last attempt to reach the Grand Canyon, his small party would probably have been cut off and annihilated.

Most of the party returned to the East, but Ives went by stage from Santa Fe to El Paso and thence to San Diego, stopping for a day or two at Fort Yuma, where he sold the *Explorer*, "the little boat that had done us such good service," to the company running the transportation on the Colorado River. Then he continued on to San Francisco, where he took the first steamer to New York.

The later career of Joseph Christmas Ives was extraordinary. Returning to the capital, he became the superintendent and construction engineer of the Washington Monument, but devoted most of his time to the raising of funds for that long-delayed shaft. When the Civil War broke out he became a captain of engineers in the Army of the Confederacy, after declining the same rank in the Union Army. He was placed for a while in charge of coastal defenses, but served from 1863 to 1865 as an aide-de-camp to President Jefferson Davis with the rank of colonel. Now Ives was a native New Yorker who had been appointed to West Point from Connecticut, but like many another good Northern man his defection was because of a charming Southern wife. In 1855 he had married Cora Semmes, a first cousin of Raphael Semmes, who became the great Confederate naval raider; and Ives and his wife were intimate friends of the Jefferson Davises in Washington before the war. They were such an elegant and attractive couple that President Davis made them official entertainers of distinguished foreign visitors to Richmond, and they showed the town to many soldiers of fortune, war correspondents and diplomats. Cora Semmes Ives specialized in amateur theatricals, and a production of Sheridan's *The Rivals*, on a stage built in her own house by her engineer husband, was considered the high spot of the somewhat difficult social life in the Confederate capital. Ives returned to New York, where he died in 1868, but his wife lived on till 1916, outliving two sons who became officers in the United States Army. A third and youngest son was a lawyer who moved to Arizona, thus returning to the scene of his father's earlier explorations.

A curious sidelight of all this was the appearance of a brother,

Malcolm Ives, in Washington during the war as a correspondent for the New York *Herald*. This erratic brother claimed to have a private pipeline to the Navy and War Departments for inside news. He was said to have had a previously checkered past as a Philadelphia banker, and, after a trip to Rome, to have been converted to Catholicism and returned a priest. He had then defrocked himself to marry and had worked in the New York customhouse. Secretary of War Stanton found him a nuisance and the *Herald* editors suspected his sanity after a wild report he sent in of a supposed interview with General George B. McClellan. Stanton then clapped him into prison, charged with espionage, where he remained for a few months but was eventually released. His brother Joseph's defection to the Confederacy must have been one reason for the suspicion directed at this unbalanced character.[1]

[1] Bernard A. Weisberger, *Reporters for the Union*, Boston 1953. pp. 130, 131, 134–136, 141–144.

CHAPTER XVI

The Mormon War

LIEUTENANT Ives mentioned meeting a small party of four Mormons while on the Colorado River and his strong convictions that they had been stirring up trouble among the Mohave Indians. He, of course, was pretty well cut off from the latest news, but he must have heard that a military expedition had started for Utah in the summer of 1857 to enforce Federal authority there, and that imminent danger existed of actual hostilities with that defiant sect.

This punitive force was in no sense an exploring expedition, for the ground it covered was well enough known, but it was the largest military force assembled between the Mexican and Civil Wars and its activities along the Oregon Trail, and on a branch to Salt Lake City, greatly increased the general use and knowledge of that route, which later logically led to its choice for the first transcontinental railroad, the Union Pacific – Central Pacific, completed in 1869. Also, it gave the military, other than the Topographical Engineers, a workout on the frontier which was a change from the constant Indian fighting and the efforts to preserve peace amidst the sectional disorders of "Bleeding Kansas." And its peaceful termination was of the greatest importance to the Union cause in the soon to follow Civil War.

One of its sidelights, the trip for supplies led by Captain Randolph Barnes Marcy through the high Rockies of Colorado in midwinter, was as daringly and skillfully accomplished, despite the worst hardships and handicaps, as any feat in the exploration of the West.

The Mormons, or more properly the Church of Jesus Christ of Latter-day Saints, after Joseph Smith had founded the sect at Palmyra, New York, in 1830, had been chevied around from pillar to post by the hostile Gentiles (as they called unbelievers), ever working generally westward except for a brief back track to Nauvoo, Illinois, after they had been brutally driven from Independence, Missouri, in the depth of the winter of 1839; ever afterwards they especially hated Missourians. In and near Nauvoo, their numbers had grown to some fifteen thousand by the end of 1844; that city was the largest in Illinois and second only to St. Louis in the Northwest, and it was growing rapidly. But once again the Mormons aroused the hostility of the surrounding Gentiles, more from their clannishness and air of conscious superiority as the chosen people of the Lord than from any overt acts; and once more they became wanderers on the face of the earth after a hostile mob attacked their city and murdered Joseph Smith and his brother Hyrum. Under the leadership of Brigham Young, they then began in 1846 the long and hazardous march, in various detachments, to the Great Salt Lake, which was in Mexican territory and so remote when their great exodus began they hoped to find a real haven of peace in their very isolation. It was while the main party was waiting at Council Bluffs, before beginning the long journey, that the Mormon Battalion was recruited from their numbers, which then marched to California under the command of Philip St. George Cooke. The hardships of some of the Mormon emigrants were extreme in making the long journey to Salt Lake, especially among a poor group of converts from England who could not afford wagons or draft animals and made the whole trip pulling their belongings in handcarts. Of the four hundred and twenty in one body of these emigrants who had started the trip late in the summer of 1856 and consequently encountered snowstorms and extreme cold, sixty-seven died on the way. Naturally, Mormon resentment was strong against the hostile Gentiles who had forced them into these dangers and hardships.

The peace with Mexico brought all the territory in which the Mormons had so hopefully settled under the jurisdiction of the United States — under the government which they had good reason to hate and from which they had tried to escape. If this land had remained under Mexico they could probably have lived unmolested for years under such a theocracy as Brigham Young and the Mormon elders saw fit to establish. But the literal irony of fate brought them once again under the authority of the United States and the discovery of gold in California upset all their hopes for seclusion. A wave of California-bound forty-niners poured through the new Salt Lake City at the western foot of the Wasatch Mountains, and while the Mormons found these unwanted emigrants a source of material profit in the selling of supplies and animals, this rampant intrusion ended the dream of an isolated ivory tower of Mormon theocracy.

To make the best of this disappointment, the Mormons tentatively organized the State of Deseret — a huge area including, besides Utah, the present Nevada, and what are now parts of southern California, Arizona, and New Mexico, and southwestern Wyoming — and applied for admission to the Union. This would at least allow them to control their own local state government. But so much opposition developed throughout the country to the entrance of such a state, which would be in effect a theocracy of the Mormon Church with its rumored acceptance of polygamy, that Congress established the Territory of Utah (with much reduced boundaries) in 1850. President Millard Fillmore, recognizing, however, the almost entirely Mormon population of this new territory, appointed Brigham Young as its governor, but also sent out certain Gentiles to fill other government positions, and this started trouble.

These non-Mormon officials complained that their authority was flagrantly flouted by the Mormon Church, which overshadowed and controlled all the acts and opinions of the people of Utah, took over the functions and duties of the legislature and the judiciary, commanded the militia, disposed of the public lands, and even coined money stamped *Holiness to the Lord* which it forced into circulation at fifteen per cent above its true value, exacted a tithe of ten per cent for its coffers from the yearly income of its members, and was in every sense an autocracy. They added that they had been personally snubbed by Brigham Young, the head of the church, and that its members were disloyal to the United States. Making their way to Washington, these officials laid the whole matter before President Fillmore.

The other side of the story, as given by the Mormons, was that these same officials were a corrupt and venal lot of political hacks who were appointed to jobs in far-off Utah largely as a means of getting rid of them. They specifically cited the case of one of the appointed associate justices of the territory's supreme court, W. W. Drummond of Illinois, who, after leaving a wife at home (probably an awful waste to a Mormon), "brought with him a harlot whom he had picked up in the streets of Washington, and introducing her as Mrs. Drummond, seated her by his side on the judicial bench. Gambler and bully, he openly avowed that he had come to Utah to make money, and in the presence of the chief justice declared: 'Money is my

God.' " [1] Others were accused of habitual drunkenness and general profligacy, and there was plenty of truth in the Mormon accusations, for but few men of good standing would have been willing to serve in such a remote place amidst such a hostile atmosphere.

Anyway, one thing led to another so that by 1857 the Mormons were in effect in open rebellion and affairs in Utah were in a pretty pass with, save two Indian agents, not a Federal official left in the territory. That left Brigham Young as absolute dictator and Utah without the jurisdiction of the United States. That was too much even for cautious President James Buchanan, and he appointed Alfred Cumming of Georgia to replace Young as governor and an entire set of new Federal judges and officials to accompany him, all to be escorted to Utah by a body of troops to act as a *posse comitatus* if necessary.

The troops, some fifteen hundred and the largest number gathered together since the Mexican War, were concentrated at Fort Leavenworth, and were at first under the command of Colonel William Selby Harney, called by his enemies, of whom there were many, the "squaw killer." However, Harney was soon replaced by Colonel Albert Sidney Johnston, a West Pointer of the class of 1826 and a former commander of the army of the Republic of Texas, who later became a sort of shining knight in white armor of the Confederacy and died at the battle of Shiloh in 1862. Johnston joined the column soon after it had started west in July, 1857.

When the Mormons received news of this small army's approach, they took immediate and effective action. The Nauvoo Legion, comprised of all men from eighteen to forty-five, was alerted for immediate duty and scouting parties were dispatched

[1] Hubert Howe Bancroft, *History of Utah. 1540–1886* (San Francisco 1890), p. 490.

to keep the Mormon leaders fully informed of every movement
of the Federal troops. By the end of September, Johnston's
advance guard had crossed the Green River in present southwestern Wyoming, where Colonel Alexander, its commander,
received an astonishing proclamation issued by Brigham Young
which forbade armed forces of any description to enter Utah
under any pretense whatsoever. This was accompanied by a
personal letter from Brigham Young demanding that the
astounded colonel retreat at once by the way he had come.
Alexander, of course, refused to obey this highhanded order,
whereupon the Mormons opened the so-called war. Orders were
issued from Salt Lake City for their forces to harass Johnston's
army in every possible way, to burn the grass to its front and
on its flanks, blockade the passes by felling trees, destroy its
wagon trains, and by night surprises keep the soldiers from
sleeping. These orders were immediately obeyed and four large
supply trains were captured and burned, as was Fort Bridger (the
trading post of old Jim Bridger, the famous mountain man, near
the Green River), and many hundreds of animals, mostly oxen,
in the Federal column were cut out and driven off. But there
were no casualties in these attacks.

The detachments of Johnston's small army finally united near
the destroyed Fort Bridger. Some of them had had tough going
from Fort Laramie, especially one of the 2nd Dragoons, escorting the new governor, Alfred Cumming, which was commanded by Lieutenant Colonel Philip St. George Cooke, who
but a decade before had led the famous Mormon Battalion to
California. His feelings must have been mixed in now moving
against a people who had served him so loyally during the Mexican War. Snow and sleet had hampered his column all the way
from Fort Leavenworth to Fort Laramie, and beyond there a
dreadful blizzard had engulfed them, so that his men arrived at

Fort Bridger almost all on foot, with only ten horses surviving of the one hundred and forty-four which had left Fort Leavenworth. It was impossible for Johnston to push on to Salt Lake City under the circumstances, for the mountain passes to the west had been heavily fortified and manned by the Mormons, provisions had been seriously depleted by the loss of the wagon trains, and the surviving animals were starving on the burned-over plains. It was a matter of supreme importance to obtain more supplies of every kind for an early spring offensive. The nearest source for provisions, animals, and equipment was at Fort Massachusetts far to the south, near what is now Fort Garland in south central Colorado. Johnston chose Captain Randolph Barnes Marcy, of the 5th Infantry, to lead an expedition for help from that lonely post, but the terrible difficulties of the trip were not fully realized, and Marcy and his men barely escaped destruction.

The Utah Expedition bogged down then for a long winter in or near Fort Bridger; in fact it stuck there for seven months. Captain Jesse A. Gove of the 10th Infantry, who hailed from Concord, New Hampshire, wrote his wife a series of letters which give a picture of conditions during that interminable wait for supplies and the warmth of spring.[2] The captain was able to live pretty comfortably, all things considered, in a snug, two-roomed tent, with sheets on his bed, and with plenty of canned provisions. He played his violin, and with some tame mice, and at a card game called "Boston," for diversion; and gave frequent dinner parties to other officers, cooked by a French private who was a skilled chef. He constantly referred, in his letters, to his commanding officer, Colonel Alexander, as an ass and old woman; and almost as often exhorted his wife to

[2] These letters were published in the New Hampshire Historical Society Collections, Vol. 12, *The Utah Expedition 1857–1858*, edited by Otis G. Hammond (Concord 1928).

keep their young son Charlie's bowels open. He was violently anti-Mormon and deplored the absence of any fighting as an outlet for his feelings. Despite the short rations of old and tough beef, the captain got by nicely on hoarded tinned goods and a large sack of salt (almost nonexistent in the camp) which he had surreptitiously scrounged somewhere along the line. The weather, while cold, was clear and bracing and there was little snow. Gove felt well and healthy the entire winter and even put on weight. He mentioned the presence of several officers' wives and children in the camp, so that the hardships could not have been too great for humans. But the animals suffered and died in droves and all the hauling of firewood from the nearby mountains was done by the enlisted men hitched to the traces of the draft animals. As Gove commented, "What a creature man is! He can exhaust all other living beings."

The resentment of the stalled and discomfited army toward the Mormons mounted during that winter of frustration, and there might have been serious hostilities and large casualties when it finally angrily moved down into the valley of the Great Salt Lake in the late spring of 1858. But bloodshed was averted by an extraordinary man, Thomas L. Kane of Pennsylvania, who, although a Gentile himself, was a true friend to the Mormons, whom he had known back in Nauvoo, Illinois. And Kane's services in finding a peaceful solution to this extremely serious situation should be measured by what a fatal diversion to the Federal government hostilities with the Mormons in the West might have proved in the shortly to follow Civil War.

Kane first went to see President Buchanan in Washington and with the President's official approval then sailed, under an assumed name, via Panama to California, whence he rode, accompanied by only one servant, across the mountains and deserts to Salt Lake City, where he arrived in February, 1858.

There he interviewed Brigham Young and the Mormon elders, calmed that bitterly resentful group, and obtained their permission to put out peace feelers to the newly appointed Governor Cumming, who was literally cooling his heels amidst the wintry blasts in the mountains to the east. The Mormon authorities gave Kane an escorted safe-conduct through their lines and this emissary of peace rode through rain and snow for twenty-six hours straight to arrive at Albert Sidney Johnston's headquarters too exhausted to dismount unassisted; he could barely say he had come from Salt Lake City. He was lifted from his saddle and put to bed in a tent and slept the clock around before he was able to confer with the governor the next day.

The news of Kane's arrival and rumors of his mission of peace quickly spread around the disgusted and frustrated troops, and Captain Gove wrote that Kane was suspected of being a Mormon spy and there was considerable sentiment for lynching him out of hand. Gove in the snug comfort of his specially built tent became very bloodthirsty in his letters, but in practice confined his energies to playing "Boston," petting his tame mice, and transposing march music for his regimental band.

During Kane's short stay with the army, however, he nearly lost his life one night when returning from a visit to the nearby Mormon lines. There was a mix-up in the identification signal which he was supposed to give when approaching the outposts. He fired four shots from his pistol, as agreed upon, but an excited sentinel believed these shots were fired by attacking Mormons and returned the fire at the mounted figure in the darkness, which shots whistled past Kane by inches. Gove morosely wrote his wife that it was a pity the sentinel missed his mark.

Kane, however, showed Governor Cumming his letters from President Buchanan and persuaded him to proceed with him to Salt Lake City with a Mormon escort. Upon arrival there, the

new governor was well received by the Mormon authorities
and was presented to the laity at a mass meeting in the Taber-
nacle, where he made a conciliatory speech in which he promised to use military force only as a last resort. This was well
received by his audience, but unhappily he threw the meeting
open to speeches from the floor and a few extreme hotheads
roused the rank and file to a pitch of excitement by reviewing
the past outrages they had suffered from the Gentiles, such
as the murder of Joseph Smith and his brother back in Nauvoo,
the ingratitude of the government for the services of the Mormon Legion in the Mexican War, and the intense sufferings
during their march across the plains. One speaker accused President Buchanan, as a final insult, of sending a hated Missourian
to govern them. At this Governor Cumming shouted, "I am a
Georgian, sir, a Georgian," but was answered by shouts of
"You're a liar!" and "Send back the soldiers!" Some of the crowd
excitedly sang, to the tune of Stephen Foster's "Camptown
Races," a verse which went:

> Old Sam has sent, I understand
> Du dah, du dah,
> A Missouri ass to rule our land
> Du dah, du dah day.

and, incidentally, this tune became a sort of national anthem
for the anxious Mormons in the tense days following.

But the forceful Brigham Young stayed the tumult and there
were no further symptoms of disorder during Governor Cumming's stay.

In May, Cumming returned to the army's headquarters, accompanied by Kane, and reported to General Johnston (he had
received his promotion to brigadier general during the winter) that the Mormons acknowledged his authority and would

not contest the advance of the troops, repugnant as this would be to them. Reinforcements shortly afterwards arrived, including a fresh supply of horses and mules which the intrepid Marcy had brought from New Mexico, and Johnston's army stirred into preparation for a descent into Mormon land.

A handful of the Mormons had good reason to be worried about the arrival of the troops, for one hundred and twenty Gentile men, women, and children, bound from Arkansas to California, had been cold-bloodedly slaughtered in the famous Mountain Meadows Massacre the previous September at a place about three hundred miles south of Salt Lake City. News of this gradually leaked out but it was generally believed, at first, among the Gentiles that the Indians were responsible for this terrible deed, and not much attention was given to it because the full horrible details were not known and because public interest was focused on the small invading army. But if one hundred and twenty of Johnston's soldiers had been killed in a fair battle, the national repercussions would have been enormous.

These California emigrants, among whom were a few hated Missourians, about one hundred and forty in all, had stumbled inadvertently into the Mormon rebellion when, about the end of July, 1857, they reached Salt Lake City, where they were astonished to hear of the troubles with the Federal government. The resentful Mormons refused to sell them any badly needed supplies and ordered them to move on at once, which they did, perforce, to the south, finally camping at a spring in a narrow valley called Mountain Meadows. There, on the seventh of September, the Indians suddenly attacked them. The emigrants quickly formed their wagons into a circle with wheels chained together, dug entrenchments, and bravely held off the savages for three days, although they suffered seven killed and sixteen wounded.

But, unknown to the emigrants, a force of Mormons was with the Indians, and these approached the defenders on the morning of the fourth day under a flag of truce to announce they would safely conduct them to a nearby settlement. The hard-pressed emigrants received and cheered these white men with the greatest joy and trustfully put their arms and their women and children in the wagons, on the promise of being escorted to safety, and started off at once in a column with these supposed rescuers. They went but a short way when, at a given signal, the Mormons and Indians fell on these defenseless people and massacred them all, men, women, and the older children, with the greatest ferocity and savagery. About seventeen of the children, from two months to seven years of age, were spared, on the belief that they were too young to tell the story, and these were scattered among Mormon families to be brought up in that faith.

It was an unbelievably brutal act with the most revolting details of cruelty and a following cold-blooded plunder of the effects of the pitiful victims. There is no doubt that this bloody and bestial mass murder was the work of a handful of Mormon fanatics who acted on their own initiative and without the knowledge of the higher authorities of the church in Salt Lake City, who, when they eventually learned the true facts, condemned it as wholeheartedly as the Gentiles. It took a few years for the details to be unearthed and many years more before the ringleader of the plot, John D. Lee, was apprehended, convicted, and shot by a firing squad in March, 1877. Lee's excuses for this dastardly act were that the emigrants had seized supplies from the Mormon settlers without payment and had poisoned some of the springs used by the Indians.

But fortunately for the great majority of peaceful, kindly, and law-abiding Mormons and for the later security of the western frontier, the facts of this massacre were not known to General Albert Sidney Johnston's army when it finally moved forward down the westward slopes of the continental divide in June, 1858. If the officers and men had known the truth of this vicious massacre, it is probable that the mass of innocent Mormons would have suffered from a revengeful soldiery whose tempers had not been mollified by the disagreeable winter they had just spent.

The troops entered Salt Lake City with their bands playing "One-eyed Riley," which must have had some significance at the time and place. They city was almost deserted — like one of the dead — for the people, beginning in March, had left it in droves at the order of Brigham Young, going ill-clad and short of food to the vicinity of the town of Provo to the south but leaving their homes filled with combustibles and a handful of men who had orders to fire all the buildings and houses in case of hostilities with the troops. Such was the implicit obedience given by the Mormons to their leader. The army moved through the city in perfect order on a day of intense heat through clouds of dust kicked up in the unpaved streets, with only the tramp and clump of soldiers and horses, the creaking and rumbling of the wagon and caisson wheels, and the shoutings of occasional orders breaking the silence of the grave which hung over this deserted city of fifteen thousand souls. Lieutenant Colonel Philip St. George Cooke, the stout dragoon officer who had commanded the Mormon Battalion in the Mexican War, is said to have ridden silently through the place with uncovered head as a mark of respect toward his old soldiers.

It was a beautiful and well-planned city through which the puzzled army passed that scorching summer's day, with fresh streams of water running down both sides of every street sloping from north to south, and with cottonwoods and other trees shading the streets with their bright green verdure. The streets themselves were a hundred and thirty feet in width and the adjoining sidewalks another twenty feet broad, a great convenience indeed in the present motor age with its attendant parking problems and for which the foresighted Mormon planners are daily blessed by the inhabitants of that lovely city today.

The army marched on to a camp site at Cedar Valley on Utah Lake, about halfway between Salt Lake City and Provo, which was named Camp Floyd in honor of the Secretary of War, John B. Floyd of Virginia, and there a force remained until the year 1860, when the few remaining troops were moved to other posts. The soldiers behaved well during their stay and brought employment and prosperity to the Mormons. Not so with the horde of inevitable camp followers, who were the sweepings of the frontier, and many of the younger Mormons were said to have been corrupted by their influence.

In early July, the Mormons accepted a full pardon from President Buchanan and moved back into their deserted homes and the strange so-called Mormon War was over, which a correspondent of the New York *Herald* summarized — "killed, none; wounded, none; fooled, everybody." Popular sympathy in the country gradually veered to the side of the Mormons and the Buchanan administration was severely criticized for the enormous expense of this seemingly useless military expedition.

The comments of the accompanying newspaper correspondents were generally favorable about the Saints, as the Mormons were often called; the representative of the New York *Herald* reporting in its issue of July 30, 1858, ". . . indeed all the principal Mormons with whom I have met, have treated me with the utmost courtesy, been very social, good natured, full of jest and fun." A similar opinion was always given by any fair-

minded visitor. This reporter went on to describe the rank and
file of the Saints as seen at one of their meetings:

They were a strange, harsh, hardy, severe-looking people. In some
respects they resembled an old Puritanical audience. The men were
tanned, hard, muscular mountaineers; they looked sombre, though as
happy and content as ordinary people. The old women were the only
persons who looked really happy; they smiled benignantly, seemed
to enjoy their religion and to be perfectly satisfied of their own perfect righteousness. The young girls, less than fifteen years old, did
not seem much more morose, or rather unanimated, than retiring
backwoods children usually do. There was a marked want of that
most interesting portion of all audiences — viz., ladies who form society — ladies from fifteen to thirty years of age. The number of
women between those two ages was few indeed, and they were the
saddest part of the audience; during the entire service hardly a smile
flitted across the face of any of them. They seemed sad, troubled,
perplexed, uncertain, unhappy. . . . This is indeed a working people
— men, women, and children work, work always; even the church
dignitaries have rough hands and hardy faces. . . . The people were
dressed very cleanly but in simple stuffs. . . . The women and children whom I have seen, however, as a whole are dressed better —
applying the word neither to style nor material, but to the cleanliness
and entirety of their raiments — than I expected to find them. The
people complain of want of clothing, but I think their dressing will
compare favorably with other people so far removed from a market
and manufactories.

The *Herald* correspondent praised the excellent music and
singing at the services, which with dancing and dramatics have
always been the emotional outlets and the strong points of the
Mormons. By their rules of health they eschew coffee, tea, alcohol, and tobacco; sensible although stringent rules, but making
for the dull life if the gates of music, drama, and dancing did
not afford release from humdrum everyday reality, and in these
things they have always excelled.

Governor Cumming left Utah in May, 1861, after the outbreak of the Civil War, and he may have regretted his excellent
accomplishments which kept peace on the western frontier when
his home state, Georgia, seceded from the Union. He departed
with the sincere regrets of a people whose hearts he had won by
kindness. The only hint of a sour note during his whole tenure
was an entry in Brigham Young's journal for May 22, 1858,
less than a month before the Federal troops entered Salt Lake
City, in which he accused the governor of making passes at
some of the Mormon girls. Probably a *non sequitur*, but Captain
Gove previously had written his wife that Mrs. Cumming was
from Boston and wore glasses.

CHAPTER XVII

Mountains and Wolves

THE Topographical Engineers may have had a near monopoly of the specialized surveying expeditions in the West, but officers of other branches certainly shared in the pioneer explorations of the 1850's. One of the most outstanding of these was an infantryman, Captain Randolph Barnes Marcy, whom Albert Sidney Johnston sent to bring help for his stalled army around Fort Bridger. A native of Hampshire County in north central Massachusetts, Marcy had graduated from West Point in 1832, had then been assigned to the infantry, and had spent most of the next thirteen years on the frontier in Michigan and Wisconsin. He saw action during the Mexican War at the early battles of Palo Alto and Resaca de la Palma on the Rio Grande. After that, he served on the southwestern frontier for some twelve years. During this time, he pioneered a trail from Fort Smith, Arkansas, to Santa Fe in 1849, when he escorted a party of California-bound emigrants between those two places. In 1852 he led an expedition which explored the headwaters of the Red and Canadian Rivers, and on this trip he was accompanied by Captain George B. McClellan of the Topographical Engineers, who afterwards married his daughter Mary Ellen. When McClellan became the commanding general of the Army of the Potomac, during the Civil War, Marcy served as chief of staff for his son-in-law. In 1854 he surveyed large tracts of land in northern and western Texas which were intended for Indian reservations but which were never successfully used for this purpose because of the hostility of the neighboring whites, who raided and destroyed the Indian settlements. At the beginning of 1857, Marcy was in Florida in one of the endless campaigns against the ever-rebellious Seminoles, or rather against the remnants of that tribe which still remained there after the great majority had been forcibly moved west of the Mississippi River, and he returned from there to join the expedition against the Mormons.

Marcy was a born frontiersman and an authority on Western life. Tall, broad-shouldered, soldierly in his bearing, he was essentially an out-of-doors man and a skilled big-game hunter. With all these virile qualities he combined a certain literary talent and wrote four books on his experiences, one of which, *The Prairie Traveler*, became the standard guide and reference book for emigrants to the Pacific Coast. This was later published in London in 1863 and edited by Richard F. Burton, the famous world traveler and translator of the *Arabian Nights*. Burton was an authority on the Moslem world and had even penetrated to the holy city of Mecca disguised as a pilgrim from Afghanistan. He once made a trip to Utah and later wrote a book on the Mormons in which he commented most favorably on that persecuted sect.[1] His editing was a bit on the patronizing side, for he probably considered Marcy's scope fairly limited, and he kept adding footnotes to the text which enlarged on and occasionally contradicted the author's advice. Two of Marcy's books, *Thirty Years of Army Life on the Border* (1866) and *Border Reminiscences* (1872), were largely a collection of rather amusing anecdotes and experiences.

Marcy, with a detachment of forty picked enlisted men, and

[1] *The City of the Saints, and across the Rocky Mountains to California* (London 1861).

twenty-five mountain men, with some packers and guides, following Johnston's orders, set out to cut south by east from Fort Bridger through the mountains to Fort Massachusetts. This meant their course was through an uninhabited and almost trackless wilderness, over towering and rugged peaks, through snows as deep as five feet, without any pathway or human dwelling to mark their way. The party left on November 24, 1857, with thirty days' rations packed upon sixty-six mules.

Like many other heartbreaking trips through the Rocky Mountains, the going was deceptively easy at first. They crossed the Green River and found a native Indian whom they hired as a guide through this completely unknown country. He led them, for a day, up a circuitous canyon to its head on the top of a mountain where the powdered snow was already two feet deep, but, after demanding his pay in advance, he eluded the sentinels that night and disappeared. The guideless party floundered on across a high tableland which ended in a perpendicular cliff some two thousand feet above the upper Colorado River (then called the Grand). As Marcy wrote: [2]

On reaching this lofty escarpment, it did not seem possible that our mules could descend it, and, indeed, I had previously been told that there was but one place for fifty miles along this cliff where the declivity was practicable for animals, and this was at a point where the Indians had cut out a narrow path along the face of the bluff, winding around over rocks and along the face of the brinks of deep chasms.

They bivouacked in the snow on the verge of this precipice with their only consolation a magnificent view to the east of the valley of the Colorado River and the towering Rockies beyond. It looked like a dead end, but fortunately one of the mountain

[2] Marcy described this terrible trip in *Thirty Years of Army Life on the Border* (New York 1866), pp. 224–250.

men discovered the downward path that night and the next morning they commenced the exceedingly steep and slippery descent. "Our pack mules had great difficulty in keeping their footing. Occasionally one of them would fall, and, with his pack, roll over and over for thirty or forty feet down the rocks, until he was brought up by a tree or projecting crag." At last, however, they reached the valley at the bottom, which to their surprise was free from snow and green with grass, and even picked up a stray, fat horse there which they afterwards used for food.

On December 8, they crossed the Colorado River, deep, rapid, and filled with floating ice, near the present town of Grand Junction in western Colorado, and rode on to the southeast to the western base of the snow-covered Rockies which rose sheer before them. Thus far the march had been pleasant enough and the animals were in fair condition from the abundance of grass and water. Here they fell in with a large band of Ute Indians, "a ragged, villainous-looking set, and we had our hands full in keeping the women from stealing everything that came in their way."

Marcy tried to persuade the chief to guide them to the summit of the impending mountains, but he refused and all the Indians pointed to the peaks and shivered as if with cold. The interpreter, as a last resort, called the chief an old woman and advised "him to go back to his lodge, cover up warm, and assist his squaw in tending the babies," but these taunts had no effect on the wise old brave, who stated that there was five feet of snow on the heights and he wanted none of it.

So the next morning the captain led his men to the long, grueling ascent of the western slope of the main chain of the Rockies. They went but a few miles before the snow became a serious impediment. On the next day it became deeper with a surface crust which seriously cut the animals' legs, and finally so deep that it was necessary to change the order of march. Up to that time the animals had broken the trail for the main party on foot, but this was reversed and now the men were placed in the van to break a track for the heavily laden pack mules. The only forage found for these suffering beasts was bitter pine needles, and they soon became weak and exhausted and began to die. Every bit of baggage and gear was thrown away except for one blanket per man and the arms and ammunition. The snow increased daily in depth as they slowly ascended and was so light and dry that the men sank into it up to their waists and could not move. They proceeded only by having the three or four leading men, one behind another, crawl painfully ahead on their hands and knees. The leading man was good for only about fifty yards of this torturing progress before he had to be relieved by another. They consumed all their provisions long before they reached the summit of the mountains and were then entirely dependent upon eating their famished animals. After consuming two of the horses, which were comparatively flavorous, they ate tough and stringy mule flesh, which they sprinkled with gunpowder in place of salt, and this lean meat only whetted their raging appetites.

Marcy, on New Year's Day, 1858, wrote in his journal:

This morning dawned upon us with gloomy auspices, far from promising to us a happy New Year. We have been engaged since daylight this morning in wallowing along through snow at least five feet deep, and have only succeeded, by the severest toil, in making about two miles during the entire day. From our bivouac tonight we can see the fires of last night, and in the darkness they do not appear over a rifle-shot distant. The leading men have been obliged to crawl upon their hands and knees to prevent sinking to their necks, and could only go a few yards at a time before they were compelled, in a state of complete exhaustion, to throw themselves down and let others take their places.

Gallant fellows! Many of them are almost barefooted, and several whose feet have been frozen have suffered intensely from pain and cold. Yet every soldier, without a single exception, has performed everything I required of him cheerfully and manfully; they have never faltered, or uttered a murmur of complaint. I feel for them from the bottom of my heart, and I should be recreant to my duty as their commander if I neglected to give expression to my profound gratitude for the almost superhuman efforts put forth by them to extricate the party from our perilous position.

To make matters worse, the mountain man trying to act as guide in these howling, snow-swept fastnesses missed the way to Cochetopa Pass, the only possible place for miles to cross the continental divide in winter. It was only fifty miles south of this famous pass that John C. Frémont attempted to cross, at about the same time of year, on his disastrous expedition in 1849, and was forced to turn back with the loss of all his animals and several of his men. Marcy's party wasted most of a day's travel in the wrong direction, but, fortunately, one of the Mexican muleteers, named Miguel Alona, had previously crossed through this pass and went to Marcy that night to protest against their route. The captain was dubious about his objections, but after the guide admitted his confusion and Miguel insisted on his knowledge, the latter was appointed to lead the party with the promise of a handsome present if he was right and of being hung to a tree if wrong.

The uncertainty of their position and the sure knowledge of their perishing in the illimitable expanse of trackless snow if they missed the pass prevented Marcy from sleeping for several nights as they wearily bucked through the enormous snowdrifts under Miguel's guidance. Even worse than the lack of salt was the want of the men for tobacco, which had all been smoked up days before. With only one blanket apiece, the men kept warm at night by digging large holes down through the snow to the ground, where a bed was made of soft pine twigs covered with a blanket. A windbreak of sticks covered the top, and with good fires at the bottom of these pits several men, by huddling together, managed to keep tolerably warm. It was on the daytime march that the men froze their feet.

It took them ten days to reach the summit of the questionable pass, with all suffering from frostbite and violent cramps caused by the mule meat. From the summit, they gazed down upon a vast plain to the east, stretching far away toward the south, and the Mexican guide informed Marcy that this was the valley of the upper Rio Grande (or Rio del Norte as it was then called), and pointed out a mountain on the opposite side of the valley which he said was near Fort Massachusetts. Three good mules still survived, and Captain Marcy mounted Miguel and another experienced Mexican and sent them forward to the fort to bring back supplies and help for the now starving and desperate expedition.

The main party slowly followed in the Mexicans' tracks, hoping for their return with supplies in about a week, but the men stumbled on through the snow for eleven days until it seemed sure that the messengers had become lost or had perished. They reached a little patch of dry grass appearing above the snow and stopped there to allow the few remaining and greatly famished mules to graze. They had not seen a human being since leaving the Grand (Colorado) River thirty-one days before and there seemed no hope to the delirious men. Into the quiet of despair at sunset, a soldier suddenly cried out, "There comes two men on horseback"; and the long-absent Mexicans galloped into camp upon fresh horses, "firing their revolvers, and making other demonstrations of joy." Marcy wrote: "Some of the men laughed, danced, and screamed with delight, while others (and I must confess I was not one among the former) cried like children." He had not slept half an hour at a time for twenty days and had lost nearly forty pounds, and as he put it, ". . . my nervous system was not at that juncture under very good control."

Right behind the returning Mexicans came three wagons loaded with supplies, including tobacco and a jug of brandy. Marcy wrote:

As I thought this a proper occasion to indulge my men in the good cheer that they had been so long deprived of, I issued to each of them a moderate drink of liquor, but, much to my astonishment, in a short time many of them were very much under the influence of it, and some even crazy drunk. It had acted upon their empty stomachs much more potently than I had anticipated, but I felt no inclination to censure them for this; on the contrary, I entertained a feeling somewhat similar to that of General Jackson when a charge of drunkenness was made to him against an officer who had rendered conspicuous services in the War of 1812, and he replied that Colonel C's gallant conduct in battle authorized him to continue drunk during the remainder of his life, if he thought proper. I conceived that my men had a perfect right to get drunk after what they had endured.

After a well-earned but brief rest at Fort Massachusetts, Marcy's column marched on to Taos, New Mexico, where he paid off the civilians, including the Mexican guides, who received a bonus of about five hundred dollars apiece; one of them promptly lost it all that night in a game of monte. Marcy gathered the needed animals and supplies and joined Colonel Johnston's waiting army at Fort Bridger in the following late spring. On the way back, this detachment camped on what later became the site of Denver and one of the teamsters discovered some gold nuggets in the bed of the local creek. Little attention was paid to this at the time in Marcy's party, but word of this find worked eastward and triggered the great Colorado gold rush of 1859 with its slogan of "Pike's Peak or Bust."

In contrast to this harrowing experience, Marcy once had a light adventure on the Great Plains which documents him (albeit innocently) as the first recipient on record of the term "wolf" as applied by a cautious maiden to a predatory male. He described this adventure in his book *Thirty Years of Army Life on the Border* [3] under the heading of "Prairie Belle."

The captain was returning, in 1854, from an exploration trip to the sources of the Brazos River in Texas when he met, near a most remote frontier cabin, an attractive young maiden picking wild grapes by the roadside. He offered her a ride in his wagon and his traveling companion, "a New York gentleman, very politely extended his hand to assist her; but, instead of accepting it, she made a sudden leap from the ground over the side of the vehicle, and landed directly by his side." This extraordinary acrobatic feat and the freedom and originality of her conversation greatly refreshed the jaded spirits of the weary explorers. The prairie belle was about eighteen and an unusually pretty specimen — "tall, erect, and lithe, but well rounded, and exceedingly graceful and feminine in outline . . ."

The New Yorker told her about some most remarkable incidents of their expedition which seemed to interest this nymph of the wide open spaces, but occasionally they taxed her credulity so that she would ejaculate, "*Oh, git out!*" or "*You go-long now*," and at the climax of the account of an exciting adventure with the savage Comanches she gave vent to her feelings by giving the narrator a violent slap on the knee and exclaiming, "*The he-e-e-ll you say, stranger!*"

She asked about their camping equipment and was most

[3] Pp. 371–373.

curious about their tent, as she had never seen one. Marcy extended her an invitation to call after they had made camp that evening to see how comfortable they could make themselves but her reaction was startlingly drastic. As he reported it:

At this she turned around, facing me, applied her thumb to her nose with her fingers extended, closed one eye, and, with her countenance assuming a most ludicrously severe expression, observed, *"I'm afraid of wolves, ole hoss."*

The nonplused captain concluded:

What significance her remark was intended to convey I have never yet learned; I certainly never for a moment imagined that any resemblance could be detected between the carnivorous quadruped so pointedly alluded to and ourselves, even had we been attired in "sheep's clothing." From the savage expression her countenance assumed, however, I did not feel inclined to press her for an explanation and changed the subject as soon as possible.

The prairie belle was almost a century ahead of her times and full credit should go to this unknown, pioneer maiden in the American vernacular.

CHAPTER XVIII

Ships of the Desert—
Afloat and Ashore

JEFFERSON Davis of Mississippi, afterwards the president of the Confederate States of America, was a very able Secretary of War in the cabinet of his close personal friend, President Franklin Pierce of New Hampshire, during the years 1853–1857; in fact, such was his influence and initiative that rumor had it he was the mainspring of the Pierce administration and the more extreme of the antislavery elements bemoaned the skill with which this ardent supporter of the "peculiar institution" of slavery seemed to steer government enterprises into channels favorable to the South. Davis was a West Point graduate who had married the daughter of "Old Rough-and-Ready" Zachary Taylor, but his wife's death, in 1835, shortly after the marriage, ended this connection, of which old Zach had not particularly approved.

Davis resigned from the army soon thereafter to become a Mississippi planter and to enter politics. But fate brought him back into the service again during the Mexican War as colonel of the crack regiment of Mississippi Rifles, an able and colorful volunteer collection of the planter young bloods of the state, uniformed in white duck trousers, firemens' red shirts, and crowned with wide-brimmed Panama hats of the finest weave. Most of the men and officers brought along their slave body servants, who performed the usual chores and housekeeping drudgeries of a regiment in the field; so that these young gentlemen of Mississippi could give their full time to acquiring military proficiency (most of them were expert shots to begin with) and to pleasant social occasions.

At the critical battle of Buena Vista, when General Santa Anna, leading a Mexican army about twenty thousand strong, attacked Zachary Taylor with a force of not over five thousand Americans in February, 1847, Jefferson Davis saved the day for his onetime father-in-law and the desperately hard-pressed Americans by quick thinking and the smart handling of his men, whom he formed into a V-shaped cul-de-sac to receive the charge of a body of Mexican lancers into its narrowing apex. These lancers had just swept all before them and actually had chased a panic-stricken regiment of Indiana volunteers off the field. The Mississippians coolly awaited the impact of these fearfully effective horsemen until the range was almost point-blank, when, at the command from Davis, they literally blasted the lancers out of their saddles with their converging fire from both sides of the acute angle and completely broke up the Mexican offensive. Davis was hailed as "the hero of Buena Vista" and soared to greater political successes on his fame. Some unkind critics, however, believe that although he may have saved the day at Buena Vista, he also lost the War between the States on the same field, for this local tactical success seems to have imbued him with an exaggerated belief in his own military ability in the larger strategic fields of the later war and to have caused him often to meddle with and overrule his field commanders, with disastrous results.

But as an administrative Secretary of War in peacetime he was outstanding. He was a sensitive and romantically imaginative man who was devoted to the ideal of expansion for the United States — to their "Manifest Destiny" — especially for the South and its institution of slavery. As a West Pointer and soldier of experience he knew all the answers usually obscured from the civilian holders of that office, and he made good use of the available brains and abilities of his trained officers, which had so often been allowed to stagnate in obscure frontier posts or in fusty, red-tape-bound offices in Washington. It was he who intelligently planned and directed the surveys for railroad routes to the Pacific about which we have read; and it was largely because of his initiative that two desperately needed new mounted regiments were formed in 1855 to reinforce the only three existing horse regiments (known as dragoons and mounted riflemen) which were almost futilely trying to cope with an overwhelming horde of mounted hostile Indians along the frontier. These two new regiments for the first time bore the official title of "cavalry," although later the dragoons and mounted riflemen were to be stripped of their colorful names and distinctive insignia and reluctantly made to adopt this same title and its markings. Davis's Northern enemies accused him of packing these new cavalry regiments with Southern officers and even nicknamed one, the 2nd Cavalry, of which Albert Sidney Johnston was the colonel and Robert E. Lee the lieutenant colonel, "Jeff Davis's Own." But like his political opponents' accusation that he showed bias in favor of the southernmost railway survey, the charge was probably undeserved. There were just simply more capable mounted officers from the South and this ratio was unavoidable in their assignments.

One of Jeff Davis's pet projects became a legend in the Southwest which has grown in romance with the telling through the years. This was the great experiment with camels in the arid and desert regions along the Mexican border. The experiment failed, not because the imported camels could not successfully adapt themselves to the conditions of Texas and points west — quite the contrary, they were enthusiastically praised by all those who gave them a fair trial — but because the Civil War disrupted our whole military organization in those regions and the camels, who had not really as yet had a chance to establish themselves thoroughly, were perforce abandoned or surrendered to the Confederates along with many military posts and much equipment. And the Confederates had neither the time nor the resources to pursue anything unproved or theoretical. So the camel experiment, after a promising start, died on the vine and the loss was a potential camel corps to the United States Army and possibly, years later, to Hollywood. Also the present young fry, who blossom forth in cowboy outfits and six-shooters, have been deprived of the colorful alternatives of the burnooses and robes of Arabian sheiks and camel riders.

The idea of importing camels into the United States possibly went as far back as 1701, when an effort to introduce camels into Virginia was reported. But the serious advocacy of such an experiment began in the 1840's when various people became interested and the idea gradually gained momentum. Among the early proponents of this experiment was a George R. Gliddon, an archaeologist who had lived for twenty-eight years in the Levant and who had been the United States consul at Cairo for eight years of that time; another was our old friend John Russell Bartlett, the Providence ethnologist, who gave the last nine pages of his voluminous book *Personal Narrative of Explorations and Incidents, etc.* to a plea that camels be imported and tried in the arid country of the Southwest, in which he had traveled so widely as boundary commissioner for nearly three years. Still another pleader for the camels was Major Henry

Constantine Wayne, a native of Georgia, and a graduate of West Point (1838), who was an artillery officer who had won promotion for gallantry during the Mexican War; and this officer was placed in charge of the whole experiment when Congress, influenced by Jefferson Davis's favorable recommendation, finally appropriated thirty thousand dollars in March, 1855, for "the purchase and importation of camels and dromedaries to be used for military purposes."

Wayne, Gwinn Harris Heap of Pennsylvania, and two officers of the United States Navy, David Dixon Porter and Edward Fitzgerald Beale (after he had resigned his naval commission), were the four leading lights in this interesting experiment, which with favorable circumstances might have revolutionized transportation and Indian fighting tactics on our southwestern frontier. It seems fitting to introduce this topic as an important example of the frontier activities of other officers of the services besides the Topographical Engineers during the 1850's; and it certainly was a reconnaissance with a new form of transportation in the arid and wild lands along the Mexican border.

Now, Major Wayne's knowledge of camels was quite naturally all hearsay, bookish, and theoretical, but he tackled the job with enthusiasm and energy, for here was an obvious chance to write his name in history. He was fortunate in obtaining two most efficient co-workers for the purchasing and importing stage of this interesting experiment and the difficult and puzzling matter of buying, transporting, and landing the camels in Texas was well handled throughout.

One of these two men was Lieutenant David Dixon Porter of the United States Navy, who later rose to great fame as a Union naval officer in the Civil War and afterwards the ranking admiral. His background was individualistic and interesting and showed a marked contrast with the staid conformity of today's officers.

His father, David Porter, was also a well-known naval officer who had fought in the undeclared naval war with France, had been captured on the ill-fated *Philadelphia* in Tripoli, and had distinguished himself in the War of 1812. An impetuous man, he had resigned from the service in 1826 after being suspended from duty for six months for violating Spanish sovereignty in Porto Rico while chasing some pirates right up onto dry land. After that he commanded the Mexican Navy for three years, and fought several bloody encounters with Spanish ships. He finally became the United States consul general in Algiers and then was promoted to be minister to Turkey, where he remained for twelve years until his death in 1843. Incidentally, an adopted son, David Glasgow Farragut, soared to probably greater heights in the navy than did his own son, David Dixon. The latter had begun his career as a midshipman in the Mexican Navy under his father's command and in a desperate fight with the Spaniards had been captured and imprisoned. When finally released, he had entered the United States Navy and had risen to the rank of lieutenant when the problem of transporting camels was dumped in his lap as commander of the United States storeship *Supply*. Fiery and impetuous as his father, he, nevertheless, showed a capacity for infinite detail and care in this assignment.

The other man making up the official trio of camel buyers and importers was Gwinn Harris Heap, a first cousin of young Porter who came from the same town, Chester, Pennsylvania. He had accompanied Edward Fitzgerald Beale, on an exploring trip, in the early summer of 1853, through the Rockies along the 38th parallel, and their pioneer path was shortly afterwards followed by the ill-fated Captain Gunnison and later, in the autumn, by John C. Frémont and his artist-photographer Solomon Carvalho.

Before following the fortunes of these three entrepreneurs

into camel land, it seems fitting to quote the opinion of an experienced British officer of the present day about these uncanny
beasts. Lieutenant Colonel W. F. Stirling in his recent book
Safety Last (London 1953), a fascinating account of his career,
largely spent in Moslem countries, writes:

Living so much with camels I became fairly knowledgeable in their
little ways and used to be employed by the Sudan Government to
purchase camels for them. . . . They certainly are most extraordinary animals and must have been left over from some antediluvian
creation. Their whole structure differs vastly from that of any other
animal: their joints work in a different way; their members are put
on back to front; the male comes in season and not the female; their
stomachs are built up in sections and they can blow several of them
out of their mouths; when travelling, and trained to it, they can go
five days without water, though normally they drink on every third
day; when grazing out in the desert and not working, they do, in
fact, go weeks without water if there is dew about. They are the
most supercilious of all animals, regarding the human being as a mere
excrescence hardly worth noticing.

And to avoid confusion in camel terminology, we should say
here that Major Wayne differed with some scientists in the naming of the different species of the breed. He placed camels into
two classes: (1) the Bactrian, with two humps, found in Tar-
tary and northern central Asia, which was primarily a heavy-set
and slow beast of burden, sometimes used in harness; and (2) the
Arabian, with one hump, found in North Africa, Asia Minor,
Arabia, India. The word "dromedary," while applying only to
one-humped camels, he used solely for the swift courser or racer
of the latter breed. The term "camel" he applied to both breeds
generally.

To begin their quest for these supercilious animals, Porter and
Wayne, the navy and the army, split their ways at first; the latter
going to London and Paris, in June, 1855, to consult various

zoölogical and military authorities about these strange beasts and then joining Porter in Italy, where the naval officer had brought the *Supply* direct from the United States.[1] From there they sailed to Tunis, where they met Gwinn Heap, who was much at home in this North African city because of his father's service there for thirty years as consul. Young Heap knew camels and their habits and Arabs and their language; so that he was of the greatest help to the expedition. He was also a pretty capable artist (as he had shown on his trip to California with Edward Fitzgerald Beale in 1853), and his fifteen camel sketches for the official report are interesting if not too artistic. Years later he returned as United States consul to Tunis, where he served from 1867 to 1878, when he became consul general at Constantinople, where he died in 1887.

Porter anchored the *Supply* off Goletta (La Goulette), then a port of Tunis, which was a small town built on the ruins of a part of the great and ancient city of Carthage, lying at the entrance to the evil-smelling (as any G. I. who was there in World War II can fervently testify) Lac de Tunis, and but a short distance from the city of Tunis itself. The intermittent connections of Americans with that place are rather interesting; beginning with William Eaton, the fabulous captor of the city of Derna during our war with Tripoli, who served as United States consul in Tunis from 1798 to 1804, to comparatively recently when a horde of Americans passed through there in World War II.

Before meeting the experienced Heap, Wayne and Porter had incautiously bought a camel in Tunis which was of dubious quality. When the Bey of Tunis learned what the Americans

[1] The complete *Report of the Secretary of War* [Jefferson Davis] *about the Purchase of Camels for the Purposes of Military Transportation, 1855–'56– '57*, is in Sen. Exec. Doc. No. 62. 34 Cong. 3rd Sess. This contains all the correspondence from Porter and Wayne about their mission.

were after, he presented them with two fine camels, both stallions, one full-grown and the other young. The bought camel and one of the stallions later developed the "itch," a common camel disease which gave the Americans much concern, and these two were quietly sold afterwards to a butcher in Constantinople for, as Lieutenant Porter reported it, "purposes known only to himself." Camel meat was generally considered as flavorsome as beef in the Near East. As can be guessed, this disposal of his gift was not reported to "His Highness the Bey."

After that, the *Supply* cruised about the eastern Mediterranean, making stops at Malta, Smyrna, and Salonica, where inquiries were made and negotiations attempted for the purchase of camels but none were bought because British agents had swept the markets and boosted prices sky-high by hiring eight thousand camels for use in the Crimean War, which they were then fighting, with their allies the French and the Turks, against the Russians.

Jefferson Davis had previously suggested that some member of the purchasing commission should go to Persia, where the finest breed of camels was reputed to be, but this was found impracticable because the approaching winter (it was then October, 1855) would make the trip too hazardous and long for a return to the United States in the following spring.

Instead, Porter sailed the *Supply* through the Hellespont into the Black Sea and on to the Crimea, where the Americans visited the allied French and British forces who had shortly before occupied the fortress of Sevastopol in the dreadfully mismanaged Crimean War; which murky conflict was distinguished by the name of Florence Nightingale and by the first use of the telegraph by an army under battle conditions. The British War Office, however, seemed to send more telegraph messages inquiring about the health of a certain Captain Jarvis, bitten by a centipede, and about whether beards were an aid to desertion, than it did about the state of the war.

Into this somewhat depressing atmosphere came the American camel buyers. They managed, however, to obtain interviews with some experienced officers, notably a Colonel McMurdo in charge of British land transport, who spoke very favorably of the use of camels by General Napier in the Sinde expedition in India, where the British employed twenty-five thousand camels, including a camel corps of a thousand men mounted on five-hundred dromedaries, with two soldiers sitting back to back on each dromedary's saddle. At a signal, these highly trained animals would quickly form a square and kneel so that their riders could fight from behind animal bulwarks, a system which might prove highly effective against the mounted Indians of our frontier. Colonel McMurdo said these dromedaries could also cover seventy miles in twelve hours for days on end. It all sounded extremely encouraging and the Americans became really enthusiastic about their mission.

For the first time they saw the two-humped Bactrian camel but found that the Arabian one-humper alone seemed to be used by the military, who esteemed them highly. Wayne reported to Jefferson Davis that the two breeds differed about as "the buffalo of our western prairies does from the common ox," but did not identify the comparison in terms of camels.

They then returned to Constantinople, which exotic city was a reminder of the past for Porter and an omen of the future for Heap. Certainly Constantinople was charged on both their scrolls of fate. The Sultan of Turkey now came forward and offered to present the United States government with some very fine camels indeed, but as these would have to be fetched from far distant in the interior, the offer was regretfully refused for lack of time. A helpful hand was given to the camel quest by several American missionaries (probably Congregationalists) in the Near East who cheerfully answered a letter of inquiry about camel conditions which was sent out by "Brother H. G. O. Dwight" from their headquarters in Constantinople. Useful replies came in from such faraway and romantic stations as Marsovan, Trebizond, and Mosul, and the missionary in the last place, W. F. Williams, excused a rather hasty answer by saying ". . . and I in the midst of lettering eight grave stones, and the stonecutters pressing me for 'copy.' "

They sailed from Constantinople in late November for Alexandria, Egypt, where they expected to buy a quantity of good camels at reasonable prices but, alas, nothing but trouble awaited them there, for the Egyptian government had slapped an embargo on the exportation of these animals without a special permit, which meant untold delays and liberal bribes to certain officials if anything was to be accomplished. After all kinds of machinations, wire-pullings, and presents to the right people, the *Supply* finally sailed with nine Egyptian camels aboard, including six good dromedaries presented by the viceroy after various skulduggeries and attempted substitutions of inferior animals by some of his minor officials. Next they put into Smyrna, in January, 1856, where Heap, the real camel expert, had gone earlier in the month, and where he had, at last, successfully bought enough good camels to fill all the remaining carefully prepared stalls on the ship.

The Americans engaged three Arabs and two Turks as "camel conductors" to accompany the animals for a year and these, with four Americans, all under the direction of the experienced "wagon and forage master" Albert Ray, a man "well known to the army during and subsequent to the war with Mexico," were supposed to tend the animals on shipboard. But the Arabs were found useless at sea and the chores of camel husbandry fell almost entirely on the American hostlers, greatly aided at all times by Porter's versatile sailors.

That young naval lieutenant deserved great credit for his care and feeding of these totally strange and peculiar animals. He had the specially constructed camel stalls on shipboard continually rubbed, scrubbed, and whitewashed until they were always immaculate; and he had the camels curried, groomed, and washed every day, until they glistened, all of which unusual treatment greatly raised the camels' standards of living and boosted their morale on the high seas. Porter wrote to Jefferson Davis that he believed most camel ailments, especially the dreaded itch, were caused by "a total absence of cleanliness. Nothing can exceed the filth of a Turkish or Egyptian 'khan' [or stable] where camels are stowed away, closely packed for the night; the filth of ages seems to have accumulated there, and the smell of ammonia is so strong that it is painful to the olfactories." He also showed his ingenuity in designing a specially built "camel car" to load these denizens of the desert, who were terrified at the sight of water, on shipboard. The floors and walls of the stalls were padded with straw and bags stuffed with straw and these, with a specially designed harness which ingeniously held the camels in kneeling position, prevented any bodily injuries in the storms and gales of an Atlantic crossing. And surely Porter's skillful breeding of these animals at the requisite time on shipboard should be mentioned, for he is certainly the only officer in the entire history of the United States Navy to have ever run a floating camel stud farm.

The *Supply* left Smyrna on February 15, 1856, with a final complement of thirty-three camels, including two Bactrian males (two humps), and a hybrid cross of a Bactrian male and Arabian female which was called by the Arabs a Booghdee, but was known among the Americans as the "mule," and which was so enormous, being seven feet five inches in height and weighing a ton, that a hole had to be cut in the deck to accommodate its hump. Among the number were four fine Pehlevans which were trained for wrestling, which Porter reported to Jefferson Davis was a popular amusement among the Turks, and might even become so in America, and he cited the case of a wealthy man in Smyrna who kept twenty Pehlevans "for the amusement of his wife who had a fondness for the sport."

The voyage home took three months and was an extremely rough one; so much so that Porter was prevented from stopping at the Canary Islands, as he had planned, to investigate the camels there, which breed the Spaniards had imported from Africa about four hundred years earlier. But thanks to his careful precautions, only one grown camel died, and that in calving. Six calves were born at sea, Lieutenant Porter acting as midwife, of which four died, making a net gain of one camel upon the high seas. One of these newborn calves showed marked ability as a wrestler under the tutelage of a Turk handler, and:

when six weeks old he was more than a match for his teacher, using his legs, neck, and mouth with such dexterity, and exhibiting such wonderful strength in so young a thing, that he became a very rough playmate, and frequently hurt the men on the deck by throwing himself on them suddenly and knocking them down.

It would probably be a safe bet to say that Porter's sailors had had their fill of camel nursing by the time the low-lying shores of Texas were sighted.

The *Supply* arrived off Indianola, Texas (a port since destroyed by hurricanes and tidal waves), which was about one hundred and twenty miles south of Galveston, about the middle of May, 1856. But it was not possible to unload the camels because of the ground swell in the Gulf of Mexico, so the ship transferred the animals to a steamer near the mouth of the Mississippi River and this craft successfully landed them at Indianola. Upon feeling dry and steady land under their feet again the camels became excited "to an almost uncontrollable degree, rearing, kicking, crying out, breaking halters, tearing up pickets and by other fantastic tricks demonstrating their enjoyment. . . ." Probably rarely, if ever, has such an emotional demonstration been made by any other living creatures upon first setting foot on the soil of Texas, but it evidently felt like home and mother to these "ships of the desert."

Porter and Heap returned almost at once to Asia Minor for another shipload of the animals and were back at Indianola the following February (1857) with forty-one more to add to the herd. And, by the way, of the twenty thousand dollars given to Wayne for the purchase of the first lot of camels, twelve thousand was returned as unexpended after paying all expenses of the trip, which was a precedent obviously soon ignored and forgotten by later government purchasing missions.

Major Wayne remained in full charge of the first camel herd and, after allowing them about a month to regain their land legs, started them off in easy stages through the dust and heat for San Antonio, which he reached in two weeks and where he encamped at the headwaters of the San Pedro River. He found, however, "this proximity to town was not beneficial to my men or animals" and moved his animals out to Medina, about twelve miles from San Antonio, to the ranch of a Major Howard; and finally to Camp Verde, near Bandera, some sixty miles northwest of the town, where a permanent camel camp was established in August, 1856.

When the camels were passing through the pretty town of Victoria on their way from Indianola to San Antonio, a Mrs. Mary A. Shirkey, but lately arrived from Virginia, managed to collect enough hair from the passing animals to spin into yarn

which she then knitted into a pair of socks and mailed to Major
Wayne with a letter requesting that these be forwarded to
President Franklin Pierce with her compliments. Wayne duti-
fully sent them on through channels to Jefferson Davis and it
can be assumed that these socks eventually graced the feet of the
"Young Hickory from the Granite Hills" of New Hampshire.

After the arrival at Camp Verde, Major Wayne worked with
his usual energy to put the herd and its new quarters into working shape. The reaction of the Texans to these exotic animal new-
comers was a mixed one of curiosity and resentment, the latter
because all horses and mules were terrified by the sight and smell
of the camels and there were many runaways and wild buckings
along the country roads and in the streets of the towns when
these queer antediluvian beasts, with their peculiar lurching gaits,
and supercilious and ruminating airs, hove into sight or to wind-
ward. Also, the Americans just did not seem to catch the knack
of packing loads on the protruding humped backs of these experimental beasts and it took much trial and error before this
could be done fairly well — although some of the handlers never
seemed to master the art. On the other hand, the camels made a
markedly favorable impression in some ways upon the populace,
as instanced by an occasion in Indianola soon after their landing.
As Wayne reported this to the Secretary of War Davis:

Needing hay at the camel yard, I directed one of the men to take
a camel to the quartermaster's forage-house, and bring up four bales.
Desirous of seeing what effect it would produce upon the public
mind, I mingled in the crowd that gathered around the camel as it
came in town. When made to kneel down to receive its load, and
two bales, weighing in all 613 pounds, were packed on, I heard
doubts expressed around me as to the animal's ability to rise under
them; when two more bales were put on, making the gross weight
of the load 1,256 pounds, incredulity as to his ability to rise, much
less to carry it, found vent in positive assertion, and as I had then

become recognized, I observed that I was regarded by some compassionate individuals as about to make a splendid failure; to convey to you the surprise and sudden change of sentiment when the camel, at the signal, rose and walked off with his four bales of hay, would be impossible. It is sufficient to say that I was completely satisfied. The circumstance was chronicled in verse by one of the poets of Texas, and published in the Indianola Bulletin or Victoria Advocate, I forget which, and in it was amusingly described the incredulity and surprise, almost dismay, I have endeavored to portray.

Unfortunately for posterity, Wayne did not include a copy of these verses in this letter to Jefferson Davis and they have probably been lost forever.

The camels also proved highly satisfactory in other local tests, such as their ability to make the round trip from Camp Verde to San Antonio in faster time and carrying heavier loads than wagons drawn by horses, and during rainy weather they could navigate with comparative ease through the sticky Texas gumbo, which was impassible for vehicles. Wayne was proud of his charges and expected great things of them when they should be tested in the arid desert country to the west, for their use in that region was the primary reason for their importation.

In March, 1857, James Buchanan succeeded Franklin Pierce as President (both were Democrats), and John B. Floyd of Virginia became the Secretary of War in place of Jefferson Davis. Floyd conscientiously tried to give the camels a fair trial, but he lacked the fire and romantic imagination of Davis and he also had to contend with other and more serious problems, such as the Mormon War. During the shuffle of the change of administrations, Major Wayne was ordered to Washington and never realized the chance to test his beloved camels across the deserts of the Southwest. The next year, however, in 1858, he had the consolation of becoming the recipient of "a First Class Gold Medal from the Société Impériale Zoölogique d'Acclimatation, of Paris, for the successful introduction and acclimation of the camel in the United States." Three years later, as a native Georgian, he quite naturally went with the Confederacy and became the adjutant and inspector general of his home state. His father, however, was an associate justice of the United States Supreme Court, on which he served from 1835 to his death in 1867, and he remained loyal to the Union and on the bench during the Civil War; and it was to his father's house in Washington that the younger Wayne went after the peace. He died in 1883.

CHAPTER XIX

Westward the Course of Camels

THERE seemed to be some kind of affinity between camels and officers of the United States Navy. Lieutenant David D. Porter had proved himself their best friend in transporting two shiploads of these animals from the Near East to Texas; during which voyages he had acted as veterinary, midwife, and general housekeeper to his charges. And it was another naval officer, Edward Fitzgerald Beale, who finally navigated a flotilla of these "ships of the desert" on a trial cruise from Texas to California which served as an acid test for their ability to traverse the arid and rough country of our Southwest. By right, of course, Major Wayne of the Army should have had charge of this trip, but he had been recalled to Washington from his camel farm at Camp Verde by one of those unexplainable quirks of military rotation.

But Beale was a worthy successor to the enthusiastic major. In fact, Beale was one of the outstanding frontiersmen of the 1850's; and was well called a "pioneer in the path of empire" by his close friend and neighbor Bayard Taylor, the now almost forgotten globe-trotter, poet, and author, but in his day a famous traveler and man of letters. Like Porter and Gwinn Harris Heap (who was a kinsman), Beale came from Chester, Pennsylvania, which town, lying just below Philadelphia on the Delaware River, seems to have been a buzzing center for camel interest and activities during the 1850's; for its sons went forth to garner, nourish, and tend those beasts all the way from the Near East to California. Beale's father was also a naval officer, who had won the Congressional Medal of Honor in the War of 1812. The son had left Georgetown University to enter the navy and had arrived off the coast of California under Commodore Stockton's command at the outbreak of fighting in the Mexican War.

He was with the small flying column under Lieutenant Archibald H. Gillespie of the U. S. Marine Corps which set out from San Diego to meet General Stephen Kearny's detachment of mule-riding dragoons who were crossing the coastal Sierras on their way from Santa Fe to California under the guidance of Kit Carson. They met the dragoons just before the nearly disastrous battle of San Pasqual, in which over a third of Kearny's men were killed or wounded in an ambush by Mexican lancers, and it was young Beale who crept through the encircling enemy lines at night, with Kit Carson and a Delaware Indian, to reach San Diego and summon a rescuing relief party of bluejackets, who arrived just in the nick of time to prevent Kearny's complete destruction. Beale became a close friend of Kit Carson and accompanied him through the dangerous Apache country to Washington with dispatches the following spring. The two young heroes from the conquest of California were lionized in the capital, but the famous scout was most uncomfortable indoors amidst a crowd waiting to shake his hand and would always somehow sidle out into the middle of the nearest street to greet his admirers. "I allays see folks out in the road," he modestly explained.[1]

Beale returned to duty in California and after the discovery of gold at Sutter's Mill he was chosen to carry the news back to

[1] Stephen Bonsal, *Edward Fitzgerald Beale. A Pioneer in the Path of Empire* (New York and London 1912), p. 30.

Washington with sample gold nuggets and dust. There is said to have been a race between the army and navy as to which branch's messenger of this world-shaking news would first arrive in the capital, and the gold-bearing Beale won the contest by landing at San Blas on the west coast of Mexico and riding overland by way of Guadalajara and Mexico City to Vera Cruz on the Gulf of Mexico. Clad in a miner's red shirt and leather breeches and boots, topped by a huge Mexican sombrero, he rode, day and night, alone, along the rough mountain paths in the torrential storms of the rainy season, over trails often blocked by uprooted trees and avalanches of stones and mud and with his way lit at night only by the almost incessant flashes of lightning. He rested only for a few minutes on the ground at the post stations while his saddle was being changed to a fresh horse until he arrived at the United States legation in Mexico City, literally caked in mud, where he at last spent two nights in a bed, while the American minister, Nathan Clifford, prepared other dispatches for him to carry. He was attacked several times by bandits and shot himself out of these holdups with his six-shooters or escaped by the speed of his mount. He made the last stage of almost three hundred miles of this epic ride, from Mexico City to Vera Cruz, in the extraordinary time of sixty hours, once escaping from a band of robbers by riding his horse with reckless daring down a precipitous mountainside where they feared to follow. He well deserved to win this race, a sort of California sweepstakes, over a more cautious opponent who chose the safer and slower route by way of the Isthmus of Panama. His arrival in Washington with the first authentic news of the discovery of gold in California and actual samples of the precious metal undoubtedly triggered the great gold rush immediately following.

In November, 1852, President Millard Fillmore appointed the thirty-year-old Beale to be General Superintendent of Indian

Affairs for California; and the next spring, after resigning from the navy, Beale left Westport, Missouri, on May 10, 1853, accompanied by his kinsman and near neighbor in Pennsylvania, Gwinn Harris Heap, who acted as an expert camel buyer on the Wayne-Porter expedition to the Near East a few years later.

This small expedition of about a dozen men made rapid time along the old Santa Fe Trail but kept on going due west along the Arkansas River, roughly following the 38th parallel of longitude, when the main trail turned southwest toward Santa Fe and the Mexican settlements. Heap wrote an account of this trip, *Central Route to the Pacific from the Valley of the Mississippi to California* (Philadelphia and London 1854), illustrated by himself, in which he gave such a cheerful description of the southern emigrants to California along the trail — in marked contradistinction to the heart-rending accounts of John Russell Bartlett at about the same time — that it is worth quoting for the reader's morale. Of course, Bartlett met this same kind of emigrants further along the southern way, possibly after the bloom had worn off, but then, the bloom had definitely worn off the ill and jaded Bartlett, who was moving East after nearly three years of wanderings and troubles along the border. Heap wrote, soon after leaving Westport:

We had already overtaken and passed several large wagon and cattle trains from Texas and Arkansas, mostly bound to California. With them were many women and children; and it was pleasant to stroll into their camps in the evening and witness the perfect air of comfort and being-at-home that they presented. Their wagons drawn up in a circle, gave them at least an appearance of security; and within the inclosure the men either reclined around the camp-fires, or were busy in repairing their harness or cleaning their arms. The females milked the cows and prepared the supper; and we often enjoyed the hot cakes and fresh milk which they invited us to partake of. Tender infants in their cradles were seen under the shelter of the wagons, thus early inured to hard travel. Carpets and rocking chairs were drawn out, and, what would perhaps shock some of our fine ladies, fresh-looking girls, whose rosy lips were certainly never intended to be defiled by the vile weed, sat around the fire, smoking the old-fashioned corn-cob pipe.

This was written on May 22, 1853, at Walnut Creek near the Great Bend of the Arkansas River, and Heap went on to say:

This is the point at which emigrants to Oregon and California, from Texas and Arkansas, generally strike this road. They prefer the route which leads them through the South Pass [the Oregon Trail] to the one on the Gila, or Cooke's route, where little or no timber or water are found for long distances.

The lack of timber for fuel on the Great Plains was amply compensated for by buffalo droppings, or *bois de vache* as the early French explorers aptly called them. As Heap wrote: "There was no wood near enough for use; but the general resource in such cases on the plains was scattered in abundance around us."

Beale's party had orders to take a direct route to California, and this they did along the 38th parallel across southern Colorado, passing through Fort Massachusetts and Cochetopa Pass (where Marcy afterwards had his troubles going in the opposite direction in midwinter), and crossing the Grand (Colorado) and Green Rivers; then on across southern Utah to California and over the Mohave Desert to the Sierras, which they surmounted through the Cajon Pass and thence descended to Los Angeles. This same way was later followed, in large part, by the "Pathfinder," John C. Frémont, on his fifth and last exploring expedition, made during the winter of 1853–1854. And right behind Beale's party came the ill-fated expedition of the topographical engineer Captain John Williams Gunnison, which was carefully and slowly making one of the famous four surveys for railroad routes to the Pacific.

Beale's party arrived in Los Angeles on August 22, with the loss of only three mules on the way, having spent one hundred days in traveling, which was very good going considering some of their misadventures, delays, and narrow escapes from the Indians. The greatest delay came when they were unable to cross the Grand (Colorado) River after a makeshift canoe, carrying nearly all their arms and ammunition, upset in that turbulent and flooded stream. Gwinn Heap then rode with a few men over three hundred and fifty miles through the roughest mountain country to Taos, New Mexico, to replenish these vital needs. With him was an invaluable Mexican guide, Felipe Archilete, an intrepid and nimble one-legged fellow called, of course, Peg-Leg, who got along amazingly well with a wooden stump, afoot or horseback or swimming the swollen rivers, and was of the greatest help in getting Beale's expedition through the rough Rockies and the country of the truculent Ute Indians.

These Utes were at first friendly to this pioneer government expedition through their Rocky Mountain fastnesses, but this feeling soon changed when the Americans were unable to make them the usual presents for the privilege of passing through their country because all the trade goods and extra equipment had been lost in the capsized canoe. The Utes then demanded the rifles of the party, which, of course, was an impossible request. At this refusal the young Ute braves really got tough and the chief's son nearly started a general free-for-all. As Gwinn Heap described it:

He [the young brave] charged upon Felipe [Peg-Leg] with a savage yell, every feature distorted with rage; his horse struck Felipe's mule and very nearly threw them both to the ground. The Indian then seizing Felipe's rifle, endeavored to wrench it from his hands, but the latter held firmly to his gun, telling us at the same time not to interfere. We and the Indians formed a circle around them, as they sat in their saddles, each holding on to the gun, whose muzzle was pointed full at the Indian's breast. He uttered many imprecations, and urged his followers to lend him their assistance. They looked at us inquiringly, and we cocked our rifles — the hint was sufficient — they declined interfering. For some minutes the Utah and Felipe remained motionless, glaring at each other like two game-cocks, each watching with flashing eyes for an opportunity to assail his rival. Seeing that to trifle longer would be folly, Felipe, who held the butt-end of the rifle, deliberately placed his thumb on the hammer, and raising it slowly, gave warning to the young chief, by two ominous clicks, that his life was in danger. For a moment longer, the Utah eyed Felipe, and then, with an indescribable grunt, pushed the rifle from him, and lashing his horse furiously, rode away from us at full speed. Felipe gave us a sly wink, and uttered the highly original ejaculation — "Carajo!" *

This was really a pretty tense situation and a close shave, for the overwhelming number of Utes would have wiped out the handful of Americans if the crippled Felipe had pulled that trigger— and the town of Chester, Pennsylvania, would have lost two citizens and the camels of the Near East two proponents in the persons of Beale and Heap.

But to return with Beale to the camel herd which Major Wayne had stabled back at Camp Verde, Texas. The second shipment of forty-one additional camels had arrived from the Levant in February, 1857, in charge of Lieutenant David Porter and Gwinn Heap, and this ended their connection with these animals. Wayne was shortly afterwards ordered to Washington and left the herd temporarily in charge of the ranking cavalry officer of a nearby post. The new Secretary of War, John B. Floyd, then selected Edward Beale to superintend the survey of a wagon road from Fort Defiance, New Mexico (now just

* Certainly not original but highly appropriate to the circumstances.

over the boundary in Arizona), to the Colorado River and to try out some of the camels on this trip.

Beale was visiting at the time in his old home town of Chester, Pennsylvania. This coming expedition was, of course, the talk of the town and its young men were keen to accompany him on such an adventurous trip. He finally chose young David Porter Heap, a son of his old companion; Hampden Porter, a son of Dr. James Porter; and two other young men, one of whom, May Humphreys Stacey, kept an interesting journal of the journey.[2]

The party arrived at Indianola, Texas, on June 5, 1857, and Stacey noted, "The town contains about six hundred inhabitants whose general character would not appear very favorably, compared with some of our neat Pennsylvania villages." Leaving here after a few days, they started for San Antonio, and young Stacey wrote his first impression of the great prairies: "A feeling of insignificance and worthlessness I felt when I gazed over the wide expanse of land — and my eyes were opened to the magnificence of Almighty God." The young Easterners were fascinated by the country and it was a shame that this enchantment was disturbed by a disagreeable incident when young Heap quit the expedition after an undeserved reprimand by Beale, much to the regret of his companions. The party reached San Antonio in a rainstorm and Stacey was most favorably impressed with that charming old town, despite his having to camp in a barnyard covered with manure and alive with fleas.

While Stacey waited for a few days in San Antonio for the camels to come down from Camp Verde to be loaded for the trip to California, one of the young men of the party had a

---

[2] Included in Lewis Burt Lesley's *Uncle Sam's Camels* (Cambridge 1929) along with Beale's official report, House Exec. Doc. No. 124. 35 Cong. 1st Sess.

sample of Texas hospitality which he seems to have received
in a rather prudish fashion. As Stacey reported it:

". . . an immense Texan came up to him, and slapped him quite
familiarly on the back, exclaiming, "How are you Breckenridge? I
am d—— glad to see you." "My name is not Breckenridge." "Well
you belong to the same Company." "Yes." "Well, let's go in and get
a drink." "No, I do not wish anything. I have duties to attend to,
and I am going to do them." "You are a saucy man, anyhow." "I can
afford to be." "Got a six-shooter there." "Yes, and by God I know
how to use it." "You're pretty spunky." "I came from a spunky
place." "Where you from?" "From old Pennsylvania." "Come in
then, and take a drink." "No, I wont."

The generous stranger finally gave up but many a man has
bitten Texas dust for less cause than such self-righteousness.

Beale soon returned from Camp Verde with a picked herd
of the camels. It was a curious meeting, according to Stacey:

The first intimation we had of their approach was the jingling of
the large bells suspended from their necks. Presently, one, then two,
three, four, until the whole twenty-five had come within range in
the dim twilight. And thus they came, these huge ungainly beasts
of the desert, accompanied by their attendants, Turks, Greeks, and
Armenians. Who would have thought, one hundred years ago, that
now camels would be used on this Continent as beasts of burden?
Our mules and horses were very much frightened at the approach
of the camels. [The usual reaction and the main reason for the feeling
against them.] They dashed around the corral, with heads erect and
snorting in wild alarm. They were so much excited that the whole
camp was aroused and put on watch. However, in a few hours they
became more quiet, and all hands were sent to bed, except the regular
guard, and soon the camp sank to silence broken only be the tread
of the sentinels.

Late in June, 1857, the party, using both mules and camels,
started west. The latter animals seemed tired at first and trav-

eled slower than the mules. Also some of the Levantine attendants refused to make the long trip to California, "alleging," as
Beale reported it, "that they had been badly treated by the government, not having received the pay due them since January." [3] And this meant that the inexperienced Americans had
to undergo on-the-job training and learn the camel business the
hard way. The members of the party were not too optimistic
about the great camel experiment for the first few days.

But things improved as they went on, as the camels gradually
got into their stride after the months of idleness on shipboard
and at Camp Verde. By the time they had reached the town of
Uvalde, Beale reported:

> As soon as they arrive they are turned loose to graze, but appear
> to prefer to browse on the mesquite bushes and the leaves of a thorny
> shrub, which grows in this country everywhere, to the finest grass.
> They are exceedingly docile, easily managed, and I see, so far, no
> reason to doubt the success of the experiment.

The party, camels and men, shook themselves down by degrees and reached the famous frontier post of Fort Clark, near
Brackettville, in good shape. On the way, a company of United
States Cavalry (probably the 2nd Cavalry) passed them, of
which Stacey noted, "They were a very hard-looking party";
which comment would have greatly pleased the troopers if
they could but have heard it. Beale's men enjoyed bathing in
the limpid Las Moras Creek, today feeding the huge swimming
pool of a luxurious dude ranch. From there they entered real
Indian country where the Comanches, and at times the Apaches,
roamed freely far and wide and where the utmost vigilance was
necessary to prevent surprise attacks and stampedes of the animals. Another strong point which Beale brought out in favor

[3] All quotations of Beale, unless otherwise noted, are from his report to
Secretary of War John B. Floyd. House Exec. Doc. No. 124. 35 Cong. 1st Sess.

of the camels was that, because of their placidity and dislike of galloping, they were stampedeproof.

The party slowly but steadily pushed westward and crossed Devil's River into ever more arid and barren country, and Beale's satisfaction mounted as he saw the camels eagerly seeking and eating with the greatest apparent relish the greasewood shrub; he noted in his report:

It is certainly very gratifying to find these animals eating, by their own preference, the coarse and bitter herbs, hitherto of no value, which abound always in the most sterile and desolate parts of every road, so far as discovered, which traverses the broad extent of wilderness between the eastern States and our Pacific possessions.

They kept passing the graves of men and women murdered by the extremely dangerous and ferocious Indians of this area and Beale quite rightly wrote of its hazards: "Scarcely a mile of it but has its story of Indian murder and plunder; in fact, from El Paso to San Antonio is but one long battle ground – a surprise here, robbery of animals there."

Stacey told of the murder of four men of a mail party at one spot. Among them was an army sergeant who had made such a brave resistance to the attacking Indians that when a rescue party of troops finally arrived they found the bodies of the other three men horribly mutilated and scalped but not so that of the sergeant; "the Indians had bound wreaths round his wrists and ankles, cut out his heart and laid it on his breast and placed a beautiful wreath around it. It was a barbarous tribute of admiration to true courage."

This report was, of course, hearsay and the chances are that the savages never went to such lengths of poetic fancy, at least in that part of Texas. The mutilations and scalpings were probably all too true.

The party moved westward, comparatively rapidly, along the

El Paso road, stopping to rest for a bit at the isolated army posts along the way. Two of the men casually made some healthy gripes about the monotonous daily grub to young Stacey, one day, and he rather sanctimoniously wrote of these in his journal:

One said that he had not had bean soup three times since he had been on the expedition, and he had not had any rice at all. He had not tasted coffee fit to drink, and swore that it was enough to kill any man. The other said that eating so much fat pork without any vegetables would give us the scurvy sure, or "shore," as he pronounced it. All this was interlarded with oaths that would make your hair stand upon end to hear. I never did, in such a short space of time, hear so many varieties of swearing.

If Stacey had been a man of experience he would have realized that this griping over the "vittles" was a sure sign that all was well with the expedition's morale. On the optimistic side, Beale waxed more eulogistic about his camels, saying of them:

As for food, they live on anything, and thrive. Yesterday they drank water for the first time in twenty-six hours, and although the day had been excessively hot they seemed to care little for it. Mark the difference between them and the mules; the same time, in such weather, without water, would set the latter wild, and render them useless, if not entirely break them down.

And a little later he wrote: "The camels are traveling finely. . . . I have never seen or heard of one stumbling, or even making a blunder."

They entered El Paso, toward the end of July, like a circus parade, escorted by swarms of curious Mexicans who had come from miles around to see the strange camels, and went into camp near Fort Bliss for a short rest. Then, turning north, they followed the Rio Grande to Albuquerque, keeping very much on the alert as reports had come in that the Apaches and Navajos were on the warpath. They passed through all the Mexican villages along the river and Stacey noted, "I have seen very few pretty women. They are generally very ugly and very dirty but very polite." The inhabitants looked upon the caravan as a sort of traveling menagerie with Beale as the head showman. One man, looking at Beale's wagon, which was painted bright red, asked:

"Dis show wagon, no?"
I [Beale] replied, "Yes."
"Ah, ha! You be dee showmans, no?"
"Yes, sir."
"What you gottee more on camelos? Gottee any dogs?"
"Yes, monkeys too, and more."
"Whattee more?"
"Horse more."
"Whattee can do horse?"
"Stand on his head, and drink a glass of wine."
"Valgame Dios! What a people these are to have a horse stand on his head, and drink a glass of wine."

The saloons of Albuquerque proved a source of trouble, after the long parching trip from San Antonio; one man was shot in the hand by a drunken companion at a fandango and Beale reported of others:

I was obliged to administer a copious supply of the oil of the boot to several, especially to my Turks and Greeks, with the camels. The former had not found, even in the positive prohibitions of the prophet, a sufficient reason for temperance, but was as drunk as any Christian in the train, and would have remained behind, but for a style of reason much resorted to by the head of his church, as well as others, in making converts, i.e., a broken head. . . . to move a stubborn half-drunken Turk give me a good tough piece of wagon spoke. . . .

The party moved on westward, about the middle of August, following the way of Lieutenant Amiel Weeks Whipple's railroad survey along the 35th parallel which we have already traced with the artist Heinrich Baldwin Möllhausen. The camels carried an average load of seven hundred pounds, which was about twice the weight packed on a mule. The men ordinarily rode mules but occasionally a camel would be used for a mount as, for example, when Beale rode a white dromedary named Seid on a special trip to meet Colonel William Wing Loring, in command of Fort Defiance. The colonel, incidentally, was an unusual man. Born in Florida to parents who had emigrated there from Hingham, Massachusetts, he was a West Pointer who had made a name for gallantry in the Mexican War, where he had lost an arm. He was a famous Indian-fighting cavalryman who later became a general in the Confederate Army. After the Civil War, he entered the Egyptian service, in which he remained for about ten years and rose to be a general of division and a pasha with the highest decorations of his adopted government. He probably little realized when Beale arrived on camelback how intimate would be his associations with camels in the years to come.

They passed the famous Inscription Rock (El Moro), on which many of the men inscribed their names, as had Möllhausen and others of Whipple's party over four years before. Then after they left the pueblo of the Zuni Indians, the way across the high plateau country was level, the weather cool and pleasant, and the forage for the animals plentiful — for this was the best time of the year to cross this tableland — so that the San Francisco Mountains, where Whipple's party had spent Christmas day in 1853, were reached in mid-September. Beale's admiration of the camels continued to mount and he wrote:

The camels are so quiet and give so little trouble that sometimes we forget they are with us. Certainly there never was anything so patient and enduring and so little troublesome as this noble animal.

They pack their heavy load of corn, of which they never taste a grain; put up with any good food offered them without complaint, and are always up with the wagons, and, withal, so perfectly docile and quiet that they are the admiration of the whole camp. . . . They are better today than they were when we left Camp Verde with them; especially since our men have learned, by experience, the best mode of packing them.

Farther along they reached an arid stretch where the horses and mules suffered greatly from the lack of water for thirty-six hours. But not so the camels. As Beale described it:

. . . one of the most painful sights I ever witnessed was a group of them [horses and mules] standing over a small barrel of water and trying to drink from the bung hole, and seemingly frantic with distress and eagerness to get at it. The camels appeared to view this proceeding with great contempt, and kept quietly browsing on the grass and bushes.

A little later, Beale launched another encomium for his camels when he wrote:

. . . they are the salt of the party and the noblest brute alive. . . They have been used on every reconnoisance [sic] whilst the mules were resting, and having gone down the precipitous sides of rough volcanic mesas, which mules would not descend until the camels were first taken down as an example. With all this work they are perfectly content to eat anything, from the driest greasewood bush to a thorny prickly pear, and, what is better, keep fat on it.

Beale kept naming various mountains, passes, and creeks after his fellow officers in the United States Navy, and if these names had stuck (which one rarely did), the geographical features of the present western Arizona would sound like a nautical roster of a century ago. Every explorer of the West seemed to indulge in this harmless pastime; it pleased their friends though the fame was usually but transitory.

About the middle of October they struck the Colorado River and were greeted by crowds of the Mohave Indians, whom Whipple and Ives had found so friendly and helpful. Beale, also, was favorably impressed and wrote of them:

They were a fine-looking, comfortable, fat and merry set; naked excepting a very small piece of cotton cloth around the waist, and, though barefooted, ran over the sharp rock and pebbles as easily as if shod with iron. We were soon surrounded on all sides by them. Some had learned a few words of English from trafficking with the military posts two hundred and fifty miles off, and one of them saluted me with: "God damn my soul eyes. How de do! How de do."

But it was an anxious time for Beale as he stood on the east bank of the Colorado River, for it had been reliably reported that camels could not swim and this was the first water crossing, on the whole transcontinental trip, deep enough to require it. If the report was true it might mean the loss of several animals in making the attempt — and the party would have to follow the river southward until a ferry was reached or go to the infinite trouble of building large rafts to float the huge beasts across. Beale wrote that "all my pleasure in looking upon this noble stream and all the satisfaction I derived in the reflection of a successful journey accomplished, was clouded by this doubt." But unfortunately Beale's pets did not let him down. As he described it:

The first camel brought down to the river's edge refused to take the water. Anxious, but not discouraged, I ordered another one to be brought, one of our largest and finest; and only those who have felt so much anxiety for the success of an experiment can imagine my relief on seeing it take to the water, and swim boldly across the rapidly flowing stream. We then tied them, each one to the saddle of another, and without the slightest difficulty, in a short time swam them all to the opposite bank in gangs, five in a gang; to my delight, they not only swam with ease, but with apparently more strength than horses or mules.[4]

Once across this water barrier, the party made spanking time across the Mohave Desert to Beale's ranch near Fort Tejon, about forty miles south of Bakersfield, which he had acquired while serving as Indian Agent for California. Young Stacey sailed home around Cape Horn to serve later, with distinction, as a captain in the Union Army. Beale made a few other trips with his beloved camels, notably one back to New Mexico the next year. The camel herd, as a whole remained on his ranch until the government transferred them to Los Angeles, shortly after the outbreak of the Civil War. They were finally sold at auction and used by the purchaser, for a time, to carry salt to the Nevada silver mines, but the owners of mules used in the same task made such vehement protests (the camels always panicked mules and horses at sight or scent) that the new owner drove his camels, with their two remaining Syrian attendants, Hi Jolly (an Americanization of his Moslem name, Hadji Ali) and Greek George, to Yuma, Arizona, where the animals were eventually turned loose on the desert.

The two camel drivers remained in the United States and became quite famous local characters. Greek George was said to have lived on in California until 1915, and was described in 1903 as wearing "a homeric beard and a thatch of hair, both so dense as to seem almost bullet proof. As a matter of fact, an Indian arrow, in a fight near Camp Mohave, had struck him square in the jaw and barely scratched the flesh through that matted beard." [5] As for Hi Jolly, he wandered for years as a

[4] From Beale's report to Secretary of War John B. Floyd, Colorado River, California, October 18, 1857. Reprinted in Stephen Bonsal, *Edward Fitzgerald Beale* . . . (New York 1912), p. 216.
[5] C. F. Lummis, *Mesa, Cañon and Pueblo* (New York 1925), pp. 80–81.

prospector over the desert and reported that he frequently saw camels around the Gila and Colorado Rivers. He was a colorful old scamp who became well known in all the saloons of that area and fianlly died in Arizona in 1903. The Arizona Highway Commission has placed a placque over his grave at Quartzsite which reads:

The last camp of Hi Jolly, born somewhere in Syria, about 1828, died at Quartzsite, Dec. 16, 1903. Came to this country Feb. 10, 1856. Camel driver, packer, scout. Over 30 years a faithful aid to the U. S. government.[6]

The camels left in Texas came, sooner or later, to about the same end. But they were first used, with marked success, on two army reconnaissances in west Texas before the outbreak of the Civil War. The first of these was reported by Lieutenant Edward L. Hartz of Pennsylvania, a young infantry officer just out of West Point, who accompanied Lieutenant W. H. Echols in charge of some twenty camels from Camp Hudson (near the present city of Del Rio) on a wandering trip through the roughest kind of west Texas country for about two and a half months in the spring and summer of 1859. Echols and Hartz, and their men, were completely inexperienced in the handling of these animals and had to go through the usual trial and error stages at the beginning. But Hartz gradually became as enthusiastic about them in his journal as Beale had been.[7] At first, they had some trouble in making fast the packs because the camels were in such "high condition" and their humps so full and round that they would not fit into the wedge-shaped cavity of the pack saddles, and the oscillating motion of their stride loosened these

[6] Albert H. Greenly, "Camels in America," *The Papers of the Bibliographical Society of America*, Vol. 46, Fourth quarter, 1952, p. 352. This article includes the most complete bibliography about the camel experiment.

[7] Hartz's diary of this trip is contained in the report of Secretary of War John B. Floyd for 1859, Sen. Exec. Doc. No. 2. 36 Cong. 1st Sess., pp. 422–441.

and caused them to fall off. But this annoyance was finally over-come by experience and time. One of the female camels was bitten by a rattlesnake on this trip but the wound was immedi-ately scarified and rubbed with liquid ammonia and the animal showed no ill effects. Hartz's final opinion was:

> The patience, endurance, and steadiness which characterize the performance of the camels during this march is beyond praise, and when compared with the jaded and distressed appearance of the mules and horses, established for them another point of superiority.

In the following summer of 1860, Lieutenant Echols took a band of twenty camels and fifteen mules, with thirty-one men as handlers and escort, on another long reconnaissance from San Antonio to Fort Davis and then south into the Rio Grande country.[8] Once they traveled for five days without water over a distance of a hundred and twenty miles; but for the water the camels carried, of which they drank nary a drop themselves, the mules would probably have died. They entered some ter-ribly rough, rocky, and steep country near the Big Bend of the Rio Grande and Echols wrote, "I never conceived that there could be such country." But when the ascent became too steep, the camels walked on their front knees to keep even the balance of their packs. Hartz had previously reported that these animals would work their way along a narrow ledge on the side of a mountain by placing their forefeet upon the slope, and keeping their hind feet on the path; they would then sidle themselves along until the way widened. Echols's party skirted the north rim of the great canyon of the Rio Grande, from which they could look directly down fifteen hundred feet to the stream below. The walls of the canyon rose vertically and as narrow as the river confined at the bottom. Echols also recommended the

---

[8] Echols's report is in Sen. Ex. Doc. No. 1. 36 Cong. 2nd Sess., pp. 33–51.

camels as highly as had all those who had given them a fair trial. But this was the last time they were officially used by the army.

The Confederates took over Camp Verde in February, 1861, with all its camels, stables, equipment and attendants, but made no reported use of the animals during the Civil War. When the United States Army resumed control, the camels were sold at auction in 1866. For a while they were used as a camel express between Laredo, Texas, and Mexico City; but this venture was a failure and the camels were eventually sold to circuses or turned loose on the desert as had been the others in Arizona. Perhaps members of both bands eventually had a reunion in that wild and lonely country. The wandering Indians gradually killed and ate some of the roving survivors, and others were shot at random by prospectors and especially by cattlemen who had always hated the beasts for frightening their livestock. So ended rather dismally Jeff Davis's experiment of introducing the "ships of the desert" into our Southwest.

Epilogue

THIS, then, has been the informal and possibly somewhat rambling account of the surveys and expeditions in the Southwest which were the high spots in the short thirteen years between the Mexican and Civil Wars. Those were "the days of old, the days of gold," and that brief period, before the terrible conflict, was probably the most golden of all.

The scientists, particularly the naturalists, may have been neglected to a certain extent in the narrative, except, of course, for the wandering ethnologist John Russell Bartlett, who, because of his comprehensive personal narrative, took the limelight for the border survey. But the others were a kaleidoscopic and confusing lot; and, often, the military men and the artists doubled in their duties to compound the confusion. Also, the official reports made by the military sometimes failed to give them what seem like their just deserts. At other times the scientific reports were made by men who stayed at home and wrote their findings from material and specimens brought to them by the actual members of the exploring expeditions. So it has been difficult to give them always the credit they undoubtedly deserve.

The military, usually the Topographical Engineers, nearly always had command, and the absence of any discord was noticeable in their expeditions. All worked harmoniously together where discipline existed and troubles only came on the civilian or semicivilian expeditions of Bartlett and Frémont. The comradeship of the frontier, the zest for new countries, and the eternal spirit of adventure held these men — soldiers, sailors, artists, scientists, and muleteers from all sections of the country and from Europe and Mexico — in a bond of good-fellowship which disappeared in the Civil War and has never since been completely recovered. Perhaps the wounds of that conflict are deeper than we realize.

Certainly the achievements of these men in that brief interim between wars were unequaled in any like period of time; and these pioneers of only yesterday, like ourselves living in the Industrial Age, merit a fame which has been denied them.

Ralph Waldo Emerson once wrote, "Europe stretches to the Appalachians; America lies beyond," and we should always remember this in a time when we are prone to spread our interests and sympathies too thin over too large a world. These men of the old West generally represented the best this country has yet produced, and may their fame grow with the mounting interest in the American frontier.

Sources

Including those mentioned in the narrative and footnotes. Only those actually consulted are given.

The general sources used throughout are listed immediately
below. The special sources are by chapters.

Biographical information about most of the individuals mentioned in the narrative can be found in one or more of the following:

Appleton's Cyclopaedia of American Biography. 6 Vols. New York
1899–1900.

Cullum, Bvt. Maj. Gen. George W.: *Biographical Register of the
Officers and Graduates of the U. S. Military Academy.* Vols. I and
II. Boston and New York 1891.

Dictionary of American Biography. 20 Vols. New York 1928–1944.

Geiser, Samuel Wood: *Naturalists of the Frontier.* Dallas 1937.

Heitman, Francis B.: *Historical Register and Dictionary of the
United States Army.* 2 Vols. Washington 1903. These contain the
military records of all officers of the period, including West
Pointers.

McCracken, Harold: *Portrait of the Old West, with a Biographical
Check List of Western Artists.* New York 1952.

Taft, Robert: *Artists and Illustrators of the Old West.* New York
1953. An outstanding work of reference.

The following were used for bibliographies and general information:

"A Bibliography of Artists Who Portrayed the Trans-Mississippi West in the Period 1819–1865." Typescript. Smithsonian Institution. Washington, D.C. (n.d.)

Catalogue of Manuscripts in the Western Americana Collection, Yale University Library. Compiled by Mary C. Withington. New Haven 1952.

Handbook of American Indians North of Mexico, edited by Frederick Webb Hodge. 2 Vols. Washington 1907.

Hasse, Adelaide Rosalie: *Reports of Explorations Printed in the Documents of the United States Government.* Washington 1899.

Reports Of Explorations And Surveys, To Ascertain The Most Practicable And Economical Route For A Railroad From The Mississippi River To The Pacific Ocean. 12 Vols. in 13. Washington 1855–1860. Hereafter referred to as *Pacific Railroad Surveys.* Vol. XI, Part II contains a list of all government explorations to 1852.

Wagner, Henry R.: *The Plains and the Rockies. A Bibliography of Original Narratives of Travel and Adventure 1800–1865.* San Francisco 1921. Revised and extended by Charles L. Camp. San Francisco 1937.

The following are special sources by chapters:

CHAPTERS I–VI

The Army of the United States, edited by Theo. F. Rodenbough and William L. Haskin. New York 1896. P. 120 about Topographical Engineers.

Bartlett, John Russell: "Autobiography." n.d. Manuscript in the John Carter Brown Library, Providence, Rhode Island.

——: *Dictionary of Americanisms.* New York 1848.

——: *Personal Narrative of Explorations and Incidents in Texas, New Mexico, California, Sonora, and Chihuahua, During the Years 1850, '51, '52, and '53.* 2 Vols. New York 1854.

Beers, Henry P.: "A History of the U. S. Topographical Engineers, 1816–1863." *The Military Engineer,* June and July 1942.

Checklist of United States Public Documents 1789–1909. Washington 1911. Vol. 1, p. 1260 about Topographical Engineers.

Conney, Peter Thomas: *A Centennial Evaluation of the Treaty of Guadelupe* [sic] *Hidalgo, 1848–1948.* Oakland, California, 1948.

Couts, Cave J.: *From San Diego to the Colorado in 1849. The Journal and Maps of Cave J. Couts,* edited by William McPherson. Los Angeles 1932.

Cox, C. C.: "From Texas to California in 1849. Diary of C. C. Cox," edited by Mabelle Eppard Martin. *Southwestern Historical Quarterly.* October 1925.

Cremony, John C.: *Life Among the Apaches.* San Francisco 1868.

Dale, Edward Everett: *The Indians of the Southwest.* Norman, Oklahoma, 1949.

Emory, Lt. Col. W. H.: *Notes of a Military Reconnaissance from Ft. Leavenworth, in Missouri, to San Diego, in California.* Washington 1848.

Gammell, William: *Life and Services of the Hon. John Russell Bartlett. A paper read before the Rhode Island Historical Society on November 2, 1886, by William Gammell, President of the Society.* Providence 1886.

Graham, Lt. Col. James Duncan: *Report on Boundary Line between United States and Mexico.* Sen. Exec. Doc. 121. 32 Cong. 1st Sess. Washington 1853.

Gray, A. B.: *Report and Map on Mexican Boundary.* Sen. Exec. Doc. 55. 33 Cong. 2nd Sess. Washington 1855.

Haley, J. Evetts: *Fort Concho and the Texas Frontier.* San Angelo, Texas, 1952.

Lockwood, Frank C.: *The Apache Indians.* New York 1938.

Magoffin, Susan Shelby: *Down the Santa Fe Trail and into Mexico.* New Haven, Connecticut, 1926.

Martin, Lawrence: *Disturnell's Map.* Washington 1937.

Mayer, Brantz: *History of the War Between Mexico and the United States.* Vol. 1. New York and London 1848.

Report of the secretary of war, communicating . . . a report and map of the examination of New Mexico, made by Lieutenant J. W. Abert, of the Topographical corps. Washington 1848.

272 SOURCES

Rodenbough, Theo. F., Compiler: *From Everglade to Cañon with the Second Dragoons.* New York 1875.

Schoolcraft, Henry R., L.L.D.: *Information Respecting the History, Condition, and Prospects of the Indian Tribes of the United States.* 6 Vols. Philadelphia 1851–1860.

Scroggs, William O.: *Filibusters and Financiers,* New York 1916. Pp. 20–50 for filibustering expeditions into Mexico.

Stevenson, Robert Louis: *Across the Plains.* New York 1887.

32 Cong. 1st. Sess. Sen. Exec. Doc. 119, contains the correspondence about the many arguments and disputes among the members of Bartlett's commission.

Thomlinson, M. H.: *The Garrison of Fort Bliss, 1849–1861.* El Paso, Texas, 1945.

Trahern, G. W.: "George Washington Trahern: Texan Cowboy Soldier from Mier to Buena Vista," edited by A. Russell Buchanan. *Southwestern Historical Quarterly.* July 1954.

Weed, L. N.: "Narrative of a Journey to California in 1849." Manuscript in William R. Coe Collection in Western Americana Collection in Yale University Library.

Whiting, William Henry Chase: "Journal of William Henry Chase Whiting, 1849." *Exploring Southwest Trails 1846–1854,* edited by Ralph P. Bieber. Glendale, California, 1938.

Wislizenus, A., M.D.: *Memoir of a Tour to Northern Mexico Connected with Col. Doniphan's Expedition in 1846 and 1847.* Sen. Misc. Doc. 26. 30 Cong. 1st Sess. Washington 1848.

CHAPTER VII

Emory, William H.: *Report on the United States and Mexican Boundary Survey.* 3 Vols. in 2. Washington 1857.

William H. Emory Papers in possession of Edward Eberstadt and Sons, New York City. For the years 1852–1855.

Faris, John T.: *The Romance of the Boundaries.* New York 1926.

Gardner, Paul Neff: *The Gadsden Treaty.* Philadelphia 1923.

CHAPTER VIII

Albright, George Leslie: *Official Explorations for Pacific Railroads 1853–1855.* Berkeley, California, 1921.

Branch, E. Douglas: *Westward, The Romance of the American Frontier* New York 1930. Chapter XXV.

Bushnell, David I., Jr.: "John Mix Stanley, Artist Explorer," *Annual Report of the Smithsonian Institution 1924*, pp. 507–512.

Gray, A. B.: *Survey of a Route for the Southern Pacific R.R. on the 32nd. Parallel.* Cincinnati 1856.

——: *Texas Western Railroad Company.* Cincinnati 1855.

Gunnison, John W.: *The Mormons, or Latter Day Saints in the Valley of the Great Salt Lake.* Philadelphia 1852.

Holbrook, Stewart H.: *The Story of American Railroads.* New York 1947.

Jackson, W. Turrentine: *Wagon Roads West.* Berkeley and Los Angeles 1952.

McCracken, Harold: "Adventure with Painting — John Mix Stanley," *Portrait of the Old West.* Chapter 8. New York 1952.

Pacific Railroad Surveys. (See general sources, page 270.)

Riegel, Robert Edgar: *The Story of the Western Railroads.* New York 1926.

Spaulding, Oliver Lyman: *The United States Army in War and Peace.* New York 1937.

Stevens, Hazard: *The Life of Isaac Ingalls Stevens . . .* 2 Vols. Boston and New York 1900.

Taft, Robert: "John M. Stanley and the Pacific Railroad Surveys," *Artists and Illustrators of the Old West.* Chapter 1. New York 1953.

CHAPTERS IX AND X

Kit Carson's Autobiography, edited by Milo Milton Quaife. Chicago 1935.

Carvalho, S. N.: *Incidents of Travel and Adventure in the Far West.* New York 1859.

Dunbar, Seymour: *The Fort Sutter Papers with Historical and Critical Commentaries*, published by Edward Eberstadt. n.d.

Favour, Alpheus H.: *Old Bill Williams, Mountain Man.* Chapel Hill, North Carolina, 1936.

Frémont, John Charles: *Memoirs of My Life.* Chicago and New York 1887. Vol. 1. This first volume was not a financial success and the planned Vol. II was never published but is now in the Bancroft Library, Berkeley, California, in manuscript form.

——: *Central Railroad Route to the Pacific*. Sen. Misc. Doc. 67. 33 Cong. 1st Sess.

Heffernan, William Joseph: *Edward M. Kern, Artist-Explorer*. Kern County Historical Society, Bakersfield, California, 1953.

Lavender, David: *The Big Divide*. New York 1949.

Letter of J. C. Frémont to the Editors of the National Intelligencer, June 13, 1854. Also printed as Sen. Misc. Doc. 67. 33 Cong. 1st Sess. under title: *Col. Frémont's Exploration of the Central Railroad Route to the Pacific*.

McGehee, Micajah: "Rough Times in Rough Places. A Personal Narrative of the Terrible Experiences of Frémont's Fourth Expedition." *The Century Illustrated Monthly Magazine*. March 1891.

National Intelligencer, June 24, 1854. Letter signed "S" (Lieut. James H. Simpson) regretting the murder of Richard Kern by the Indians and giving a brief summary of the careers of the three Kern brothers.

Nevins, Allan: *Frémont, Pathmarker of the West*. New York 1939.

——: *Frémont, the West's Greatest Adventurer*. 2 Vols. New York 1928.

Ruxton, George Frederick: *Life in the Far West*, edited by Leroy R. Hafen. Norman, Oklahoma, 1951.

"The Story of a Famous Expedition," as told by Thos. E. Breckenridge to G. W. Freeman and Charles W. Watson. *The Cosmopolitan*. August 1896.

Taft, Robert: *Photography and the American Scene*. New York 1938.

CHAPTERS XI AND XII

Barba, Preston A.: *Baldwin Möllhausen, the German Cooper*. Philadelphia 1914.

Möllhausen, Baldwin: *Diary of a Journey from the Mississippi to the Coasts of the Pacific*. 2 Vols. Translated from the German by Mrs. Percy Sinnett. London 1858.

Pacific Railroad Surveys. (See general sources, page 270.) House Exec. Doc. 91. 33 Cong. 2d. Sess. Washington 1856. Vol. III is Lieutenant Whipple's official report.

SOURCES   275

A Pathfinder in the Southwest, edited by Grant Foreman. Norman, Oklahoma, 1941. Lieut. Amiel W. Whipple's diary of his railroad route survey.

Simpson, James H., A.M.: *Journal of a Military Reconnaissance from Santa Fe, New Mexico, to the Navajo Country* Philadelphia 1852.

Sitgreaves, Captain L., Corps of Topographical Engineers: *Report of an Expedition down the Zuni and Colorado Rivers.* Exec. Doc. unnumbered. 33 Cong. 1st Sess. Washington 1854.

Taft, Robert: "Heinrich Baldwin Möllhausen," *Artist and Illustrators of the Old West.* Chapter II. New York 1953.

CHAPTERS XIII, XIV, AND XV

Clay-Clopton, Virginia: *A Belle of the Fifties.* New York 1904. Pp. 173–177 about the Iveses' life in Richmond.

De Leon, T. C.: *Belles, Beaux and Brains of the 60's.* New York 1907. Pp. 116–120 about J. C. Ives and his wife.

Freeman, Lewis R.: *The Colorado River, Yesterday, Today and Tomorrow.* London 1923.

Hardy, Lieut. R. W. H., R.N.: *Travels in the Interior of Mexico, in 1825, 1826, 1827, and 1828.* London 1829.

Ives, Lieut. Joseph Christmas: *Preliminary Report of First Lieut. J. C. Ives, Topographical Engineers, to Captain A. A. Humphreys in charge of the Office of Explorations and Surveys, War Department, November 1858.*

———: *Report upon the Colorado River of the West. Explored in 1857 and 1858 by Lieutenant Joseph C. Ives, Corps of Topographical Engineers.* Washington 1861.

Macomb, Capt. J. N.: *Report of the Exploring Expedition from Santa Fe, New Mexico, to the Junction of the Grand and Green Rivers of the Great Colorado of the West, in 1859, Under the Command of Capt. J. N. Macomb, Corps of Topographical Engineers.* Washington 1876.

Phoenix, John: *Phoenixiana or Sketches and Burlesques.* With an introduction by John Kendrick Bangs. New York 1903.

Stewart, George R.: *John Phoenix Esq., The Veritable Squibob.* New York 1937. A life of George Horatio Derby.

Waters, Frank: *The Colorado.* New York 1946.

CHAPTER XVI

Bailey, Paul: *Jacob Hamblin — Buckskin Apostle*. Los Angeles 1948.

Bancroft, Herbert Howe: . . . *History of Utah. 1540–1886*. San Francisco 1890.

DuBois, John Van Deusen: *Campaigns in the West, 1851–1861. The Journal and Letters of Colonel John Van Deusen DuBois, with Pencil Sketches by Joseph Heger*, edited by George P. Hammond. Arizona Pioneers Historical Society. Tucson, Arizona, 1949.

Dunn, J. P. Jr.: *Massacres of the Mountains*. New York 1886.

Gove, Jesse Augustus: *The Utah Expedition 1857–1858*, edited by Otis G. Hammond. Concord, New Hampshire, 1928.

Thomas L. Kane Papers, William R. Coe Collection in Western Americana Collection, Yale University Library.

McGavin, E. Cecil: *U.S. Soldiers Invade Utah*. Boston 1937. The Mormon side of the troubles.

McMaster, John Bach: *A History of the People of the United States*. Vol. VIII. New York 1913.

New York *Herald*, July 30, 1858.

The John Walcott Phelps Papers — Letters and documents of Col. Alexander, Lt. Maynadier, A. G. Brown, Col. Crossman, Lt. Bennett, Charles Brewer and others On The Mormon War. 1857–1860, in William R. Coe Collection, Western Americana Collection, Yale University Library.

Stansbury, Capt. Howard: *An Expedition to the Valley of the Great Salt Lake of Utah*. Philadelphia 1852.

The Utah Expedition. Containing a General Account of the Mormon Campaign by a Wagon-Master of the Expedition. Cincinnati 1858.

CHAPTER XVII

Foreman, Grant: *Marcy & the Gold Seekers*. Norman, Oklahoma, 1939.

Marcy, Randolph Barnes: *Border Reminiscences*, New York 1872.

——: *Exploration of the Red River of Louisiana in the Year 1852*. Washington 1854.

——: *The Prairie Traveler*. New York 1859.

——: *Thirty Years of Army Life on the Border*. New York 1866.

Parker, W. B.: *Notes Taken during the Expedition Commanded by Capt. R. B. Marcy . . . through Unexplored Texas, in the Summer and Fall of 1854.* Philadelphia 1856.

CHAPTERS XVIII AND XIX

Beale, Edward Fitzgerald: *Wagon road from Fort Defiance to the Colorado River.* House Exec. Doc. 124. 35 Cong. 1st Sess.

Bonsal, Stephen: *Edward Fitzgerald Beale, A Pioneer in the Path of Empire.* New York and London 1912.

Carroll, C. C.: *The Government's Importation of Camels: A Historical Sketch.* Washington 1904.

Emmett, Chris: *Texas Camel Tales.* San Antonio 1932.

Greenly, Albert H.: "Camels in America." *The Papers of the Bibliographical Society of America.* Volume Forty-six. Fourth Quarter, 1952. This article has the most extensive bibliography of the camel experiment.

Heap, Gwinn Harris: *Central Route to the Pacific from the Valley of the Mississippi to California.* Philadelphia and London 1854.

Lummis, C. F.: *Mesa, Cañon and Pueblo.* New York 1925.

Report of Lt. W. H. Echols between El Paso Road and Rio Grande from Camp Stockton to Ft. Davis. Sen. Exec. Doc. 1. 36 Cong. 2nd Sess.

Report of Lt. Edward L. Hartz between Pecos R & Rio Grande. Sen. Exec. Doc. 2. 36 Cong. 1st Sess.

Report of the Secretary of War about the Purchase of Camels for the Purposes of Military Transportation, 1855-'56-'57, by Jeff'n Davis, Feb. 24, 1857. Sen. Exec. Doc. 62. 34 Cong. 3rd Sess. This contains all the official correspondence and reports about the camel experiment.

"The Ship of the Desert," *Harper's New Monthly Magazine.* October 1857.

Stirling, Lt. Col. W. F.: *Safety Last.* London 1953.

Uncle Sam's Camels, edited by Lewis Burt Lesley. Cambridge, Massachusetts, 1929.

Index

Index

Needles, Calif., 154
Nevins, Allan, 111
New Almaden quicksilver mines, 63
New Mexico, southern boundary, 56, 82, 89
New Orleans, La., 12
New York Historical Society, 8
Newberry, Dr. J. S., 176, 181, 193, 198
Nightingale, Florence, 238
Nogales, Ariz., 99
North Platte River, 101
Northern Pacific Railway, 104

OATMAN MASSACRE, 71
O'Donoghue, John, 44
"Old Fitzwater," 146
Opate Indians, 54, 55
Oregon (mail steamer), 60
Oregon Trail, 4, 29, 76, 101, 103, 106, 110, 139, 204
Orphan Creek. See Huerfano Creek
Oto Indians, 139

PAH-UTAH (PAIUTE) INDIANS, 106, 159, 160, 191
Paiute Indians. See Pah-Utah Indians
Parke, Lt. J. G., 108
Parowan, Utah, 134, 137
Parras, Mexico, 87
"Pathfinder, The." See Frémont, Col. John C.
Paul William, Duke of Würtemberg, 139
Pecos River, 16, 144
Perry, Comm. Matthew C., 123
Pershing, Gen. John J., 81
Petrified forest, 150, 151
Phoenix, Ariz., 71
Phoenix, John. See Derby, Lt. George Horatio
Pierce, Franklin, 88, 93, 230, 244, 245
Pimas Indians. See Pimos Indians
Pimos (Pimas) Indians, 71, 73
Pindray, Marquis Charles de, 58
Platte River, 101
Pluton River, 62
Polk, James, 113
Pope, Capt. John G., 5, 102, 108
Porter, David, 235

Porter, Lt. David Dixon, 234–239, 241–243, 247, 253
Porter, Hampden, 254
Porter, Dr. James, 254
Pratt, Henry Cheeves, 11, 40, 43, 45, 52, 53, 54, 64, 67, 83, 100
Pratt, John, 40
Presidio, Texas, 70
Preston, Texas, 108
"Prince John." See Magruder, Col. John Bankhead
Providence Athenaeum, 8
Provo, Utah, 217
Pueblo Indians, 143, 145, 150, 165

RAILROADS TO PACIFIC, 103, 113, 126, 176
Raousset-Boulbon, Count Gaston de, 58
Ray, Albert, 240
Red River, 105, 108, 220
Red Sleeve. See Mangus Colorado
Redding, Calif., 135
Rhode Island Historical Society, 8
Ringgold, Comm. Cadwalader, 123
Ringgold Barracks, 88, 89
Rio Bravo, 18. See also Rio Grande
Rio Colorado. See Colorado River
Rio del Norte. See Rio Grande
Rio Grande, 4, 10, 16, 18–20, 23–27, 32, 39, 45, 64, 70, 73, 82, 83, 85, 89, 90, 96, 97, 99, 108, 118–120, 124, 129, 142, 160, 258, 265
Rio Grande City, Texas, 88
Rio Grande Valley, 117
"Rock of Chickamauga." See Thomas, Maj. George H.
Rocky Mountains, 3, 5, 37, 43, 101, 106, 111, 112, 114, 117, 126, 128, 136, 137, 139, 148, 205, 222, 223, 235, 252
Rodgers, Lt. John, 123
Royal Gorge, 106
Royal Society of Northern Antiquaries of Copenhagen, 8
Ruxton, G. F., 116

SACRAMENTO BATTLEFIELD, 85
St. Louis, Mo., 139, 205
St. Paul, Minn., 105
Salazar, José, 98